Good Works Review

2018

Editor-in-Chief
Robert S. King

Associate Editors
Ruth Bavetta, Jesse Breite, Sara Clancy, Joan Colby,
Marie C. Lecrivain, Rachel L. MacAulay

Production Editor
Diane Kistner

For More Information
www.goodworksreview.futurecycle.org

A Good Works Project of FutureCycle Press
www.futurecycle.org

Cover photo, "Splashing Wave from Within" by Tim Marshall
Cover and interior book design by Diane Kistner; PT Serif text with Macondo titling

Published by Good Works Review (a division of FutureCycle Press)
Athens, Georgia, USA

ISSN 2576-8166
ISBN 978-1-942371-98-4

Welcome to Good Works Review

Good Works Review is a Good Works project of FutureCycle Press. Introduced in 2013, these projects are altruistic collaborations of creative souls (like us) willing to give of their time, talents, and any profits to help improve our world. They have no source of monetary funding other than occasional sales of *American Society: What Poets See,* our first Good Works project.

With *Good Works Review,* we give struggling authors a way to submit their work without the necessary evil of reading fees, and all proceeds from sales are donated to charity. For this reason, the press gives contributors a Kindle edition of the issue in which their work appears upon publication, although on written request contributors can ask for a rebate on their paperback purchase. Clearly, the more copies purchased at full price, the more we can donate to worthy causes. FutureCycle Press has given an aggregate of several thousand dollars to the Malala Fund, Friends of the Earth, and Action Against Hunger for sales of *Malala: Poems for Malala Yousafzai, Weatherings,* and *Kentucky Review.* The ACLU is the beneficiary of all proceeds from *Good Works Review.*

To find out more or submit your work, visit www.goodworksreview.futurecycle.org.

Poetry

Fiction

Essays

Poetry

"The Alchemist," photograph by Fabrice Poussin

"Study of the Future," photograph by Fabrice Poussin

Roy Bentley

John Lennon Bitches about a McCartney-playing Violinist

It's *The Dick Cavett Show*. John and Yoko for the hour.
Yoko is chain-smoking. Wearing a leather mini-skirt.
Fishnet stockings. Cavett tries to light her cigarette.
She waves him off, saying how there is never a man
around when you want one. The smoke is a carnation
then a starburst of silence Lennon watches disperse.
This is 1971, years before her husband's murder,
so the guarded eyes are jewels. And a reminder
of the power of tenderness to rout subjugation.

Lennon is wearing a British Army uniform shirt.
Non-commissioned officer chevrons on each sleeve.
He pulls a cigarette from a pocket. His smoke entwines
Yoko's and they each notice. After reminding the camera
and the studio audience that the British invented penicillin,
John sings "Rule, Britannia! Britannia rule the waves!"—
soliloquizes: *In a restaurant in Spain, the violinist*
insisted on playing "Yesterday" right in my ear.
Says, And then he asked me to sign the violin.

Roy Bentley

The Stockinged Woman

Because the past is a destination too,
a limousine pulls up. Stops at my door.

This lady needed a ride, the driver says,
talking in conspiratorial tones. Shaking
his head as if confronting something new
or new again like the assertion that we are
bodies and some of the bodies are beautiful
corsetry into which he may never cinch words.

She wears a skirt. A red smolder of fabric.
It's the fire shoveled by envious angels.

The windows are down. There's a zephyr.
Marilyn's ballooning dress comes to mind
as the declaration of independence she is
catches the driver's eye in the rear-view.
If this were a dream, no time would pass.
But I watch her work the clasp, the silk.

The hour quickens, a pulse. The leviathan
Lincoln is moving. Her hand commences

a pilgrimage to the bordello-themed shrine
cast in consensual shadows and in lightplay.
On a night this clear, you can see the skin
above a garter shine like one light burning.
She knows what she's doing. And smiles.
Generations of the dead know that smile.

Byron Beynon

Byronic

I am walking from Marble Arch
parallel with the rigours of city traffic
towards the dark statue of Byron.
The anniversary wreaths and flowers
have already gathered at the base
with a family of cards
from the mayor of Nottingham and the Society.

At thirty-three he carried
a heavy heart,
his midnight regret felt
the sharpness of winter's grasp.
"An Italian frost" in January
the birthday month,
with the castle clock
awake in his turning mind
at three minutes past twelve.

George Bishop

Constable

—for George Bishop (Unknown–1899)

He was Quaker, didn't believe
in gravestones. I don't believe

in graves. Yet, I'm sure we would've
found something to talk about, say,

the soul, how it's often confused
with a conscience, which is always

confused with the truth. And then
there's what qualifies as a heart,

that colorless stirring toward
possession. However, we'd both

know to leave love alone, its
trappings, how it's defined by

what we can't explain and explain
anyway. We lived a hundred years

apart, barely connected by a trace
of blood that slowly evaporates in

the same name, by the desire to be
lost in the certainty of what we believe.

George Bishop

Natural

The chill of tiny bones cracking
high in abandoned barns trickles

down the spine of a field mouse,
unaware he's been chosen to live

another night, to breathe through
a useless world of whiskers until

the hawk awakes to the thunder
of hunger and escape escapes

to the darkest reaches of reason
where my most important ideas

are waiting to put a few choice
skeletons together another way.

Jesse Breite

City of Roses

"What must strike a stranger here, is the apparent indifference to what we call personal comforts." —George Featherstonhaugh on Little Rock, 1834

Gov. Pope's wife took the rifle to find her runaway sow,
left directions to the tavern
where you find *bits of pork fried
in lard, bad coffee,
indifferent bread...*

The senator'll be there.
He'll bum the cash you got, promise a payback
when the coffers come in.
Neither the bed, nor the women are soft,
nor to be expected.

The river down yonder is very fine and runs
through all our generations.
You could get a catfish near 20lb
if you got some bamboo.
Up north, the foothills rise.

Course, the highway aint safe near sunset.
Some place always given to
the elder powers
till it goes for the takin.
This a mighty king country.

Make sure your knife's thick for a fight
when you crossin West Markham,
or headin to the county cause anything's
liable to stick or slash you good
round the way.

It's a haven for the fleet of hand, the ceaseless.
They serve whiskey and whist
till dawn. Or you can sleep
on the ground whenever you decide
to go down, *oh, to go down.*

Jesse Breite

Cutting

Rain spotted down the driveway
into the backyard.
It tiptoed through the gut bucket,
over the cutting board.
The instruments, now still, waited there—
whispering on the silent clutter,
the glamorous fortes.
Water blunted the dried blood,
edges of the Bowie,
the long, thin slope of the fishing knife,
the scythe leaning on the wall,
the machete, the butcher,
the curved shaft of the amputator,
the quick airless stab of the boot knife.
You can feel the disemboweling
of the rabbit, the squirrel, the fish,
the cleansing of the viscera.
This is where we change
the plan, redesign bloodlines.
We find new beds to place
the strange knot of the animal heart.
What to call it—surgery, another kind
of warfare or atonement?
No human is left, but you can hear
the swift hollowing bass
of clay hearts, electric lungs, muscles
invisible in their flexion.
The song whistles through each
bladed instrument,
wet with the sky's weeping.

Wendy Taylor Carlisle

Full Wolf Moon

      the First Nations named it. Tonight it rose
in Cancer, frost mottled the walkway,

      and a jumped-up breeze blew us weather
in the low forties. Tonight someone is dying.

      It's a flat fact. The Moon rose
at 6:42 this morning to follow

      his last day across the sky. They say
a Cancer moon pulls unstable water into its restless

      self, encourages drowning. Tonight
a man is drowning under a moon he can't see

      from the windows of his room.
His lungs are awash but his eyes are the sun

      and when he drowns he will drown
like a new-plowed furrow in a flash rainstorm.

David Chorlton

Forest

A wooden house moves slowly through the forest,
imperceptibly at first, yet forcing trees apart
to let it pass. To the ones who live inside,
this is the great adventure
they have waited for through all their years
of staring into the density of leaves
and listening to the noises
whose origins they could never fathom. With their faces
pressed to the windows, they watch as branches snap
and thrill to the spectacle of earth
ploughed by their own, familiar walls. For days on end
the house carries them to the taller growth
they had only heard of in stories, until firs block out the sky
and they light candles to illuminate their faces,
which are suddenly old, suddenly those
of the grandparents who used to read to them at bedtime.

David Chorlton

The Journey

At first it was the city I wanted
to escape from, so I waited at the station
until the right train
stopped and I bought a ticket
for any destination. The other passengers
were tired, and seemed
to have been traveling for a long time.
The train sped into the night
and as nobody ever got off
the corridors filled with people standing,
leaning on each other to rest
from whatever it was
they were leaving. When daylight
returned, we stopped in open country
and a signal passed from each of us
to the next that we had reached
our final stopping point. One by one,
we said our goodbyes, the only words
ever exchanged, and went off
into the hills. I sometimes wish
we had said more, spoken
of whatever lay behind us, or arranged
to meet when we were finally
content and could sit together
bound by the memory
of that night on the run, the clicking
of the wheels, the blurred lights
at every town we passed through,
and the stars reflecting
in the final river we crossed.

David Chorlton

Tiger

As the stripes fade on a tiger's pelt,
he follows the scent of a mate,
although his forest tightens its grip on him.
As he sharpens his claws on bark

someone drawing a plan of his territory
imagines a city in its place. Only a shadow
remains of the tiger, rippling across ground

shaved of its trees. Only a shadow remains
of the Earth, passing across the face

of the bone white moon.

Barbara Crooker

Journey

at the Tyrone Guthrie Centre, Annaghmakerrig, Ireland

Blackbirds chuff the dull sky,
color of roof slates on this grey day.
Yesterday, sheets of rain lashing
the bus going north. In the bus station,
lashings of tea. After the rain stopped,
out for a walk; autumn, and chestnut
and oak leaves litter the ground brown
and gold. The quiet, broken only by
swans, whose startled wingbeats,
low notes of a cello, stir the air.
Above the lake, firs murmur
their resinous dreams.

Gareth Culshaw

I Was There Yesterday

I rub coconut oil onto my mother's feet.
They are swollen and as hard as bricks.
The dead skin on her legs is sandstone rough.

Her knees won't straighten anymore
and keep her from reaching the height
she should be.

She is like a garden wall around an estate.
Left to the sun, left to the rain. Allowing
the tongue of frost paint her until the cracks

weaken everything she's ever been.

J. P. Dancing Bear

Oracle of Rust

Let me bathe in the sweet rust of lies, in the trickle-
voice of old leaks and seeps of groundwater. I
love to feel each word well up and vine, snake around
my limbs, my torso, like the arms of a lover I know better
than to let near. The old gods look into you, see the thing
wriggling within and what they riddle you to, is this root
where that which is beckoned calls, that little flush
of old browning blood, that smear of vision, *look,* they say:

even if you find a god that will have you, there's still so much
confessing for you to do. Then they make me breathe
the vapors and the fumes of forgetting, they make me
fall into the stubble field of our collected griefs, ground
cracking, aching for tears, they make me fall to my knees
so you might know the ways I have already forgotten.

J. P. Dancing Bear

Oracle of the Virga Fields

In the silence of the day you can ask yourself if you know where
the music of the world comes from. Is it the virga that looks
like clouds dragging strings across the sky? Is it the tight lines
between the ghosts of telephone poles? All those voices trapped
inside twisting wires, humming in transformer boxes, mingling
with the whine of insects filling the fields. Even way out here, on empty
roads that connect empty towns—where heat rises watery
like reverse virga—you can hear the origins of a choral coming together.

These fields have seen too much future, too much progress, not
to have a song. They still hold a memory of trees rooting deep into
the ground. They remember being unfenced, how their animal souls moved
freely through the land. You can see them now and again, sad eyes
looking for something gone, something removed—they stalk the scars
of asphalt and moan something raw and very close to prayer.

J. P. Dancing Bear

Oracles of Vanity

Don't be silly, only nothing sees nothing, because everything
is in the act of seeing itself. The future is a catwalk where
the body flounces several gauzy colors, round after round
until the consuming self picks a fabric, possibilities, potentials,
the kinetic energy locked in a cell, the chemical processes
of a devourer's life: entropy: breaking: dividing: cuts: slices,
sections: cleaves: slit: tear: fragment: piece: parse: bite: byte:
bit: one: zero: on: off: proton: electron: lepton: dark matter.

When Macbeth's three witches brailled their palms along
the Pacific Rim, they dreamed they wore rings of fire. Does
the outward eye completely boil away to reveal the basin
of a brilliant future? Or an insufferable desert? Where the missing
consume the soul—a collapsed star; a beacon for strange attractors.
I felt attraction once and have regretted the results ever since.

Mike Faran

Autumn in Iowa

She told me that her
name was Maura Flowers and
that today was her 91st year

on Planet Earth.
We spent the afternoon talking
Spanish architecture,

then discussed theories on how
the pyramids were built

But I wasn't there, you bastard!
she joked, but her voice was
gentle and

her eyes beautiful blue

At 5:00 pm I wheeled her to the
rear of the med-line
then to the dining-hall

where we had dry meatloaf and
decaf

Nobody knew today was her birthday—
no cake or balloons—
I was the only one she had told

then we talked of abstract art and the
night-life along the Danube

Mike Faran

A Crown of Stars

I don't remember being
eleven—it's such a strange
number

A strange *sounding* number
with three
off-balance syllables

E-LEV-EN

It sounds like a little girl's
name—
a little girl from across the

world
who milks her goats in the dark
frost of morning

wearing a stained burgundy
overcoat
her blonde hair full of stars

Michael Gaspeny

One Smart Pig

Strain as I did to talk to you, I could only grunt
or squeal. Now on my way to the blade,
a strange truffle has given me syllables.

You do consume everything but the tail.
You coo, "This little piggy went to market,"
summoning death to tickle a baby's toes.
You sing with Bing Crosby, "He's got no manners
when he eats his food. He's fat and lazy and extremely rude."

After Christ stuffs a lunatic's demons into 2000 of us,
you celebrate our drowning as the Gadarene miracle.
The Manson Family kills Gary Hinman and scrawls
"Political Piggy" on the wall next to a Black Panther paw,
hoping to incite race war... For Valentine's,
you buy a card depicting a couple of us swapping tongues.
Beneath the caption HOG HEAVEN, you write LOVE,
        hoping for some.

I've heard your scholars expound as they rove the farm,
And I can tell you true: My eyes exemplify Aristotle's definition
of tragedy—"incidents arousing pity and terror
to accomplish a catharsis of these emotions."
My frozen left eye bears the terror; pity smears the right.
The catharsis will be my scream and your meat.
        Know who you cat.

Andrew Gent

Bird on a Wire

One point on the graph
of an otherwise perfect curve.
Comma with an actual tail.
A single note of music
you can see but not hear.
The way the dead stand
perfectly still on the horizon
never getting any closer.

Andrew Gent

Sparrows

If my heart was burnt to a crisp
and the ashes of that fire
rising from the heat
escaped the chimney
and scattered over the city
finally coming to rest
in corners among the litter
of old newspapers
and fast food wrappers,
those ashes would be sparrows.

Randel McCraw Helms

Koko Enters into Heaven

*(Koko, the lowland gorilla who learned American Sign Language, mastering
more than a thousand expressions, died in her sleep June 19, 2018, at age 46.)*

Imagine a heaven of gorillas,
Imagine Koko's sudden appearance there
With her wordhoard, more than a thousand teachable signs.

Imagine delighted lessons in hand-speech,
Imagine a manumission of the mute,
A joy like Beethoven's at hearing again,
As outward-spreading rings of her portable gift
Transfigure immortals into visible hymns.

Imagine a manual choir, a myriad
Innocent digits awave in unison,
Moving the nutritive empyrean air
With gales of unheard but understood song.

Imagine speechless fingers of eternity
Awaking like Lazarus into praise.

Mike Horan

Homecoming

If not for death I would not have come
back here at all.
Somehow it all looks smaller than I remember,
the wood of the house as rough and full of splinters
as the man who occupied it for fifty years.
Softer now, it seems to sag in the middle like
his will was the only thing that made it solid.
The wind rises and
the house makes a sound like the banging of a drum or
a heart on the verge of beating its last.
Underneath the rattle of windows I can hear, can feel,
the hum of power lines that slice through the farm,
their towers looking down on the house, standing in judgment.
I pull open the door and step inside the shell
of my father's life.

Joseph Hutchison

Sounds Over Broken Fields

Rattle of dry
    cornstalk leaves
        the mottled
oyster-shell white
    of death-bed linen;
        other leaves,
too, ticking
    as the wind
        flicks them
over like Tarot cards; and those
    wild Canada geese
        a few yards
above your head—how
    their honks
        are the sound
a mill-wheel makes,
    groaning
        on its worn
axle, like the Earth; and
    let's not forget
        the young
fox's bark, dampish
    at dawn,
        and at dusk,
the year's last
    cricket as it
        ekes
out its
    pinched complaint.
        Listening so
hard, who
    could help but
        feel this harsh
music must be the world's
    only music?

Paul Ilechko

The Metal Years

Nickels melt and clump together   a cluster
of finance like a tin pot Wall Street   we live
enclosed in metals   we live in a land of killing
weeds that devour the grain that we rely
upon   our land is stained with cadmium
our land is poisoned with lead   this place
where we diminish   receding into the
terrible vista that spans what little universe
we ever understood

pretend that we came from ocean   pretend
that our worlds were never so constrained
that we escaped across the open sea   to
places where there might be monsters
pretend that when we journeyed back to
our weed-stricken gardens   sun-tanned
and muscular   with the rolling gait of a
sailor   pretend we were no longer
overgrown   nor trapped by metal fences

we slept throughout so many generations
our people never noticing the changing
cadence   as the mountains turned to scree
our grandmothers' grandmothers'
warnings gone unheeded   their eyes closed
tight inside the wooden boxes where we
stored their bones   the metal rings that
closely cinched their waists   the blue-green
flakes of copper rust that stain what little
remains.

Mike James

Ghazal

You might have heard, the alphabet is a grand palace with
Many rooms. I'll let you guess my least favorite letters.

I love words, but once feared religion. Thought the Devil was
Just God in long pants, hiding behind a fern in the next room.

Some mornings, I step away and walk in the woods. I look for
Rooms as large as an acorn, large as the spider's crystal palace.

Most days I feel split between two worlds. I'm a small bird in a
Grain silo, circling towards cracks of light as if they are other rooms.

One of these days, like everyone, I'll go away without packing.
I don't expect a humble palace, just cushions in an unlit room.

Mike James

On Hedonism

Desire is an easy chair. A place to rest in the hunger of yes. One of the things my legs can do is wrap around. There's a blank after *wrap around* that can be filled in or erased. It's this way year round, especially in spring. As whoever dances alone hears music a different way. Emptiness is never like rapture.

George Kalamaras

Hound-Dog Beautiful

Based on a photograph of a coonhound climbing a tree—"This canine
'Davy Crockett' didn't wait for the hunters but started after his own raccoon"
—near Richardson, Maine, November 19, 1927

Coonhound means barking up the right tree, not the left

Coonhound means one word or two

Three. Coonhound means give me three tablespoons of salt

Three branches in the tree to wound out the boar coon

Dear mother, possum-stink father, is what a coonhound means

Coonhound is hoarse gutters at the back of the throat, the base of a sycamore

Coonhound is hoarse and throat and all light long

Meaning, quick-salt and pond-scum the moonlit willow-sway of the blood

Coon means hound means shiver my spine

Coonhound bark in the tree at the *base* of the tree

Red oak. Sassafras hollow. Elm

Coon the coonhound tree coonhound baying the coon up the coonhound tree

Coonhound means droopy ear bloodshot eye

Meaning how a face can be odd before it is beautiful

How we are all *oddly* beautiful

Drop the needle on the record, and coonhound means 1961 thick Indiana woods

Wind in a northern Indiana holler, in sassafras shiver, in acorn print in the knee

In the way we pray in woods, or the woods pray through us

Or bark print in the south country, in an ankle, as we move through gray scaly shin oaks

In the way we bark up the right tree sometimes wrong

The way we wrong way right, sometimes jumping around

Coonhound means tracking through *many* layers of woods, of words, of woods of words—
   how such jumping is good

Coonhound means sweet milk and crumbles of cornbread in the glass

Coonhound means meaning my face, eating a name

Call it *lost* call it *George* call it *moist-now-my-mouth*

How a name can be odd breaths before it turns beautiful

How a possum can be an *opossum*. A stink-badger, a *skunk*

Say the word *offal* properly, and it should sound like *awful*

Which sounds awful if you talk about the inside blight of this organism or that

Scooped out like hulling a possum

How things odd can be ugly in the norm of the mouth

How it were a wonder in the tongue's fiddling

How a face can be strikingly odd before it is beautiful

Coonhound means *Reprise* or *Atco* or *MGM* or drop the needle into childhood before
   the tongue and all its salt

Coonhound means play the record again. All things revolve

Even the past Saturn-turns the present

Spare the coon coonhound really means. It's the thrill of the hurt

A boar coon quitting the tree till leaves break and thunder

Black ash, basswood, butternut, and birch

Follow the wound and lead where it sees, back-dancing glance at us like Lot's lie

Spare the lie, it is written, *and spoil the vile*

Coonhound means reverse the course, let oneself loose, hurt-hunting the woods

Meaning, coonhound your coon-startled self

Some coons track fast, some soul

If the coonhound *scents* your soul, fog-climb the highest branch. Coon-shiver weight

Sourwood, sweetgum, hackberry, oak

If you risk the use of the word *soul* in a poem, make sure it bleeds

How what is moist is most beautiful before it is odd

How what is odd is hound-dog beautiful

How all hounds *are* hound-dog beautiful

Meaning—nose in the switchgrass—coonhound your coonhound weight

Meaning, let the branch shiver and shake. Let the hounds loose to bark apart the dark, bark
    apart the tree

Clyde Kessler

Marsh Wren

A breeze scours a wren from a stone,
sing-song ice for its voice, swamp-crazed
with bulrushes clacking against machines,
and a shytepoke beaking an April toad.

Music is hauling its warped guitar
against the clouds. It props the flurries
in the frets, and says the soloist has rolled
dope in a john-boat, and rattled the song.

This might be me I imagine, more
like the mud tracked in, more the wren's
blind shrub for the song's echo, and less
the creature the sky is tearing away from.

Steve Klepetar

Confession

Forgive me for pleasures
I've spoken about out loud,
and for failures I've kept

hidden. I couldn't help it,
living too long in the throat
of the wind. All those photos

I took of rough coasts
and skies drenched with light,
the forests of gigantic ferns,

it's true, I loved those places
with a hunger born of mortal
fear. In all my wanderings,

I came near the shoreline
of shadow and loss.
I stretched my blanket

where sun crept to the edge
of shade. I ate the fruits
of abundance by the valley

of no return, where birds
wheeled away and night frogs
sang in the tangled roots of trees.

Timothy Krcmarik

Son,

the sun will bloom into a red giant
five billion years from now,
gobbling up Mercury and Venus like wild radishes,

and the last sentient life on earth,
whether a gentle race of gardening bipeds
or a grumpy purple lichen

named Stan,
will have a front row seat
to the absolute end of things,

the clouds running for cover, trees screaming,
oceans hot enough to fry an egg.
And that will take a lot of grit,

something like the grit your mother showed
laboring to bring you from her womb
until your hearts began to wane

or the grit of the obstetrician
who drew you through her belly
unwinding the cord

from your neck and wrists and feet,
or the grit you showed on the warming table,
five seconds old

when you pushed yourself up
on both hands
and took a long, furrowed look

at the sapling world,
which for just that moment
was your sap of a father weeping.

Timothy Krcmarik

Apple

It's not every day the city
you serve as minor functionary
throws you the keys

to an unmarked police cruiser
with a Corvette engine
and paint black as the Madonna of Toulouse

to ferry yourself
from one official duty or another
until the humble mule cart

you're regularly assigned
is resurrected
at stupendous effort and expense,

but should you find yourself
by the curious interstices
of sloth and zeal,

which dictate life
in any thriving bureaucracy,
approaching the land-speed record

on a stretch of wildflowered highway
in wine country
and under sunny skies no less,

be ready for a grin
that hasn't stolen across your face
since the night it unfurled steaming green wings

and fled the ashes of your virginity,
or that other time some years later
when your beloved gave you a bite

of her apple
and the two of you were ushered from Paradise
by a giant Angel

whose meaty hands on your shoulders
meant she was sorry
but had a man and kids and a job to do.

Timothy Krcmarik

Passion

The wall beyond this window
is purpled in bursts
from the sprawling southern family,

Passifloraceae,
green with the sting of August
and helixed in honeybees

harvesting a thousand bruised nectaries
of this late wet-summer bloom,
droning with a timbre

honed by several million years
of outmaneuvering meteor strikes and ice ages,
wildfire, hungry bears, glyphosate.

And they will be droning still
tomorrow, a week from now, maybe a century,
certainly after the asphalt gang

smoking and eating sandwiches
in the shade of my front oak
have finished laughing themselves silly

at a story the fat one told
about what his girlfriend
tried to do to him last night

with a cucumber
and how he outmaneuvered her
with a trick of the tongue

he guarantees will make any woman
forget all her troubles
going so far as to demonstrate

his secret
with the remnants of his ham and cheese
to applause so thunderous

even I have to run to the window
drawing back the curtain
to see how the thing is done.

Jennifer Lagier

Matriarchal Messaging

Friends tell me of dreams
during which deceased family members
return, impart comforting messages
to their survivors.

My obstinate matriarchal precursors
rampage through recurrent night terrors,
a dead grandmother who interrupts sleep
to claw my mouth open, crawl inside,
appropriate my voice and fingers.

Mom, recently departed, appears
amid dark, restless hours,
a frail, wasted baby I am forced
to carry, continually resuscitate.
First light shocks me awake,
gasping and grieving.

Marie C. Lecrivain

The Secret Behind Imogen Cunningham's
"Self Portrait on Geary St, 1958"

(to Viola Weinberg)

For you, it was all about triangles;
equilateral, scalene, isosceles.
You found them where
sunlight meets shadow,
bent into the crevices
of knees, elbows, breasts,
and hands shaded over faces
lit by wonder of your gaze.

And here you are, caught in
the reflected pillar of a storefront
window on Geary Street. The flare
of your coat suggests the pleasing
symmetry of a Mayan temple
before the fall, and the smile lines
on either side of your
amused face form the capstone.

Kevin J. McDaniel

1973

Mama lost her firstborn
in a trailer fire.

Naked wires ignited when Grandma
opened the door

for the morning paper.
God or fate one

had put Mama and me, her baby son,
in a car on a roadway

as flames shot from the rooftop
like shrieking skyrockets.

Grandma on arthritic knees wept.
Firetrucks drove away.

A bottle nipple leaking milk
is how she marks the day.

Mama hardly ever whispers
my big sister's name.

Kevin J. McDaniel

1977

When I moved in
with your daddy,

Grandma Mary
scared me shitless.

She got mad
when I packed his lunch.

To make her happy,
I let her do it.

Your daddy came home
grubby and burnt

from the welding job
he footslogged to.

At night, we bathed you
on an unwanted table.

Little Michael's rabid pup
got hit on that road.

Cars flew like bats in hell.
Only ashes now,

merciful fire burnt it all down.

William Page

Almonds

We walked slowly along a shore in Santorini
watching a rose bloom red on the blue horizon,
as we thought it would, but for that it was
no less a marvel. We wandered in Venice,
where clacks of skiffs' bows striking one another
sounded like squawks of grackles in Austin,
a city we loved, its lights we'd seen dazzling
through our plane's window as we rode
through the black air holding hands thousands
of feet above concerns of faith or faithfulness.

But now I don't know where you are, if you're
sleeping between cotton or silk sheets in Madrid
or you're somewhere else planting rows of poppies.
You may be in Athens sipping wine with an older man
in shadows of an arbor of purple grapes or sitting
naked before a mirror with a blush on your breasts
as you brush your long brown hair that smelled like almonds
that first morning we awoke so close together
you said we were one.

William Page

Homage to Andre the Giant

Andre wrestled with his fate from an early age.
The bones of his body grew to such proportions
pain grasped him in its hammer lock.
Though his body grew too fast and large,
his shoulders the width of house beams,
his arms the length of ship staves, it was his heart
big as a mountain those who knew him praised
saying it was his gigantic abiding grace.
He pleased the crowds, straining at the ropes
for all he was worth. A colossus who had
to consume a case of beer to cop a buzz,
his laugh was happy thunder, his shoes big
as the houses of your neighbors' pit bulls,
his hands the size of Agassi's retired rackets.
We who are not freaks of nature, who cried
because our pony rides were not longer, gave
no thought to the little horse grown weary,
to the saddle made from an animal's life.
Andre was not so petty and thoughtless.
He rode on the back of nothing; he carried
the weight of his life as if it were a handful
of feathers to be cast aside when wind
came to carry them aloft.

William Page

Fame

 I was once a world-famous cinema director.
You have seen my films of bloody men and beasts
and screaming women with admirable décolletages,
but I chose as well to direct little girls in pinafores
strolling by the Seine and sailors dancing up walls,
assassins screwing shining silencers onto their pistols.
It could have been a blonde debutante stepping
out of her yellow convertible, a teenage
prostitute just pulled from a slop in China
sitting on the floor eating a steaming bowl of rice
or a race driver speeding through the Pyrenees
before he crashed in a cloud of steel and glass.
But all this is misleading. My glossy forte
moved toward elegant drawing rooms
of the wealthy and highly educated, who spoke
French in languid syllables of mink, and caviar
eaten with tiny forks as they sailed
down the Riviera. Of course, you
may have guessed I'm just an old man lying,
who's done nothing to gain fame or fortune.
I merely took the measurements of men
at Macy's. For forty years I rode
the subway back and forth until I retired,
living with my spouse who whispered gossip
as we sat at our kitchen table stirring our
bowls of broth or chewed sandwiches sliced
into triangles, then stood to feed our spaniel
wagging its tail into a question mark.
I drank my coffee and watched TV
and saw the sun rise up like a freight elevator
that brought coats and hats to my floor.
But it was pleasant on icy nights to climb
into my warm bed with my aging wife, a comfort
to think I'd wake again to see her wrinkled face
among morning shadows and listen for the phone
to ring to learn our son or daughter was coming
or just an old friend, or yet no one at all
to break the silence of our mediocrity
which I wore like a familiar coat I'd learned to love.

Simon Perchik

(Untitled)

Afraid and the wall
follows behind though you
point, know all about

descent and hammer blows
as the distant cry from home
—you sift between

as if this ready-mix
no longer cares about stone
broken open against one finger

retracing some caress
lost and the others
with no end to it.

Clela Reed

Black Box

Planes fall from the sky
and yet we fly.
What else can we do
but plan the trip, choose the flight?
It's always worked before.
The shattered dead
would have scoffed at caution,
rolling their luggage into the rain,
hailing a cab for the airport—
everything on schedule.
How can it be otherwise?
Unless set free,
the yearning heart
lies caged in its hangar
of bones and regret,
powerless to soar—or to falter,
falling perhaps,
breaking into a million pieces,
black box of answers missing
in the deep.

Marvin Shackelford

Wyvern

The gravel disappears into woods,
a throat closing over
our passage. It's not quite a dragon,
less death and flight than the light and scales
of a viper, but this isn't
quite a mountain either. The foothills
spilled just enough fire to birth me,
end of a warped and spindled line,
and have cooled since. But still they lift us
from creek bottom to sky. Ivory
beeches rise and clatter like teeth.
Cedars curve like spiked tails, a stinger,
poised to strike but only dropping
to the side, amiss. No flame or frost
breathes out on us. Why are we here?
Look out. All this falling land
I'll make yours, these kingdoms of stone
and drying water, of bruised sight
and hungry, vanishing soil.
It's all inside me, a small
hole in the landscape, and when I'm gone
I want it to fill again.

Bobbi Sinha-Morey

Autumn

Holed away in my cabin
by the river some mornings
I'll wake from dreams ripe
with the lingering scent of
fall's leaves, their golden
dusk rippled by the rub of
river across rocks tense like
thumb and forefinger to
test the silken slip of leaf;
and beyond the blue pages
of wind and water, I scoop
a handful of seeds, scatter
millet and sunflower on
the ground. What I sow here
will soon blossom in a flush
of wings—the flash of brown
in towhee, sparrows descending
from the branches of a blue
beech lofting from their nests
of down. On a slab of stone
I left a slice of prize melon.
They poked holes in it, and
a hummingbird came to join
the feast; my breath lifted,
admiring its iridescent chest
and ruby throat. I'd entered
the world of autumn, my
shadow left not too far
behind me.

Christopher Stolle

Prisms

Dangling crystals
a mousetrap for sunshine
a mirror for shadows
a minaret for gazing

into the night sky
and the rainbows
stuck inside stars

yearning for birth
aching for admiration

when spectacles explode
like supernovas

and showers telescope
with limpid babies
crying for gravity

Christopher Stolle

Tomatoes

Vines curl around rusted wire
Plump fruits hang like tight fists

Follow each view to its root
Guess why this tendril survived

Twist quickly for best separation
This makes tragedy less bloody

Drop them into boiling water like lobsters
Skins peel like summertime sunburns

Cone-shaped colander acts like a sieve
Wooden pestle serves as a gruesome murderer

Ladle steaming flesh into Mason jars
Seal with boiled vacuum pressurizers

Invite folk and friends for dinner
Serve them sauce you executed

Carine Topal

Mementos

I would save them again, the bromide of eastern postcards, bracelets and amber rings of my lost marriage. I'd save those Sunday afternoons reading Tsvetaeva and Mandelstam across the long pine table, eating garlic cloves on black squares of bread. I'd save this to remind me of how it was when he arrived, when we were young.

Then the memory of the throwing back of iced vodka, the long repetitious toasts to ourselves, the downing of pickled mushrooms and sprats wading in oil. The taste of salmon on my tongue, beets with their sweet boiled blood from the stove. And it was I who peeled their skin once they cooled in their juices until they swelled.

And throughout our days, the language he spoke—inside the English he grew into—filled his speech with war and drink. But that's how Russians stride through the world. And this I save to remind me of how it was when he arrived and how he began when we met and why he left me for her. He wanted her for her fingers, like his mother's, dicing the dill, the pickles, the peas.

Vivian Wagner

Winter in Ohio

is all about monster trucks
and coal-rolling, black
smoke filling the air,
hoping to warm it
against the losses of
meth and heroin,
as muddy rivers
wait to melt, the sun
waits to come out,
and the woods wait for
people to see the magic
in their pine needles,
their maple roots,
their loam.

Martin Willitts Jr.

Medic in Rain or Shine

And when the winds come from the hills,
I do not mind if they bring the rains
along for the ride. The sky is reflective—
black as the Vietnam Memorial Wall
where my face, mirrored, had names written on it,
but my name, thankfully, was not present.
It could have been engraved. I checked—twice.
I was that close. War and bullets are inches apart.

A person could have been rubbing my name.
I've seen them do it. Someone asked if I knew
anyone there, pointing to the massive list. I heard
bullets and rain, almost the same, with
red skies exploding. I pulled out many
of those names, feeling failure, seeing them die.

Martin Willitts Jr.

Not Yet

All plants tremble in the fall sadness. Not yet.
Not yet. This way, that way, thrashing in gusts,
flinging loose leaves and petals, piece
by exotic-green changing piece. Not yet; please,
not yet. Rough tastes of wind pluck the plants apart,
making liver spots, rustic burnt sienna, yellow
jaundice, wrinkled. Not yet. No, not yet.
The fallen scuttle, settle, exhausted, then tremble
in strangling wind, calm down yet again.
Yet again, not yet. Every winter some might liquify.
Every snowfall, branches scold the season
for ravishing every leaf this way and that.

I know, I know, not yet. Yet we all end eventually.
We all head towards a home, this way, that,
trembling in sadness with exhausted breath,
not yet, not yet. I know my settling is coming,
spiraling downwards like leaves, that way, this,
and I am thrashing and loosening from this world
towards...not yet! Not yet, I am not falling, not yet.
I am not taken yet by the wind, this way, that way,
where seasons leaf by, pages of ravished endings.

Jesse Wolfe

93301

You cut a perfect circle in the bread
Stood in silence as it fried
Tapped the egg a dozen times—
Immensely delicate!—
And dropped the yolk in the hole

For years I fooled myself
Imagining illustrious crowds
Gathered on the platform in your mind—
Chaucer, Milton, George Eliot, and Joyce—
Your thoughts awash in sonorous sentences

But I, the resenter, had been adrift:
You'd jettisoned London long ago
Coalesced in your flesh in Bakersfield
Flipped your toast on its back in the grease
Fatter, mediocre, and almost at peace

Fiction

"Bedstand," photograph by Roger Camp

"Table Setting," photograph by Roger Camp

David T. Anderson

Noble Jack and Pretty Bev

Jack scrounged the County Valentine's Auction for a sweet deal, something he could resurrect and sell to cover the shortfall of Bev's Medicare. He was an old machinist who loved tools and anything mechanical. If you took care of them, they'd serve you well or, if needed, you could sell them and make a buck. Jack found a 1998 GoldTek printer, a real steal at $25, and he told Bev it was old and cheap like them, so he grabbed it.

Jack wedged the printer into a corner of their trailer, a cramped rental near Interstate 10. He slotted in cables, snapped in new ink cartridges, and loaded a stack of paper. Jack set up a test document and tapped print. The machine roused and winked its green lights, sucked in a sheet, and went to work. He grew impatient with the surprisingly slow printing. The paper edged out showing thin bands of green, not his test document.

"Damn thing might be a doorstop, after all." Jack drummed his fingers on the table.

"Maybe it needs a new driver." Bev wheeled close with effort. She looked frail and bent in the black and chrome wheelchair. Her skin was sallow and her expression pinched. Over the two years she'd used the chair, her body had sagged and settled within the sturdy frame.

"It has nothing to do with the driver. Christ's sake, you don't know."

Jack reached to cancel the printing, but Bev ignored his irritation and put her hand on his. "Let's see what it is."

Three filigreed green bands grew as the printer chattered.

"It's money!" Bev said.

"Damn." Jack squinted through his glasses. "It might be." He laughed. "So, that's what they're doing at the County!"

The printer spat out the sheet and there lay three five-dollar bills like green apples waiting to be picked. The paper was wrong, but the reproduction seemed flawless. Jack turned the paper over and there were the bills' flip side. All he had to do was cut them out. Jack felt strongly that he was being invited, encouraged, to take the money; he imagined a voice saying, *Help yourself, Jack, you deserve it,* and he glanced up at Bev to see whether she'd read his mind. He shook his head to clear the foolishness.

"They look so real." Bev felt the sheet between thumb and forefinger. "With better paper, you'd never know."

"But, it'd be wrong?" Jack didn't intend to ask a question, it just came out that way. "Maybe we should call the cops?" What was he thinking? Of course he should call the cops, no "maybe" about it. When he was sixteen, he'd found a purse holding hundreds of dollars and returned it; he'd been rewarded and featured on the local news for his honesty. That's how everyone saw him. That's who he was.

"Well...I suppose," Bev said.

Jack and Bev looked long at each other. Jack saw a dare in her eyes; the wild, beguiling spark that had always pulled him out of himself, made him feel more alive, and let him do things he'd never do alone. He hadn't seen that look since...he couldn't recall when.

Bev held the bills to the light. "You'd have to cut the edges carefully. I mean, if you wanted to see how good they were. Hypothetically."

"*If* you were to actually use them...hypothetically."

"You could always say you got them from someone else, which is certainly true. I mean, *you* didn't make these."

"Yeah...I guess that's true...in a way." Jack saw excitement grow in Bev's eyes. But this wasn't like Bev swiping some waitress's two-buck tip; she'd done that kind of thing when they were first married, and he'd been shocked and told her so in no uncertain terms. She'd never done it again, so far as he knew. This was different. Even if they weren't stealing from some person, counterfeiting was a major crime. Jack wasn't a criminal, but after a lifetime of low wages and no savings, scrimping along on Social Security and losing their house, small as it had been, he felt the temptation. When bankers stole millions, what was fifteen bucks?

"Do you think it was a fluke?" Bev said. "Will it print more?"

"Don't know." He smoothed his thick hand over his lined face, knowing what was next.

"Let's see." She looked eager, eyes bright in her tired face.

Fiddling with the printer was easier than thinking, and he set it for five copies, just to please her and keep that lively look a bit longer. He punched the button, and five sets of three bills slid slowly and neatly onto the tray.

"Seventy-five bucks," Jack said softly. "Just like that." The money would cover the cost of the printer three times over. He felt like he'd made a profit, even if it was phony. It felt good. Like Monopoly with hotels on Park Place and Boardwalk. Like a billionaire. He distrusted the feeling.

"Ninety. It's ninety with these." Bev held up the first three.

Jack shook his head. It was so easy. But it was wrong. Besides, they'd get caught.

"Everyone knows how hard it is to get along now," Bev said. "What with prices always going up, it isn't fair. We've always worked hard and played by the rules. And look at us! It's just so unfair."

"That's God's own truth." His company pension had been cut during the recession, but the CEO got a golden parachute. They lost their small house, and the CEO bought an Italianate villa near Monterey. Jack still burned when he thought about that.

"Besides, they only check new twenties."

"We'd need better paper..."

"Soft, strong paper that we could rough up..."

"But not too much..."

"No, just enough...we *could* try it once. You know, buy coffee? That wouldn't be so bad, would it?"

Jack and Bev passed their first bogus bill at Beanstalk Coffee. They never bought fancy coffee, but the store was small and local, and they thought the teenaged barista wouldn't be suspicious. Jack was nervous and glowered at his thick hands, which were everywhere in the way, but Bev chatted brightly to distract the girl. As Jack rolled Bev across the parking lot, they shared a look of triumph that arced between them like lightning. He put his hand on her shoulder, and she stopped the chair and stood up shakily to kiss him.

"This seems to agree with you."

"Mmm." Bev insisted on taking a couple wobbly steps holding Jack's arm. "Must be the caffeine."

Jack and Bev passed three bills at a strip mall thrift shop. Bev browsed too long for Jack's liking, but she'd brought her cane and insisted on standing to hold up to her shoulders a fuzzy, white sweater with iridescent spangles. Jack grimaced to get her moving, but she smiled back with a look so stirring and seductive that he momentarily forgot what he was doing. The longer she poked through the clothes racks, the stronger she appeared to feel. Jack slouched forward to be less visible and put his hand on her back to ease her along, help she didn't seem to need, which pleased and puzzled him.

Remember, he whispered, this isn't a shopping spree, it's a feasibility study. Bev pressed close and breathed in his ear that she liked doing this; it was like being a secret agent; *you* know what's up, and *they don't*. Without thinking, Jack let his hand slip to her bottom, still enchantingly curved and surprisingly firm. He squeezed gently. She gave him a look that said, you *bad* thing. Jack flushed and pulled his hand away before anyone saw. He felt slightly delirious and wondered what had come over them. They stood in the checkout line, and Bev, leaning on her cane, held up the blouse for the woman behind her to see, shifting it back and forth to make the spangles flash. Bev continued to stand, though she teetered precariously, and Jack crowded close behind her with the wheelchair. The cashier wore a T-shirt decorated with puppies, and Bev bubbled with enthusiasm for dogs. Jack squirmed at the way she drew attention to herself, but he admired her coolness and composure. He hadn't known she had it in her, but she was good.

"I should have been an actress!" Bev said outside as she sank into the wheelchair. "That was such fun! Isn't it beautiful?" She waved the blouse so it sparkled in the sun.

"Let's not push it, okay?" he said, though he knew they would.

"Let's do something for you."

"No. That's all right."

"You need to enjoy this, too."

"I enjoyed it just fine."

"We'll stop after that."

Jack grumbled half-heartedly, but this seemed good for Bev in some way he didn't understand, so he gave in and drove to Ken's Pre-Owned Shop Goods, a ramshackle maze of metal shelves and battered tools. While Bev sat up front, Jack browsed, nudging a grinder or hefting a sledge, until he found a honey of an impact driver. It cost $49.95. Jack cradled the driver in his arms as he considered whether to risk buying it. Paying with ten five-dollar bills might look suspicious, but the longer Jack held the driver, the more he wanted it. In his head, he knew this was wrong, but...the thing was used, beat up, and Ken jacked up his prices so outrageously it would make a saint burn with anger. Jack struggled with the temptation, but finally yielded and the yielding felt good. He couldn't look at the clerk for fear he'd appear guilty. He frowned at the driver as though undecided, like maybe he'd put it back, then slid the thing across the counter. Bev and the clerk bantered about vacuum cleaners as he took the bills, faced them one direction, tapped the stack even, and slipped the wad into the cash drawer.

"That was close," Jack said, as they drove home. He didn't understand how Bev could feel so easy.

"It was a breeze, such a nice man."

"A breeze, huh?" Jack had sweated through his shirt.

"Would you feel better if we mixed in some real money?" She put her hand on his thigh.

He covered her hand with his, and her warmth calmed him.

"Did you see that power sander? Damn thing was like new." Remorse rose like bile as soon as he spoke. "But we can't do this. I feel terrible." He didn't feel quite so terrible after he said it.

"You know, tens, twenties, whatever," Bev said, gazing out the window, the furrow between her eyebrows deepening with thought. "It'd be like a senior discount, which I think is perfectly appropriate, and it'd be safer. Like, 'Those couple bills were bad? Really?'"

"Well, we would be paying for it, just not as much. A senior discount, like you said. The bastards wouldn't get to gouge us so much, and that is fair, our being on a fixed income and all." He bobbed his head with a righteous jerk, like he was all in, though he didn't know if he was. He could barely keep up with himself.

"How could we know?" Bev practiced looking helpless and wide-eyed; a sweet, old lady dismayed by the wicked world.

"How much of a discount?" Jack said. "I'm thinking 10 percent, we use a five for every $50."

"No! Too low!"

"Twenty percent? A five for every $25? I think that's still prudent." Jack pursed his lips and felt momentarily judicious and conservative.

"Prudent... Okay, I can live with 20 percent, since we're being prudent." She laughed, and he did, too. He reached over and patted her leg.

"Keep your hands on the wheel, Mr. Prudent." She nailed him with a coy smile.

Jack and Bev didn't touch a thing on the printer, didn't even consider turning it off, and they came to enjoy its contented humming and glowing green eyes. Jack wiped away dust with a soft rag every day and took to speaking to the machine as he did.

"You're talking to your machines now?" Bev laughed.

"Well, you talk to your plants."

At first, they ran fifty or sixty dollars every so often, afraid to spend too much at any one time, but Bev seemed to like the excitement as much as the merch, and she grew stronger and stronger. Jack noticed that she was gaining weight and her pale skin was regaining color. On July 4th, she abandoned the wheelchair. They went to see the fireworks. They had sex.

Jack kept a tally of their spending, and when they had passed $1,000 in fake bills, Jack decided they should stop. Bev had dumped her cane and signed up for Dancercise For Seniors at the Y, which Jack thought too much, even though she'd danced as a young woman. Now she was happy to lurch around to Bruno Mars songs, the clumsiest and most passionate dancer in class, and her lame and neglected muscles swelled and freshened like flowers after rain. She felt so healthy and vibrant, she told Jack, this had to be God's reward for their hard life. Jack wondered how they could ever stop. Would that put her back in a wheelchair? And just to ease his moral qualms? No one got hurt, and Bev got better. Where was the harm? When he put it like that, he couldn't stop, but it still felt wrong.

When Jack opened their September bank statement, he was startled to see their balance $1000 more than it should have been. He examined all their past statements, but he couldn't account for it. Bev peered over his shoulder and shook her head silently, apparently baffled.

"Well..." Bev gazed out the window. "I did deposit $100 last Tuesday. But not $1000. I don't know what that's from."

"There's no $100 deposit last week. Just this $1000 on Tuesday. What'd you do? You didn't use the funny money, did you? Did you?"

"This is embarrassing, and I didn't want to bother you. It was the Danskins…"

Bev confessed to buying a closet full of colorful Danskin tights and leotards, which she really, really regretted because she looked like a shrink-wrapped bunch of grapes, but she'd bought them anyway. When she realized their account would be overdrawn, she'd printed and deposited $100. She said she told the printer she was going to feed the bills into her bank's ATM and it'd be risky, so please do a really good job. Talking to the machine felt like praying, she said, and she'd had a spiritual intuition that there'd be no problem. Even so, she wore a floppy hat and shades, kept her head down, and fled the ATM so fast she'd left the receipt. Bev knew she was weak, and she was sorry, but she had no idea how $100 had become $1,000. Maybe her prayers had been answered?

Jack checked their balance every day, and when the October statement arrived it still showed a $1,000 overage, and they'd had no bank notice. Jack knew that one day the bank's computers might catch this mistake, and he told Bev *never* to do that again because they'd surely be caught.

The November statement arrived along with three new statements addressed to Bev from different banks.

"What have you done, Bev?" His sense of dread told him exactly what she'd done.

"It's so simple!" Bev said. "I opened a new account at Wells Fargo with regular money and then went outside and put $100 into the ATM. And guess what?" Bev went to two other banks and the same thing happened. It was meant to be, she said. She fed in $100, and the ATM receipt read $1,000. Bev could hardly contain herself. Life was so good, so generous; they were blessed. Jack agonized.

"Your receipt said $1000?"

"Yes! I think it's something with our printer…some code or something. It's like a gift from God to make up for our tribulations."

"We've had no more trouble than lots of others. You've got to close these."

Jack followed her as she walked from bank to bank. He saw her find her reflection in the windows and looked pleased, like she saw someone who was shaping up nicely.

Bev put makeup on for the first time since…neither of them knew. She'd rarely used the stuff. When Jack saw her in front of the bathroom mirror smoothing on lipstick, he slipped up behind and wrapped his arms around her to pull her close. He nuzzled her skin, so smooth and firm; how young she appeared. Bev leaned into him, looked up, and kissed him, a full, inviting kiss. He felt how much he'd always loved her vitality and headlong high spirits, how much she had lost and how much regained. He looked over her shoulder at her reflection to tell her he loved her and saw his face leering back at him, haggard, creased as a dried walnut with worry lines; a greedy, old satyr, a billionaire with a trophy. He leaned back in dismay.

"You know, I think I'll get a makeover." Bev leaned forward to examine herself in the mirror. "I used to think I looked like a bulgy mess, but I think I'm better."

"Shrink-wrapped, you said! I'd love to see that, but grapes don't come to mind. Melons, maybe…"

"All right! All right! I shouldn't have mentioned it." But he knew she was pleased and so was he.

Jack drove her to The Salon at Grande Mall. He paced the three glitzy, half-empty levels four times and stopped to lean on the third floor balustrade. A sparrow streaked past, soaring up to the vaulted ceiling. He heard birds chirping though he saw few. He wondered if the birds fluttered around up there until they died and dropped to the ground floor. Maybe they got lucky and bolted out a door with a departing customer.

Voices from all three floors floated to the ceiling and echoed back down, distorted and jumbled. Jack's hearing wasn't good, and the faint, dislocated voices seemed to hover like arguing angels over the silent, impassive shoppers. He felt a twinge of vertigo. Bev was taking forever, and he returned to the ground floor and sat on a bench across from a branch of their bank.

A woman behind the counter worked with her head down like she was counting money. Jack considered asking her about their account. Just ask. Was it all in order? His conscience nagged him that eventually the bank would notice, and waiting for the ax to fall made his stomach hurt. He'd probably get an ulcer, maybe he had one already. He bit his thumbnail. Or, he could stroll into the bank and act like he'd just discovered this silly mistake; they had given him too much money. Ha, ha. Must be an accounting error, some computer glitch? Noble Jack, he thought and snorted. Honest Jack. But, one thing he could never mention was the Goldtek. Never. Not to anyone. They'd go to jail. What would happen to Bev? It would kill her. He resolved to end this whole thing as soon as they got home.

No one was near when Jack heard the clack of heels echoing among the sparrows and lost voices. At the far end of the hall, a woman walked toward him in a yellow dress with blue accents that drew his eyes to her wonderfully swaying hips. Bev was gorgeous, like a luscious fifty-year old. Her hair was dyed so it didn't look dyed, and her skin gleamed. She laughed at Jack's wide-eyed gape and waved. By the time she stood before him in an ironic model's pose, his resolution was forgotten. Jack reached out toward her and was embarrassed by the sight of his rough, veined hand. He let the hand fall.

"My God! You look like a movie star!"

"B list," she laughed. Bev knew lusty exaggeration when she heard it and was happy to be hearing it again. Jack drove the starlet home.

The makeover artists had promised Bev a wonderful "sense of well-being," and she felt it. Bev fizzed with energy and rattled around the trailer restlessly until she announced to Jack that she had a great idea. She would share this "sense of well-being."

"Whatever. But no more funny business," Jack said. He sat on the sofa staring at his feet while she paced. His work boots were so thick and wide he thought they looked like hooves.

Her business model, she said, was to invest their "unconventional money" in a project that would make real money and let them ease away from the not-so-real money. He could relax, enjoy life, and let her take care of things. She'd already developed her product called Bev's Herbal Refresher: a cocktail of turmeric, ginger, cardamom, molasses, tap water, and a hefty slug of grain alcohol. She'd sell it in homey Mason jars from the trailer carport.

"Doesn't that sound yummy, Jack?"

"Bev! That's called money laundering."

"Oh, nonsense. We aren't the Mafia."

Jack clutched his stomach. "This is giving me an ulcer."

"You have an ulcer?" Bev flumped down next to him. "Oh, no! You poor thing. Are you sure?"

"No, I'm *not* sure. I just *feel* like it is. I worry, you know?"

"Of course you do. And you were thinking about your ulcer when I told you the plan, and it clouded your judgment. But, really, this will let you relax. I know it. Don't I make you happy, Jack? You make me happy."

"Oh, Christ," Jack groaned. "We can write each other love letters in jail."

"Oh, don't be silly," Bev said. She left the room and returned with a jar of Refresher. "Care for a snort? It'll perk you up."

Jack held the sluggish, orange murk in the Mason jar up to the light. He sighed. He took a small sip and nodded. "Not bad for snake oil, I guess."

"You see?" Bev pumped her fist in the air.

"No."

Word of Bev's Herbal Refresher spread uncommonly fast, and women from outside the trailer park began dropping in to buy two or three Refreshers at a time. Bev sold it cheap and people soon returned for more.

Jack watched anxiously as Bev chatted with Donna, a neighbor and notorious drunk. She clutched two jars with one arm and tipped back to drink from a third. Her husband, Cesar, a city cop, marched up the drive, shouldered past the waiting customers, and pulled the jars of Refresher from Donna's hands. He sniffed the open one, then emptied all three on the ground. He yanked Donna by the arm, and she staggered into him, startled and protesting.

"What're you doing selling this shit to a drunk? You're gonna be in a world of hurt, you don't quit. A world of hurt."

"It's just an herbal remedy," Bev said, but Cesar was quick-marching Donna away. The others scattered.

Jack's brain felt scrambled and sluggish with panic; he felt short of breath. "Christ. We're busted. This is it. We're done."

"People love my Refresher, and it's doing them a world of good. We can't stop. It makes good money. Honest money."

"No! It's not. It's fraud for Christ's sake. It's all kinds of stuff, I don't even know what. Food and drug...whatever." Jack waved his hands. "We've gotta dump it all."

"No, you're not! It's free enterprise, and there's nothing wrong with that." Bev cradled a box of Refreshers, flung the door open, and went inside.

"Can't you see where we're heading?" Jack felt like an idiot yelling at the trailer.

That evening a cop car cruised slowly down the trailer park drive, turned, came back, and slipped away on Buena Fortuna Road. Jack watched from between the curtains. His stomach cramped.

"Bev, I'm leaving tomorrow morning early. The cops are coming, you know they are, and I'm not going to be here when they do. You can stay if you want, or you can come with me. But I'm done. This is killing me."

"I'm not going anywhere! This is good. This is the best we've ever had it and you want to go back to the way it was? I won't. I'll fight for my life!" She went in the bedroom and slammed the door.

Jack yelled through the door. "I'm not going to jail! And I can't watch you go to jail."

"No one's going to jail. That's stupid. Refresher doesn't hurt anyone."

"It could make people sick."

"Sick?" Bev flung the door open. "I was sick. I was almost dead." She raised her arms as though on display. "Look at me! I'm alive. What's wrong with that? You seemed to like it, too. Why do you want to take it away? Do you want to kill me?"

"Listen. It's simple. What we're doing is wrong, totally illegal, and when the cops come, and they will, we'll go to jail. That could kill you."

"That's ridiculous. We aren't going to jail. Can't you just enjoy life? You've been a drag on me all along. This's wrong, that's wrong. Everything I want is wrong. You think life is wrong." She slammed the door and didn't answer anything Jack said. He gave up talking to the door, and the rest of the evening passed in cold silence.

Jack tried to sleep in the lounge chair, but failed. He got up at four o'clock, went to the printer, took a deep breath, and switched it off. It felt like an execution. The lights winked from green to red, and Jack turned away. The lights stayed on. He slipped quietly into the bedroom to grab some clothes. The room was dark, but the dim light from the living room window touched Bev where she lay. She was staring at him, but Jack couldn't read her expression. He wanted to say something, but he was too upset to trust his words. He stuffed his things into a duffel and went out to the truck.

He felt a longing for the new tools, but had to break clean. Jack slipped the key in the ignition. The trailer was dark. He started the engine. He felt the clunk of something dropped in the truck bed and turned as the passenger door opened and Bev climbed in. She slammed the door shut and sat silently with her hands clasped over a large grocery bag. Jack looked at her; Bev stared straight ahead.

"What are you waiting for?" she said. She was quiet, like cooling lava.

"Nothing." He put the truck in gear and rolled away.

Jack and Bev drove the deserted streets to the Interstate as the sky turned dusty rose in the east. He turned the radio on softly to fill the silence.

"These damn wrinkles!" Bev whispered fiercely and rubbed the back of her right hand with her left as though brushing away cobwebs.

Jack looked over at her. The grocery bag had opened and a jumble of bills pushed over the top.

"Oh!" was all he could think to say.

"Being prudent." Bev smiled without looking at him. She turned up the radio to hear "Uptown Funk," and softly sang along with it, nodding her head, "'Don't believe me, just watch!'"

Jack smiled, accelerated up the on ramp, and merged with the traffic rushing west.

Z. Z. Boone

Tremors

The three of us were watching Dancing with the Stars when the phone in the kitchen rang. Somebody who identified himself as Father Campos from Our Lady of the Mist. "I'm calling at the request of Lillian Feld," he said. "Is this Robert?"

I told him it was.

"You might want to come down as soon as you can," he told me. "I'm afraid Lillian's time with us is limited."

"Shit," I said, mostly to myself.

"She has something she wants to tell you," Campos said. "It's important you hear it directly from her." When I hesitated, he promised it wouldn't take long.

"Who was on the phone?" my wife Dana asked when I stepped back into the living room.

"Some priest," I told her. "Ma's dying and he thinks I should go down to Florida while I still can."

On TV, an ex-football player was doing the rumba with a woman in a very revealing gown. My sister Kelsey was in her rocker, trying to keep up. I walked behind to steady the chair.

"I don't know," I said. "Maybe this is good."

Dana shrugged. "Watch out for alligators," she said.

I immediately called my supervisor at home and told him the story. On the internet, I found an open flight to West Palm. I hardly slept and the next morning Kelsey—recognizing a disruption in the everyday routine—cried and clung to me as if I were leaving for war.

"He'll be back on Friday," Dana kept telling her. "Three days."

"I'll bring you a surprise, Kels. How 'bout that?"

My sister clutched me at the front door and hugged with such force that I was afraid we might both tumble to the floor. Kelsey is not a small woman. Five-nine—just an inch shorter than me—and around 180 pounds. There are things she's perfectly capable of doing, but keeping her emotions in check is not one of them. She can shower and dress herself, make toast, and boil water for tea. She uses the bathroom unaided. Her speech, though, is halting and slurred, and she walks with a decidedly pigeon-toed gate. Frequent tremors make it difficult for her to perform simple manual tasks like buttoning her coat. She's also has cognitive impairment but —if her doctors are to be believed—she's beaten the odds by lasting this long.

•••

I got in just after noon and Campos was waiting outside the security area like he said he'd be. He had a cardboard placard with my last name printed on it, and he stood among the cabbies and limo drivers holding up similar signs. I wouldn't have recognized him as a priest. He looked to be in his mid-forties, athletic, a full head of curly brown hair. No cassock. Light gray slacks and a maroon sports shirt, slip-on shoes with no socks. He cupped both my hands when we shook.

"First time in southern Florida?" he asked. I nodded. He grabbed the handle of my carry-on and wheeled it toward the exit. "Follow me," he said. "I'm parked in short-term."

Campos drove a black Cadillac Escalade and hit I-95 like a participant in a demolition derby. "You have a place to stay?" he asked.

I told him I reserved a room at the Marriott.

"Why don't we visit the hospital?" he said. "You can get settled later."

He asked how the fall weather was back in Baltimore, if I was an Orioles fan, if I knew that both Tom Clancy and Mama Cass were originally "Baltimorons." He smiled as if he was trying to sell me something, and I disliked him almost immediately.

•••

Ma and I never got along particularly well. Her first husband, my dad, shot himself during a hunting trip a few weeks before I was born. This was the reason, according to Ma, that Kelsey's "wires got all twisted." Not true. My sister never attended a day of regular school, never learned to ride a bike, never had a sleepover with a giggling crew of adolescent friends. She was diagnosed with ataxic CP at eighteen months, a fact I later found verified in her medical records.

Ma remarried after a year of widowhood. Kelsey was sixteen, I was one. We were kept pretty much apart not because of the age difference, but because—again in Ma's words—"The girl doesn't know her own strength." By the time I was nine, I was considered the "older brother." Ma took care of her and was protective, but her resentment was obvious. "The things I could have had," she'd say some nights after Kelsey was asleep. "The things I could have done."

Roy, husband number two, was a locksmith who ran his own business. He was successful, a decent provider. Roy and I got along fine, but Kelsey never warmed to the man. He died from a pulmonary embolism when I was eighteen; I got the news only six days into Army basic training, and Ma raked in everything the guy owned.

For the next four years, I came home only when I had to. Just before I was discharged, Ma invited me to move back in. I accepted, considering it a temporary landing spot until I found something better.

"I want you to take over the house," Ma told me my first night back. "Pay it off and it's yours."

"What makes you think I want it?"

"What you want isn't important," Ma said. "What's important is for me to get down to Florida and see the sunshine for once."

"What about Kelsey?" I said.

"What about her?"

"I can't take care of her."

"You're an adult," Ma said. "You'll be surprised what you can do."

Shortly after Ma left, I got married to the woman who did the books at Advanced Electronics where I still work. That was thirteen years ago. In that time Ma, for some reason, turned Catholic, and kept in touch with ridiculously ornate Christmas cards sent every December. The one I got last year had Baby Jesus—halo aglow—administering Holy Communion to the Wise Men. "Good luck in the New Year," was written inside. "They tell me I have cancer."

•••

Ma was in a semi-private room on the fifth floor of Boca Raton Regional Hospital, separated from her roommate by a folded-closed partition. I hadn't seen her since the day she left and now, hooked to hoses and IVs and I-don't-know-what-else, she was as pale as a catfish flipped on its back.

"Hey, Ma," I said.

Her eyes were blank but her mouth quivered.

"You have to lean in," Campos said.

I expected the odor of death, but when I lowered my head all I smelled was bleached linen and rubbing alcohol.

"Kelsey," she said.

I waited for more. There was none.

"Kelsey sends her love," I said. "So does Dana."

"Robert made it all the way down from Baltimore," Campos said in a voice much too cheerful. "Quite a fan you have here."

No response from the prone body on the bed. Finally Campos said, "Perhaps we should let her rest. Come back in an hour or so." I nodded because there wasn't a place within the known universe I wouldn't have rather been.

•••

Love for Ma was not why I was here. I came because Dana, after a dozen years of trying, had finally gotten pregnant. Our problem was money. Money and Kelsey. My sister needed assistance and supervision, both of which Dana had unselfishly provided while I went to work. We'd checked out a number of facilities where we could place Kelsey, and found one called Hedgewood that seemed perfect. "A thriving community," is how the brochure described it, "where special people learn their own inner worth." But Hedgewood, even with financial aid, would go through my paycheck like Pac-Man.

Thirteen years ago, Ma had been either very lucky or very smart and had bought a townhouse near the beach in Boca Raton. I don't know what it was worth then, but I checked the current real estate market on the flight down and figured it has to be in the three- to four-hundred-thousand dollar range. I hoped maybe she'd pass it on to me—along with whatever other goodies she had—if I held her hand and played the role of the selfish and unappreciative son who's finally come to his senses.

That's why I was here.

•••

Campos and I both ordered iced tea and grilled chicken salad in the hospital bistro. He asked about the family, calling them by name. "Dana's doing well?" he said. "How about sister Kelsey?" As the waitress refilled our coffee cups for the third time, Campos got down to the subject of money.

"Allow me to lift a burden," he said. "When Lillian passes, Our Lady of the Mist will cover all expenses. Funeral service, requiem, full burial."

"No disrespect," I said, "but why so generous?"

"Least we can do," Campos said. "Just know that she made me executor of her will, and everything she owns goes to the Church."

Ah! I thought to myself. Now I get it! But before I could say a word, Campos' cell went off

••• 73

to the tune of "Thank You for Being a Friend." He got up and walked toward the door and out of hearing range. Maybe a minute later he returned.

"I'm afraid we lost her," he said.

"You've got to be kidding," I said.

"Let's go up."

Ma was in the exact same position as when we'd left, except now the room was still. No labored breathing, no electronic machinery. The partition was open, but the other bed had apparently been rolled someplace where death was less evident. Campos made the sign of the cross, kissed the fingertips of his right hand, and touched her forehead. I found the gesture both pretentious and overly dramatic, and under different circumstances I might have thrown him out on his ear.

"At least you got to talk to her one more time," he said.

"It wasn't exactly a conversation."

"I'm sorry, Robert," he said, a hand on my shoulder.

You're sorry? I wanted to say, but instead I just walked out.

• • •

He drove me to the Marriott, asked how long I planned to stay in town. "I'm out of here ASAP," I told him.

"Have a drink with me," he said. "I need to show you something."

We went into the Marriott bar. I noticed Campos had brought something with him, a leather folder that I pictured holding a check. I figured he'd maybe try and pay me off, get me to agree not to contest the will.

The place was empty, but Campos went to a booth in the back. A bartender came over and took our order. Two pints of Guinness. "Lillian wanted to do this herself," Campos said, "but that doesn't look to be in the cards." He opened the folder, took out a manila envelope, handed it to me. It had some heft to it; I was thinking maybe cash.

I lifted the flap and was about to slide the contents free when Campos reached over and stopped me. The waiter put the beers down, and as soon as he was back behind the bar, Campos removed his hand and sat back.

Inside was a photograph with some paperwork. A woman in a bed not unlike the one I'd just seen Ma in. I recognized her immediately; it was my sister Kelsey in a hospital gown, holding a baby wrapped in a blanket. She had this look on her face. Supremely pissed off.

"The child is you," Campos said. "There's a copy of your birth certificate in there."

I unfolded it. According to the Baltimore City Health Department, my mother was Kelsey Feld, age fifteen, the father simply recorded as "unknown."

I looked up at Campos, who sipped at his beer. "No way," I said. "I have a copy of my birth certificate. This is bogus."

"The one you have is bogus," Campos said. "They weren't hard to fake back then."

"This is bullshit. My sister never even went on a date."

"She didn't need a date," he said. "She had your goddamn father."

• • •

That night I called the airline and moved my flight to the morning. It was the soonest I could get out. In the Marriott gift shop I bought Kelsey a stuffed raccoon that zipped open so you could put a pair of pajamas in there. The rest of the time I sat in my room with a bottle of scotch I bought from the ABC store at the end of the block, and I studied the photograph. Saw something different and realized my mistake. It wasn't anger in the eyes of my sister, it was defiance. Because she knew what happened next. The photographer would lower the camera, her baby would be taken from her, she'd be medicated, and everything she knew— everything she suffered through—would be hammered flat and adjusted to fit.

Around eleven, I called home. I told Dana the full story, everything. She stayed quiet for a good amount of time, then said, "Look. We'll handle this. Whatever happens, I'm onboard."

How can you help but love the woman?

I asked her to wake my sister and put her on the phone, and when Kelsey finally picked up, her voice was loud and sleepy.

"Hello?!" she said.

On the white wooden dresser, the stuffed raccoon pecked its masked face out from the plastic bag.

"Hey, Kels," I said. "Guess what?"

Bill Carr

Transitions

It's Sunday. I'm standing at the ballfield entrance to the schoolyard. Just surveying. Now it's a ghostyard. The concrete fields are absolutely empty. It used to be that even on the most depressing day of late fall—when the sky is gray and the temperature dips to close to freezing—there were always a couple of guys throwing a football around or some little kids running around playing tag. On a normal spring or summer weekend, there were at least two, maybe three softball games going on simultaneously. The left fielder of the game at the right was in imminent danger of being run into by the second baseman of the game to the left. Now there's a rumor that the entire ballfield is going to be turned into a parking lot.

Across the field there's the basketball court. At one end there's three guys shooting baskets, waiting for a fourth to come by so they can play a two-on-two half-court game. I know all three guys. There's no one on the other half-court. It used to be that on the week-ends, there were five, six, seven, sometimes eight teams at each end of the basketball court, waiting their turn to play half-court, three-man ball. Three baskets, winning team stays on the court, winning team gets the ball to start, team that scores a basket gets possession. If you don't get a defensive stop, you could be off the court and back waiting on the sidelines without ever touching the ball.

And now we're down to three guys—soon to be four.

The brochure I received upon being discharged from Army active duty, titled "Readjusting to Civilian Life," cautioned that "...people and environments may have changed in your absence." I guess that's true.

I have wondered where the young hotshots have gone. I'm curious but in no way motivated to find out. That may be the most curious thing of all.

I walk across the empty ballfield and join the basketball players—what's left of them. Orville is the only one who gives me a normal greeting. Orville is a big, redheaded kid who may be the most normal of us all—except for his shot. He likes to take this one-handed ten-footer, back to the basket, not looking at the basket. If not guarded closely, he can actually make that shot.

We may be down to the social misfits. Waterbug Joe mumbles something inaudible when I arrive, and The Monster doesn't say a word. Waterbug Joe looks like he's about fifty, which makes him at least twenty-five years older than anyone else who ever came down here. He's short, balding with gray hair, and has an inconsistent, two-handed outside shot. He's determined to prove he can run with the kids. Most of the kids, at least the ones who are left, readily concede that he can run us into the ground. Whether it's a half-court or full-court game, he puts on his own version of a one-man, full-court press.

The Monster—I shouldn't call him that because he doesn't like it—Dan is a loner. At six foot eight, he's always been the tallest guy to frequent the schoolyard. He's well-proportioned—just big, with blond, curly hair. He comes to the schoolyard late on Saturday and earlier on Sunday afternoons. I first saw him there when I was a senior in high school. Other than making layups, he has no offensive skills. But he's a definite plus for your team for rebounding and shot-blocking.

It turns out we don't even have four. Orville says he has to leave early. He vowed to his wife he'd mow the lawn today. I didn't even know he was married.

Unless we can corral someone for a two-on-two game, it's shoot-around time.

This is the first time since I learned to play that I haven't been on a team. When I was in summer camp, we played other camps around the lake. In college, we had a team that went around the borough, playing in gyms in all sorts of neighborhoods. In the army, I played on a Fifth Army Headquarters team.

It's good to have a sport that's not inherited from your parents. My father played basket-ball—twice. He told me the first time he played in a gym with a bunch of his friends, he couldn't miss. The second time he played, he couldn't hit. He never played again.

I wanted to tell him that the game is about more than just scoring. Of course most of the guys down at the schoolyard don't exactly buy into that. I don't buy into it myself when I start gunning up jump shots. Instead, with typical teenage arrogance, I told him, "Well, you should have tried it once more. The deciding round."

Supposing he took my advice and decided basketball was his sport. What position would he have played? Point guard, I guess. He's five foot five. I'm six inches taller.

The problem with this scenario is that my father does not have the temperament of a point guard. He's a conciliator and a negotiator. He's a lawyer specializing in negligence cases. He settles almost all of them. At the temple that he and my mom belong to, he's the president of the Men's Club. He also does comedy routines there. He has this Jewish-style sense of humor that can turn any tragic situation into a comedy routine.

When he was five years old, he came to the United States with his mother, father, grand-mother, older brother, Sol, and four other sisters and brothers. They came from a small town in the Ukraine called Romny.

"In 1905," he explains, "the Cossacks came through our village and murdered half the Jews. They promised to get the other half the next year. We had the feeling we weren't wanted there."

My grandfather traded a successful life as a lawyer and innkeeper in the Ukraine for one of economic misery in the U.S. I guess you could say that here he at least managed to stay alive—for a while, anyway. He couldn't practice law here, so he tried various businesses such as ink-making and fruit-peddling. All of these failed. His sister, my father's aunt, had a more transferable skill. She was a dentist, which was unusual for a woman at that time.

"He was in his early forties when he died," my father relates. "He took the easy way out. He had a stroke. Right in Aunt Sadie's dental chair. That was very bad for business. She never forgave him for that."

It occurs to me, almost like a revelation, that my father's older brother, Uncle Sol, would have made a perfect point guard. Why? What do point guards do? The job of a point guard is to run the offense, to make things happen. He probes the enemy's defenses, finds weaknesses in the seams. And then attacks. The ball whizzes around the perimeter, then inside, maybe back out, then maybe to a back-door cutter. Or maybe there's a deft pass on a pick and roll. Suddenly someone's wide open for a jump shot or a layup.

There are some problems with this scenario. Uncle Sol was shorter than my father. There have been some good five-foot-three point guards, but they tend to be wiry and can jump a ton. Uncle Sol was flabby, pear-shaped, and earthbound.

There's another problem. Uncle Sol never played basketball. He probably never had time. My grandfather, known to my second cousins as "the one who died young," left a wife and seven kids. Uncle Sol, as the oldest male child, had to quit school at the age of thirteen and go to work to help support the family. He had a tough life. He became an insurance salesman. My father says he was the best in New York, but Uncle Sol never seemed to have any money.

Basketball was still a relatively new sport then. My father's sports were tennis, handball, and baseball. When he was younger and much thinner, he was a track star. At the time he and my mother married, he was five foot five and one hundred twenty pounds. The prevailing philosophy at the time was that skinny people don't look prosperous. They look like they just got off the boat. So my mother "fattened him up." Even with the extra thirty-five pounds, he still moved around the tennis court really well.

Still only three guys, counting myself. I guess I'll stay another half-hour and then head for home. As soon as I made this decision, I saw a group of guys walking diagonally across the baseball field. They were obviously taking a shortcut to the Bedford Avenue exit of the schoolyard. Maybe we could convince three of them to play a three-on-three game.

I recognized one of the guys. It was Arnie Nelson. I hadn't seen him for seven years. Arnie was not a regular at the schoolyard, but when he did show up on the weekend with his friends, he and I would spend the time waiting for a game talking about economics and politics. I walked toward him to say hello and realized, to my surprise, that they were headed toward the basketball courts. To my further surprise, I knew all these guys. They were all Arnie's friends from high school. They'd had a reunion and decided to walk over to the schoolyard. There was Arnie, Al, Kent, Larry, Matt, and Jonathan. Rick Gross wasn't there but his kid brother, Robbie, was. Al started counting. We had exactly ten.

It was nice. We spent the next half-hour just shooting around and catching up on what we were doing these days. Arnie was working for the Fidelity Mutual Life Insurance Company. Larry had a job with an engineering firm. Kent was in a management training program. Al had just passed the bar exam. Matt had a job with Newsday out on Long Island, and Jonathan was working as a cab driver until he could find a better job.

Rick Gross had always been pretty close with these guys but couldn't make it today. He was a serious guy and I liked him. Robbie, who looked a lot bigger now, was, as a kid, short, fat, fussy, and generally unpleasant. He always wore a fatigue jacket at least two sizes too big for him. He still had this freckled, cherubic face. I asked him what he'd been up to.

"Just got out of the Marines," he said.

I think I registered the normal reaction: astonishment. "You were in the Marines?"

"Yep," he said, his face brightening. "Airborne too."

"Wow," I said. "Impressive."

During the shootaround I walked over to Arnie. "Was Robbie really in the Marines?" I asked.

"Hard to believe, isn't it," he said. "How about you? What have you been doing for the last seven years?"

"College, army, recovering from a busted romance, and trying to find a job."

"That might be the resume for most of us," he said. "Still looking for a job?"

"Just found one a month ago. A firm called Computational Consultants."

Arnie's face brightened. "Sounds like a great area."

"Good area, strange company. They're actually into publishing. Don't know a thing about computers."

"Still great," Arnie said.

"How about you?"

"I'm not sure about the insurance game," he said. "No one tells you anything. You have to find it out all by yourself."

"Don't they have training programs?"

"Useless," he replied. "They tell you how the business is supposed to work, not how it really works. But how about the romance? You over that?"

"Yes. In fact, I just met someone new."

"Promising?"

"Maybe. But there may be problems."

"What kind of problems?"

I didn't feel like talking about the problems.

•••

Bobbie and I attend Henry Grant's wedding in Englewood Cliffs, New Jersey. It's only our third date. Grant invited all four guys who went with him from Basic to Fifth Army Headquarters in Chicago. No one else showed. There's a huge crowd there. I know all of two people: Bobbie and the groom. That's twice as many people as Bobbie knows. It's not a problem for her. She's outgoing and vivacious. We find the large, round table to which we are assigned. The drinks are already poured. Some guy in a tuxedo lifts his glass and takes a sip. "Hmmm," he beams. "Manhattans." I'm studying the amber color of my drink when I see a slender, sleeveless arm a few inches from my glass. I thought Bobbie was talking to the woman on her right. "Are you going to drink that?" she asks. I notice her glass is empty. "Nah," I say. "Go ahead."

Bobbie is the only child of upper middle class parents who live in Memphis. Most people, especially adults, describe her as "cute as a button." She's also a stickler for etiquette. When I see her tilting her head back, holding her nose, and chug-a-lugging my drink, I almost burst out laughing. I don't have time to comment. "Let's dance," she says. En route to the dance floor, she deftly plucks another Manhattan from a tray-wielding hostess, chug-a-lugs that one, and replaces the glass on the tray before the hostess can get away. She has two more drinks after we get back to our table. She does not seem drunk. She just seems relaxed. But that's a lot of drinks in succession. As we drive back to her apartment, I want to say some-thing like, "Together we can fight this thing," but that seems totally incongruous—especially while she's contentedly sitting in the front seat of the car, scanning the entertainment section of the newspaper and planning what movie we should see tonight.

•••

"What kind of problems?" Arnie repeats.

This guy is tenacious. "Nothing serious," I smile. "She's rich."

"That's not a problem."

"Correction. Her father is rich."

"Still not a problem."

In elementary and high school, Arnie and his friends were a half-grade behind me, which seemed to have enormous significance at that time. That importance gradually declined until my senior year at high school. I decided I could finish in three-and-a-half years. Suddenly I was the equivalent of a year older than them and about to graduate in a few months.

Arnie and Larry were best friends. However, I do remember one afternoon at the school-yard when they got into a fight. Larry was a skinny kid; Arnie was bearlike. Confrontations at the schoolyard are not unusual. When it gets physical, other guys break it up. This time the onlookers couldn't figure out if it was physical. Until the two were separated, Larry was snarling, citing a litany of past wrongs, throwing combinations of rights and lefts. However, he was backing away; most of his punches were missing by at least a foot. Arnie was boring in, arms outstretched. It was hard to tell whether he wanted to reason with Larry or just crush him.

The atmosphere on this day was far more mellow. You know it's mellow when you try to make fair sides rather than shoot foul shots to determine the teams. Dan and Kent couldn't be on the same side because the other team wouldn't have any rebounding. The jump shooters, Al and I, had to be on different sides. Because of their bulk, Arnie and Matt were deemed power forwards. As I recalled, Robbie Gross wasn't particularly good at any position. However, we realized that after the Marines, he should have a lot of stamina, so he and Joe were placed on different sides. That left two guys as point guards: Larry and Jonathan.

The feeling was that these were remarkably fair sides. The teams were Dan, Al, Arnie, Jonathan, and Robbie against Kent, Matt, Larry, Joe, and myself. In a brief huddle Kent said he would stay outside on offense. He wanted to practice his outside shot. Besides, that would draw Dan away from the boards. No one but Kent thought this was a good idea.

I felt a little insulted that our opponents decided Arnie should guard me. As I ran down the court on our first offensive sequence, he followed a few steps behind, jabbering nonstop something I couldn't understand. Trash-talking was very unusual in a game like this, especially one that is essentially a reunion of old friends. When I got in the front court, I rubbed Arnie off on a pick, got a pass from Larry, started to drive, and still heard his voice.

"This policy is so good I think they're going to realize what they've done and withdraw it. This is really unbelievable. It's whole life insurance—the best kind."

I stopped and passed off to Matt. I couldn't figure out whether Arnie had gone nuts over the past seven years and was talking to himself, or he was talking to someone else. On our next trip down the court, he started in again.

"It not only pays dividends but interest on accumulated dividends. You can withdraw the dividends any time you want. And, if you need money, rather than cash in the policy, you can borrow against it at really low rates."

This time I tried to tune him out. Joe got me the ball in the high post. I faked left and Arnie went for it. I turned right, had real good elevation, and got off a soft, arcing shot. *Clang.* Off the back rim.

On offense Arnie was not a factor for his team. He'd shuffle and pivot in one position, still talking away.

"What do you think?" he asked as he got the ball and quickly passed off to Al.

"About what?" I asked, a little annoyed.

"This policy."

"Arnie, I may have aged a little in the army but I'm still very young. I don't need life insurance."

"That's the point. Life insurance is really just a side benefit. The real beauty about this policy is that it's a good investment."

Our next time on offense, I came around a double pick. Arnie was nowhere to be seen. However, I didn't get the pass. Arnie popped out from behind Kent and looked at me reproachfully.

"What's the matter?" I asked.

"I asked you how old you were."

I sensed a put-down. "Twenty-three," I said suspiciously.

"Twenty-three! That's perfect," he said as we started to run the other way. "Do you know what your annual premiums would be for a five-thousand-dollar policy? Ninety-two bucks a year. For whole life insurance."

True to his word, on offense Kent hovered around the outside, mostly in the right corner —about twenty feet from the basket. He had the ball and was alternately faking a shot and a drive. The problem was there was no one within ten feet of him. Dan was anchored under the basket, looking out in the direction of Kent, holding up a big hand as if he was waving good-bye to someone about to leave on a cruise. Finally Dan moved out a few feet. Kent was still alternately faking the drive and the shot. I slipped in behind Dan, and Kent got me the bounce pass. I didn't see Arnie but I could hear him. "Ninety-two bucks a year. In thirty years you'll have a five-thousand-dollar paid-up policy. And you won't have put in anything near that…" Al was racing over for weak-side help, but he was far too late. I put up a soft jumper off the board. It rolled around the rim, dipped into the basket, and popped out.

Matt was scoring a lot on garbage underneath. That was keeping us in the game. Larry called time out. Arnie, with a pencil and small pad, was right in the center of our huddle. Larry outlined his strategy for pulling out this game. "Look," Arnie said quietly to me, "you put in ninety-two dollars a year for thirty years. That's a total of two thousand, seven hundred sixty dollars. And you've got a paid-up five-thousand-dollar policy. Plus you get dividends each year and interest on those dividends." Kent and Matt leaned over to see what we were talking about.

"Nelson!" Larry exploded. "Get out of here."

Arnie motioned me to the periphery of the huddle. I suggested we talk about this later. Actually, I was getting pretty frustrated. This is a rinky-dink schoolyard game; I'm being defended by a lumbering insurance salesman who is much more interested in selling me a life insurance policy than in guarding me. And I can't score a goddamn point.

I've always felt that shooters have to shoot their way out of a scoring slump. Faithful to this philosophy, I proceeded to miss my next eight shots, the last of which was an uncontested fast-break layup. No one was within ten feet of me. The closest defender was Arnie, gasping for air, shouting something about surrender values.

I'm not sure what happened right after that. Something about surrender values seemed to click in my mind. The next thing I knew, I was at our foul line, right in Arnie's face. Kent and Al came over to intercede. They stopped, looking bewildered.

"Look, Arnie," I said furiously, "it sounds like a very good policy. I'll take one."

Arnie raised his eyebrows and backed up a step. "I think five thousand dollars would be the one you'd want. Give me your home address. I'll send you the application form tomorrow."

I felt certain that Arnie understood that this was not an unconditional surrender. Implicit in this transaction was his tacit agreement to keep his mouth shut about insurance policies for the rest of the game. Arnie demonstrated that he understood perfectly. He took a couple of deep breaths and started guarding me real closely. I hit three straight jump shots but it really didn't matter. The game was over. We were just going through the motions.

Robbie demonstrated his Marine Corps stamina by embarking on a series of one-man fast breaks. Joe was the only one on our team who could get back to defend. What had been an occasional exchange between Al and Larry as to exactly what the score was now began to involve everyone on the court.

"Do you agree," Al began, "that approximately five minutes ago you and I had a conversation about the score, and you stated that—"

"'Stated that'?" Larry interrupted. "What am I, on the witness stand?"

Behind Larry, Jonathan staggered to the sidelines and slumped down against the chain-link fence.

"I've had it," he said. "I haven't been getting enough sleep."

"All right," Larry said. "I'll sit out too. You guys can still play four-on-four."

Arnie sat down next to Jonathan. "I'm bushed," he said.

This was my cue to collapse against the fence.

"Maybe we should get going," Larry said.

Arnie looked at his watch. "Oh boy, you're right." He turned toward me. "So, Computational Consultants," he said approvingly. "Sounds like a winner."

I waved good-bye as Arnie and his friends trudged toward the East 24th Street exit. I headed toward the Bedford Avenue gate. Dan and Joe stayed to shoot some more baskets.

I never saw Arnie again, at least in the flesh. Twice I saw his image on television, making some analysis about the insurance industry.

As promised, the proposed policy and application arrived at my home three days later. I guess I could have backed out, claiming I agreed to take the policy under duress. But the policy sounded pretty good. I figured I'd check it out with my father.

The front porch of our house has some good and bad features. It's enclosed. It's a very bright room: there are sixteen windows. Those panes are a pain to keep clean. The room is not heated, so we can't use it in the winter.

But you can use the room right up to mid-November. It's a very pleasant room. That next Saturday afternoon, my father sat on the porch at the bridge table, glasses on the end of his nose, looking over the policy Arnie sent.

"It's a good policy," he said. "That is, if they pay the dividends they say they'll pay. The surrender values are lousy, but that's probably true of any policy you get at your age.

"You're at the perfect age to get life insurance," he said, a little wistfully, I thought. "The premiums are dirt cheap. What made you decide to get it now?"

I told him the story of the basketball game. My father smiled, putting his hands behind his head and leaning back in his chair.

"The kid shows promise," he said, sounding like a basketball scout evaluating a high-school prospect. "Of course, the best insurance salesman in New York was your Uncle

Sol. Not that he ever got rich from it. He had too many other problems. He was an alcoholic and a diabetic—not a good combination. He was also in a state of denial over both those conditions.

"One day he went into a diabetic coma. Aunt Ruth was frantic. She didn't know what to do. She called the police. They sent a squad car over, and they dumped him in the back seat.

"On the way to the hospital, Sol regained consciousness and saw the cops in the front seat. He immediately tried to sell them a policy.

"'Look,' he said, 'how much life insurance do you guys have? Not much, I suspect. Listen, you could be me. And you guys have a dangerous job. I bet you're both married with young kids. Am I right?'

"The cops looked at each other and nodded in agreement. They each took out a large policy."

I'd heard this story before, but I didn't remember the end. Was this the time Uncle Sol died or was it later?

"Did Uncle Sol make it?" I asked.

"That's just what I was thinking when I went to the hospital that evening. Will he make it? They had Sol in intensive care. Surprisingly, they didn't have too many tubes in him—just an intravenous line. He was lying on his back, eyes closed. He was a little more pale than usual. But, you know, he has that high color, so he actually didn't look that bad.

"For a few minutes I just sat by the side of his bed, looking at him. Then he turned toward me, opened his eyes, lifted up the side of his pillow, and showed me a bottle of scotch he had there.

"By now I was really confused. I went looking for his doctor. I found him by the nurses' station.

"'Doc,' I said, 'give it to me straight. I can take it. How bad is my brother?'

"'Mr. Danielson,' he said, 'there are three hundred patients in this hospital. Your brother is the sickest of all of them.'"

When I hear this story, I don't know whether to laugh or cry. When faced with this dilemma, I usually laugh. It's a shaking-your-head-in-disbelief type of laughter. Maybe it's the way the story is told—that combination of irreverence and sincerity. Uncle Sol's death two days later seems almost out of context.

The story ends and I've got work to do. Lately, I've taken some freelance writing jobs to make a few extra bucks. They pay only $50 each, but I can knock off an article in about three hours. I've got one due on Monday.

My father takes the newspaper and turns to the bankruptcies page. "Let's see who failed," he says thoughtfully. The story ends but the show continues.

When I start up the stairs to my room, the sadness sets in. Once, at my grandmother's house, in one of the rare somber moments between joke-telling at those family gatherings, I heard Uncle Sol tell his brothers that he never got over the death of his daughter. I've seen the grave at our family plot. It's got a small, sorry-looking headstone. The lettering is eroded like the stone was from the previous century. She died when she was six years old. It's hard to imagine my cousins Dave and Jeffrey with an older sister. Jeffrey is my sister Greta's age, but Dave, six years older than them, seems incredibly removed from my sphere. And Sol's daughter would be two years older than Dave.

Sometimes I get these episodes after Dad's stories. But the sadness doesn't last long. I have the feeling that for him, the pain is much more intense.

In the middle of winter, three months after I mailed in my first premium, I got a call from Ronald Riddick of Fidelity Mutual. Arnie had been promoted out of sales, and Riddick was taking over all of his accounts. Riddick wanted to stop by my home, just to introduce himself.

Although I was still a novice as a life-insurance owner, I immediately recognized this as an attempt to sell me more insurance. I was not exactly averse to this idea. After all, I'd just gotten a five-dollar-per-week raise and had already received two checks, admittedly small, for my first two freelance articles.

I thought Riddick might want to stop by my office during lunch hour. He might even enjoy the socioeconomic discussions that occurred daily around the bar of the cramped lunchroom. Since no one except management could afford to go to a restaurant for lunch, we always had a pretty good crowd of brown-baggers.

Ironically, even though every one of the debaters was mired at the lowest rung of the wage-earning ladder, the discussions usually involved the majority railing against all government programs except unemployment insurance.

Riddick politely declined my invitation to show up at work. I wondered if he was familiar with the environment at Computational Consultants. More likely his training course recommended making the pitch in the cozy comfort of the client's home. I told him to come over on a Saturday afternoon. It did occur to me that Uncle Sol and Arnie would not have operated in this way.

Riddick was about six foot three and two hundred fifty pounds. Fidelity Mutual seemed to like beefy insurance salesmen. It was far too cold to sit on the porch. In the semi-darkness of my parents' living room, he went through a scripted routine of why I should increase my coverage. First, he said, at my age insurance was dirt cheap. That was true. My father had said the same thing. But, for some reason, my sales resistance hackles were up. He said that should I need money, for a wedding, for example, borrowing against an insurance policy was the cheapest way to obtain cash. This was also true. However, Bobbie and I were currently drifting away from matrimony rather than toward it. Finally he asked if I could increase my coverage by $2,000 since he could really use the extra commissions.

At least he was honest. Under any other circumstances, I would have felt sorry for the guy. I got up, shaking my head.

"This is not in the tradition of Uncle Sol and Arnie."

He looked confused. "Do you think your Uncle Sol might consider buying a policy?"

"Maybe two years ago, but very unlikely at this time," I said, walking toward the door. "But you might want to see Arnie, as a potential mentor rather than as a customer."

What would Uncle Sol and Arnie advise? It would certainly not be to say, "Please buy this policy as a favor to me." Maybe it would be something like, "Find out your client's weakness. Confront him in an environment conducive to exploiting that weakness. Then attack. Attack, attack, attack."

Douglas Cole

Memoriam in A-Flat Minor

News came—Bruce had died. It was not shocking news. He had battled Big Death in his bones for the last three years, coming out victorious in that fragile way a war survivor emerges with radiant clarity and eyes that glow. No fooling around anymore, not that he was a fool-around type. He was a shaggy-headed Bostonian with a big Irish laugh and jazz love and basketball handler's hands and an ivy league memory. Stories of scholarship rides and semi-pro days. But he knew and we all knew he'd entered the land of borrowed time. But happy. Outwardly. Hit by occasional, weird side effects and glancing blows: thyroid went out, he lost much weight, a snap of the femur. He rolled around in a wheelchair for a while. But happy at least to be in the world. His favorite riddle: "What do you get when you throw a piano down a mineshaft?" He was even still ambitious to go up the administrative stream. A good soul, if anyone can judge.

A heart attack. That was it. Magnificent. Just allow that for a moment. If you think about it—the prospects? We never spoke of the possibilities, but I imagine and imagine I'm pretty close that he'd had a few dread dark nights looking down the barrel of his own imagination at tubes and hospital bed and withering limbs and fading air and languishing nightmare—but instead, heart attack. I thought he'd hit the lottery. I envied him. What a death!

Still, there were those of us who were stunned to get the news. Death, even most inevitable, still comes as a surprise to some people.

•••

Testimonials at the funeral captured bits and pieces of the man. But how dead the room was even full of people. The green carpet of the foyer as some kind of cold pastoral. The perfect blond wood of the chairs. The purple upholstery of the benches—a space so generically non-denominational, hinting in its tilted way towards church synagogue and maybe mosque—floor-to-ceiling windows along one wall and a Zen garden on the other side with koi pond and stone pedestals and paperbark maples dripping with rain. Up front the casket with body, and I caught the glimpse of his profile there.

Here are my colleagues, Bruce's friends and family. I took a spot in the back near esoteric Steve with his phlegmatic heavy brow and eyes of authorial intent. I placed my hands on my knees. The speaking began.

Good Man
Good Husband
Smart
PhD
Athlete
Jazz Buff

Those labels hit the air, coming like cartoon anime arrows through a buzzing fly-cloud of miasmatic black stuff. Somewhere, it slipped into a talk-show routine, microphone going around to sincere leaden student remembrances saying how much they learned from him, tears whipped away with the edge of a finger. Family members, gratitude, moments caught in flight. I was pretty sure I'd never draw a crowd this big.

I was slipping into a different space—rain drops out the window were bouncing on the pond—one two three—boom!—diminishing with each landing and leaving their reverberations on the surface—wonder. How had I missed that before?

...I remember working at the radio station with him and he was always smiling and I thought he was interested but he never asked me out until I took another job...

Then I was looking down at my feet as more memory unspooled itself. What is an eggshell doing here on the ground near my toe? Who put that there? How does it arrive?

...Jokes, more jokes, he could list them off alphabetically, and operas and TV shows...

The eggshell—I picked it up. It was just big enough to fit on the tip of my finger like a little helmet. And look, you, see how its smooth white surface is really quite rough, how going deeper reveals it's really a lace of spongy ropes like a ball of rubber bands—rich and strange.

...and my favorite...Beethoven's last movement...

And the minister said in his sanguine voice: a man known for his humor, his generosity, his dedication to teaching...

All true. You can say just about anything about a person and it's true. At some point—some point—everyone shows humor, generosity—and their opposites. But to be known for one particular aspect? How much did you have to have to be known for it? Where is my heart in all of this? In us. Of us. Maybe I'm only talking about myself—there is no progression without contraries.

I see it as that light in the basement of my grandmother's house. She's been gone a long time. She straddled three centuries. Family from the old country. They had tickets on a great liner that went down, but they missed it. Missed it! Those tickets hung around in hope chests for years like entry to a theater of ghosts. The next ship carried them and they plucked the survivors out of the constellation of bloated white bodies floating in the void. And it hung around her—that sense, that feeling that disaster averted had disaster to pay. And after that everyone around her died: both parents when she was young—mother by a mis-filled prescription, father nobly in a streetcar accident stepping back to allow two ladies to board before him, though he was known as a con man, brilliant but devious and always on the run from the police...stepmother who hanged herself in madness, goiter bulging from her neck... first husband drowned...she wondered if there was some kind of curse. Who wouldn't be superstitious about that? You could see it in her eyes for years and years she made herself iron hard working nights as a nurse to take care of her two children—add into that my drunken Irish grandfather she married thinking the children needed a father, who was a dashing man at the time with well-heeled family—he owned a warehouse at the city market that carried produce and was making money hand over fist as they said then—then she had my mother—and he slipped or revealed his weakness for drink and came home nights falling blind drunk in the yard broke-broken after a few years—so my sister was her favorite was herself carbon copy sent down the line of life, you see how it works?—she had shot her choleric energetic epigram deep into my sister's code and I could see it unfolding year after year as she violently staco-stabbed at perfection on her violin playing and triumphed in school mathematics and athletics—that iron will directly transferred through some hidden intent—my uncle and his first son my cousin were two fragments of her beloved first husband—and I—I was a fragment of the lout the ne'er-do-well drunk fool evil loser and her glare let me know it at every thanksgiving dinner as I watched The Wizard of Oz looking back and forth between the wicked witch of the west and her and knowing my grandmother was far more scary—then—the—you see because she outlived herself she outlived those patterns—lived long enough to lose its visceral meaning and become like the cards she played solitaire with so worn you couldn't see the numbers those years we played double solitaire and on the few occasions I won she'd say no one likes a cheater—then—the—she looked blinking and smiling into the dusty rays of afternoon light while she swept her sidewalk those memories still there but hollowed out like shadows so far away her heart was pure if you can believe it and her spirit was clean and fresh inside the husk of the old body and occasionally some mad person from the neighborhood—we never discovered who—descended on her in her near deaf blindness and slapped her hard and set her ear bleeding and screamed at her—die you old crone die!

...a man known for his intelligence and wit...

I see that light in her basement and I avoid the basement and that energy balled up like rotgut anger and fear and poisonous ether stuff it's like even going near it sets my nervous system in grind and yet and yet I know I have to do it and so I go right into it right into the heart of it yes I do yes and ah really truly ah it just flat-out evaporates like a melancholy exhale and is gone and I am standing there in nothing now because what it was is just an echo and a ball of psychic laundry left behind gone now and good and she was gone before that anyway so maybe it was just my own.

Anything you say about a person is true. Just as anything we don't say about a person is true. Who said I contain multitudes? Who said I am legion? Who said therefore I contradict myself?

And now the service was over. So much easier to be among you all in a ritual, a ceremony, however broken sterile packaged, rather than mill about trying to think of something to say.

Hey...

And I hugged my friend Phebe. Gave that sad smile to Roger. Stood among the colleagues.

We getting together at Lila's?

Who's going to head up to Marianne's next week to help with the yard?

Food schedule?

Yeah, meet at Lila's.

OK.

I know...I know...it's going to be rough for a while...

I don't know, we'll have to talk about that later...

Who needs a ride?

Roger with his porkpie hat, bird-furtive Cindy, rock of all ages Jed, Midwest solid and practical Sheri. Why was Karen glaring at me? Why does that look say she wishes I were dead?

I've got to get out of here. I've got to get out of these dead rooms. That casket over there with Bruce's gray face—God, the weight of that space, that black hole gravity—he's gone and in his leaving is a vortex like a sinking ship taking those free-floating bodies down with it—goodbye sad prince.

I made it to my vehicle and immediately took several blasts to get my balance. The gray world of the gray day. Light rain gray on my windshield. People filing out and driving away. Cherry blossoms plucked from the trees and wet-pressed like little flat faces on the glass. And as I leaned back, I could see the innumerable great black carbon bowling balls of infinite space all lined up in the sky above and hanging in the elastic steel threads of the vast spider web—raindrops bouncing and diminishing, bouncing and diminishing—sound waves moving on.

Part Two: Lila's Bar and Grille

Lila's is a great place for enlightenment, because if you can't escape the dream, go deeper into it. Harold and Edgar are going head to head on the issue of time.

Edgar: Einstein said you can only go back, never forward.

Harold: The other way around.

Edgar: I'm pretty certain about that.

Harold: Even so, if you can break the time barrier at all, why would there be any limitations?

Edgar: Mathematics, man. It's gotta work out in the math, or it won't hold.

Harold: Math is just a symbol set, too.

Edgar: Combined with the scientific method, though, it's pretty sound.

Harold: The finger pointing at the moon...

Nothing as it seems...the taxidermied fox, the Jesus with eyes that follow you. Even those shuffleboard players are phantom shadows—out back a secret courtyard in the rain where the dead congress like golfers in the lounge after the eighteenth hole to boast about handicaps and lie about the score. Hey, Bruce—I knew you; I didn't know you. Did you have a good world when you died? Enough to base a movie on?

Marcia—hey, Marcia, I said. She gave me that big body embrace. What a warm soul. I think that, at least. What do I know? She's the head of the philosophy department. She knows. She knows how to deconstruct those assumptions!

Good to see you, she said, and sad, though...sad.

I was having a hard time locating my emotion on this. So I said, I know. Ironic, isn't it?

I hardly see you anymore, she said.

Well, you escaped to the Fine Arts building. Who do you see?

No one...

And you teach mostly afternoons, right?

That's true.

So...

Yeah...

I didn't mean to interrogate her. It sounded like an interrogation as I replayed it in my head. How often was I playing a role no one recognized? I thought it was all pretty obvious kabuki. Or No.

Old people. We sound like old people, now. Ah, Marcia...you're looking older, grayer, heavier with time and gravity. I have no idea what to make of it. Where is the moon?

You know, I said, I often think of that weekend we stayed with you out at Ragsdale's place...

He loved you guys.

He was amazing. What a life. And what a place!

That was in another country, and besides...another life! Another marriage. My young son. What a crazy, ramshackle place old Rags had made—out of driftwood, scrap wood, found pieces, woodstove, collectables he'd accumulated, not one straight line, not one square angle, ramps up to loft rooms, ratty wood-bare out-cabins on sticks over the water—his stories of the news days, covering political upheavals, changing of the guard, regimes shuffling, waves of change, celebrities, world beat, madness, truth beauty—old school newsman (look up the old footage and you'll see him there in the background, taking it all down) then in his Xanadu compound of piece by piece castle domain on the island shore—Marcia's old friend, she brought us into the fold, my ex, my son and me—a lifetime ago, another name, another reality—Marcia, my old friend, here and now, fading as we go, Ragsdale out on the secret patio with the lords, the ghost crew—

Another whiskey, please...

God, the server's arm is smooth and those tattoos—a line for every lover, a star for every year in recovery. Did I linger too long in my admiration? Did I fall in love and lose my way?

Nash, there, moving in slow motion. He's got a time-frame of his own. We're surrounded by things we can't see, he sees. He sees grass lifting leaves. He sees ivy slithering up a tree. He sees the fried rose and the slime molds on the move—decades of dates logged in for your perusal.

Why is Karen glaring at me and looking down at her machine?

Whatcha doin? I said across the universe.

I didn't know ignoring could be so violent.

Jeb appears—hey, he said, how are you doing? I don't know why he looked so worried.

I live in the slime and the muck of the dark age, I said. He laughed. Jeb always laughs. My good friend, my colleague, maybe the only one who still gets the sacred geometry:

ASA

NISI

MASA

You okay, he said. You look a little...

Ah, I said, to all my friends... And I lifted a glass to no one in particular, then leaned into him and said, by cock's crow thrice will you deny me...

He laughed. He always laughs.

I'm just trying on reality, I said.

You might want to be careful...

What? Now? Now? I'm burning off the deception!

You're not planning on driving, are you?

And I thought, oh...it's come to this? So, I thought, then said, Only bison over the cliff.

He laughed.

And ignorance, materialism, hypocrisy, the black fog—vas is los? Look you—And I pointed to old Phil who most mornings could be found at the Bauhaus composing notes in his leather ledger of cosmic music for his self-made instrument that resembled a parch-ment. There he was now walking—I saw him once at the Good Shepard Center performing his compositions so complex and cascading they seemed simple and I'm not sure I could really hear them as much as—out there now in the rain, lotus flowers springing up from every step.

Seriously, are you okay?

Wine is proof that god loves us and wants us to be happy.

He laughed.

My colleagues there, the remaining few, spread out at the table like the disciples at the last supper, and me—I'm no Jesus, nor was meant to be—But I'm entering the resurrection just the same, here at Lila's, where the old men sitting in the periphery look out through their eyes and the spiders spin their webs from elbow to hand and back again, those sinister little gods!

John Danahy

A Kiss to Build a Dream on

I can't get used to the empty bed in the morning. After a scotch at night, I fall asleep quickly so I don't focus on being alone. But I reach for her when I wake, and she's not there. She won't ever be there. As I boil the water for tea in her kitchen, I think of how much I miss Carmen.

The headline in the *Gazette* jarred me out of my early morning doldrums: MAN FOUND DEAD IN HOUSE OF GLASS. Succinct as always, the *Gazette* relayed the unadorned facts. At approximately nine thirty Monday night, the body of James Hemple, an employee, age thirty-one, was discovered in the lower level of a local shop, the House of Glass. The exact cause of death was not yet known, but foul play was suspected.

I retired three years ago as captain of the Homicide Squad, but the old excitement of a murder case pumped through me now. I hadn't felt so alive since my wife died. I realized what I'd been denying since I retired—I missed being a cop.

And this case—this was a lot more than the curiosity of a retired cop. As a customer of the shop, I'd known Jim Hemple casually. I wanted to find out who killed him. And I wanted to know if Hemple's death had anything to do with the Mackinaw *Mushrooms*.

While browsing in the House of Glass last week, I'd spotted a particularly beautiful piece: red and brown mushrooms rendered against a background of brilliant, sunshine-colored rippled glass. The distinctive colors, delicate shapes, and smooth flow of the lines in the foreground were extraordinary.

"What can you tell me about the mushrooms?" I asked Jim Hemple. His tiny, globular black eyes peered out through wire-rimmed glasses, so he always appeared suspicious.

"What mushrooms?" he said. He fidgeted with a glass box, then almost dropped it as he slid it under the counter.

"The stained glass piece leaning against the back wall in the other room."

"It's not for sale."

"Oh? Why not?"

"It's, uh, it's on consignment." He turned as if he wanted to rush away.

"Then it is for sale. How much is it?"

"Look, I'm busy right now." He headed quickly down the basement steps.

Even as I shrugged off the incident, Jim's reaction bothered me. How would merchandise be on consignment and not be for sale, and why would the shop take merchandise on consignment when they hadn't in the past? Was Jim trying to make money under the table? Nothing pointed to wrongdoing, but why was he so nervous?

Retirement affords me the time to indulge my whims, so the next day I spent a few hours in the library looking through craft books and magazines until I found a picture of the piece. Done by Ian Mackinaw, a Welsh artist and sculptor, it was called *Mushrooms*. Part of a private collection, the piece was not quite of museum quality, but would command a higher price than merchandise commonly carried at the shop. I wondered how it had found its way to the House of Glass.

The next day I returned to the shop. *Mushrooms* wasn't in the back room where I'd seen it, so I browsed around. As far as I could tell, the piece was gone. I asked the other clerk, Felicity Ward, if it had been sold.

Mrs. Ward has bright red hair, a ruddy complexion, and dark green eyes. In her early forties and of average height for a woman, she appears to be fifty pounds or so overweight and, as on that day, often wears clothing that calls attention to her large bosom and ample hips.

"I'm not sure," she replied. "I don't think I've seen it."

Jim wasn't working that day, so I didn't get to ask him about it. Now I never would.

•••

Carmen and I were regular customers at the House of Glass. Since her death, I've continued to visit the shop and have become friends with the owner, Edna Burwick. Perhaps it's because she's a widow, or maybe because she's stirred within me some semblance of longing I thought I'd never feel again. Edna listens patiently when I need to talk about Carmen, or about my years on the force, but in spite of my tenuous attempts to bridge the distance between us, she maintains it. I can't even get her to call me Ira instead of Mr. Steinberg. Edna is ten years younger than me, and I don't have the nerve to express my feelings. I feel guilty about Carmen, I guess, and I feel like a foolish old man yearning after a younger woman. Mostly, I can't bear the thought of being spurned.

As I read of the killing in Edna's shop, my protective instincts bubbled and boiled—along with a faint ray of hope. I've been a cop all my life, and in that time I've helped hundreds of people. If I could help Edna, see her through this, maybe she'd think of me as more than a lonely, sixty-three-year-old widower.

•••

When Captain Patrick O'Rourke, the C.O. of the Homicide Squad, had been a beat cop fresh out of the academy, I'd been the desk sergeant at the Twenty-First Precinct. O'Rourke had treated me well since then, repaying the many favors I'd done for him and the interest I'd taken in his career. When I asked to see the file on the Hemple killing, he smiled.

"Old horse can't get out of the harness?"

"I knew the victim, or at least I've talked with him in the glass shop. Let's say I'm curious."

"That's good enough for me, Ira. I was just studying the pictures of the crime scene." O'Rourke handed me a stack of color enlargements.

Jim Hemple's body lay facedown, a pool of blood encircling his head. The contents of an overturned table were strewn around the floor, as if he had grabbed the table while falling. Bits and pieces of glass of every size lay scattered on and around the body.

"The M.E. puts the cause of death as a blow to the back of the head from a sharp instrument," O'Rourke said as I looked through the pictures.

"What kind of instrument?"

"Like a chisel maybe: trapezoidal, sharp, and very narrow. Something with significant mass."

"Hmm. Time of death?"

"Between eight thirty and nine thirty. Probably closer to eight thirty, based on the degree of rigor."

"Anything stolen?"

"The owner, uh, a Mrs. Edna Burwick, says she'll do a complete inventory, but it looks like nothing is missing. And no unexplained latents, no indication of a break-in or an intruder, no physical evidence of any kind."

"Any connection with the person who found him?"

"A tourist killing time while his wife spent his money in another shop. But we did find a few interesting details about the victim."

O'Rourke paused, waiting for me to pry it out of him. I kept silent for a few moments, but finally gave in.

"Well?" I asked. "What did you find out?"

"Hemple dropped out of Lombard, a small, private college back East, only seven months from graduation. He was asked to leave by the campus police, who suspected he'd helped himself to drugs from the infirmary. Also, he and several friends were picked up a few times for suspected marijuana use. No formal charges were filed, though, and he has no record since college."

"I'd never have pegged him as a drug user."

"The shop owner came up clean. What do you know about her?"

I wondered if O'Rourke was baiting me, if he knew I was friendly with Edna.

"She's a pleasant woman, friendly and efficient in running the shop, and a skillful hand with stained glass."

"That's all?" O'Rourke asked. "Goddamn it, Ira."

"Edna got married right out of high school and stayed that way for almost thirty years," I added. "Seven years ago she lost her husband to cancer."

A question formed on O'Rourke's face, but he looked down at his desk, avoiding my eyes.

"Yes," I said, "like Carmen. Edna took it hard, very hard. Now she's alone, and at that awkward age for a woman."

"Awkward? You mean turning fifty?"

"No. Actually, I think she's fifty-three. I mean still attractive, but old enough so the lines and sags are public knowledge."

I remembered how hard it had been on Carmen, when both youth and old age stared simultaneously back at her from the mirror. She had struggled to hold on to what she had been, and I sensed Edna was in lonely, solitary combat with the same demons.

"When her husband died," I continued, "she was devastated, emotionally and financially. She worked hard and built her business from scratch, without any training or experience. She's not well-off, but it gives her satisfaction and it pays the bills."

"You think she'd have anything to do with dealing drugs from the shop?"

"That's way off base," I said, shaking my head vigorously.

"You seem to know a lot about her."

When I didn't rise to his bait, he asked, "What about the other clerk? Mrs. Ward, I think."

"I don't know much about her." I smiled at the mental picture I had of Felicity—a gaudy, fleshy flower.

"We ran a routine check on her," O'Rourke said, "and turned up several domestic beefs. Black-and-whites were called to her house a few times to break up family squabbles that got out of hand."

"She doesn't seem the type who'd stand for abuse from her husband."

"People are full of surprises. Got anything else?"

I paused. Jim Hemple's reaction to *Mushrooms* proved nothing. His background wasn't spotless, but that didn't necessarily mean anything, either. Before I revealed my suspicions about *Mushrooms,* I needed more hard facts.

"No," I said. "Mind if I ask a few questions, check a few details?"

"Okay, Ira, but keep me posted. Personally."

"Is Reardon still the in-charge at Robbery?"

"What the hell does Reardon have to do with this? This is a homicide case. My case."
"Oh, just want to say hello, that's all."

"Look," O'Rourke admonished, shaking his finger in my direction, "you've got no official status. You can snoop around, but I want to know exactly what you're doing, and I don't want you to get in our way."

"There was a time when you'd have been grateful for my help," I groused.

"I don't need your crap on this, Steinberg, and you know it. Let me do my job, and if you can help along the way, I'll be damned grateful."

"Thanks," I said, grinning.

"And for Christ's sake, remember you're not wearing a badge, and you're not carrying a piece."

"How could I forget?" I walked out of his office quickly, headed for my next appointment.

• • •

Over coffee at the Metro Cafe, a greasy spoon a block from the precinct house that's a regular stop for beat cops coming off their shifts, I learned more than I had hoped from Marty Reardon.

During the investigation of a series of break-ins of private residences over the last year, his unit had become convinced they were dealing with a ring that had a pipeline for the distribution and sale of stolen property. The ring specialized in art objects, crafts, and antiques. The stolen items were professional, one-of-a-kind pieces—expensive, but not highest-ticket museum quality, which would attract more attention.

"These guys know their stuff," Reardon said as he passed me the case file. The waitress poured him a half cup of black coffee, which he topped with milk and measured in five heaping teaspoons of sugar.

"How do you stand it so sweet?" I asked.

"Can't stand it at all. It's the sugar I'm after."

The case file was half a foot thick. I skimmed through a few inches before stopping dead. The Mackinaw *Mushrooms* jumped at me from the list of property taken in a break-in two months ago.

"Have you cross-checked for a connection between the victims?"

"You think we're brain dead since you retired, Ira? Some of the victims were widows, but there were no connections. Other than that, nothing panned out."

Martin Reardon had eighteen years on the force, the last seven as commander of the Robbery detail. He knew his job, and I had no business questioning his thoroughness.

"Sorry," I said. "Old habits, Marty. Second-guessing everyone."

"Forget it," he replied with a shrug.

"So you have nothing?"

"Why are you so interested in this case?"

"I'm just an old cop scratching an itch."

Reardon studied my face, gauging the lie. I wasn't ready to tip my hand to him, though, as O'Rourke would surely find out. I finished my coffee and got up.

"It's on me this time." I flipped a five on the counter and walked away.

•••

After leaving Reardon, I went to the House of Glass to speak with Edna. As I went down the basement stairs, I saw her slicing a square of glass with a Raven cutter. I thought it odd she wasn't using the distinctive Fletcher cutter she normally used.

Edna looked girlish and unsullied in tight jeans and a starched white cotton shirt. Her chestnut hair gleamed, and her face was radiant. Visible under the partially unbuttoned shirt, her breasts rose and fell gently with each breath.

After exchanging hellos and expressing my sorrow about Jim, I asked a few questions. She answered without hesitation, telling me when she'd hired Jim, his previous employer, and the names he'd listed on his application as personal references. When I asked her what time she'd left her shop the night of the murder, her face froze.

"Why are you questioning me about this, Mr. Steinberg?" Normally soft and full, her voice quivered with anger. "I thought we were friends."

"We are friends. I'm trying to help."

She studied my eyes. I had the feeling she was wondering how much to tell me, or whether to talk to me at all.

"Edna, please. Our friendship means a lot to me, and if my digging into this case bothers you, I'll drop it."

A breeze blew in the window, carrying the smell of baking bread and the sounds of muffled voices from the bakery next door. Several strands of hair blew across her forehead, and her expression softened. She put the cutter down and reached for my hand.

"I guess this whole thing has upset me more than I realized," she said. "I'm grateful for your help—Ira." Her lips parted slightly with the beginnings of a smile.

My other hand covered hers, and my heart began to beat faster than makes sense at my age.

"No more questions, for now," I said. "If you feel up to it later, perhaps we can finish this, say, over coffee."

"Deal," she replied, and agreed to meet me at three that afternoon at a nearby coffee shop.

•••

Over steaming cappuccino with whipped cream and nutmeg, Edna related the events of the night of the murder. I could see she was nervous, so I held her hands to soothe her anxiety, or so I told myself. She looked even more beautiful than at her shop, and she seemed more attentive than she'd ever been. A young couple at the next table stole a few glances at us, but I didn't care. I tried hard not to break the mood with an awkward question.

Jim and Felicity had been scheduled to work until nine thirty that night, closing time. Edna had been doing paperwork since lunch and had developed a nagging headache. When she left the shop at seven thirty, Jim and Felicity were both waiting on customers. She went straight home, took a hot bath, and was in bed by nine.

Done with questions, we lingered over coffee another half hour; then I walked her to her car. After saying good night, I turned to leave. She touched my shoulder, stepped toward me, and kissed me gently on the cheek. Walking toward my car, my heart and mind racing with excitement, I realized I didn't care that I had learned very little about the case.

•••

"I've already told the police everything I know," said Felicity Ward. She pressed her fists against her ample hips and pursed her full lips. Her breasts, struggling against the low-cut dress she wore, were as rosy as her cheeks. When I had told her I had no official status and was merely trying to satisfy my curiosity, she eyed me as if I were a zoo creature whose origin she couldn't quite place.

"What time did you leave the shop that night?" I asked.

She rubbed her lips together several times, then arched her eyebrows sharply. "Around eight."

"Oh? Did Jim often close the shop by himself?"

"How should I know?"

"You worked with him three nights a week."

She gulped a deep breath and held it, like a pearl diver preparing for a dive.

"He did close alone once in a while," she said. "So did I. It was foolish for both of us to be there when there were no customers."

"Did you go home when you left the shop?"

"That really is none of your business."

Her breathing became more rapid, as if she were struggling for air. A bit embarrassed, I averted my eyes from her heaving chest.

"No, it isn't," I said, "and I appreciate your patience. You've been very cooperative. Could you answer just a few more questions? It would certainly help a great deal."

She emitted an elephantine sigh. A customer on the other side of the shop appraised us both, then turned back to a glass butterfly he was admiring.

"I stopped for a drink, if you must know," Felicity said. "At the Boar's Head Pub."

"One last thing," I said, deciding to press my luck a bit further. "Mrs. Burwick told us she left at seven thirty, and I was wondering—"

"No, she didn't," Felicity interrupted. "Edna left a few minutes after six thirty. I know because when I got back from supper, we, ah, had a few words, and she left right after that."

"Words?"

"That old prude and I had another argument about my clothing." She hunched her shoulders and tilted toward me, exhibiting her cleavage. "You don't mind the way I dress, do you?"

I glanced away and cleared my throat, wondering how or if I should answer. "Thank you for your help, Mrs. Ward," I said, then turned away quickly and left the shop.

•••

Something about Felicity's story nagged at the edge of my consciousness, so I decided to tail her. At seven thirty that night, waiting in my car a block from the shop, I spotted her as she came out the front door and strode quickly up the street. When she stepped into an alleyway that led to the next street, I lost her.

Turning my car onto the parallel street, I saw her getting into a red convertible, some sort of English model. As she shifted back and forth, adjusting her body, the driver kissed her playfully on the cheek. When she had settled into the seat, she turned to him and kissed him full on the mouth. The driver shifted into gear and sped off, too fast for me to follow. But with glasses, my eyes are almost what they were twenty years ago, and I jotted down the plate before I lost sight of the car.

I drove back to my house, phoned headquarters, and asked to have the plate run.

•••

Felicity and the man in the red convertible occupied my thoughts as the phone rang the next morning. The desk sergeant on days, Al Goldstein, had picked up the DMV sheet from the night shift. Al and I go way back, and he knew I'd want it right away.

"Are you up to something on this?" Al asked.

"You know me better than that," I answered.

"Yeah, I know you. I know you good. Got a pencil?"

"Shoot."

"Ninety-two red MG convertible. Registered to Mr. Austin Cloud, age thirty-two, apartment 3F, 1904 Brick Hill Road."

"Okay. I got it. Any wants and warrants, or priors?"

"You asked to have the plate run, not get the guy's life history."

"We both know you never ran a plate in your life that you didn't check the outstandings and priors." I could hear him breathing softly into the receiver, probably waiting for me to make the next move. "I'll owe you one for this."

"It's on the house," he said and chuckled. "Besides, I figure you've still got some of my markers."

"This'll clean the sheet."

"Your boy has a past," Al began, "going back to his college days at one of them snotty places back East. Him and his playmates were tumbled a few times for smoking weed. And he was politely asked to leave before graduation—something about missing drugs."

"What was the name of the college?"

"Uh, it's here somewhere. Lombard College. But there's more. The Bunko boys have him near the top of their list of gigolos who prey on little old ladies. Austin's a pretty boy who specializes in widows. He flashes his smile, and who knows what else, then bilks the admiring women out of whatever isn't tied down."

"Does Bunko have anything solid?"

"None of the victims will talk. Bunko thinks he threatens them after he gets the goodies. A real charmer, your boy. Oh, yeah, and one more thing. Bunko says he's got a kink—a letch for fat broads—the fatter the better."

"He singles them out to victimize?"

"Kink, I said. He bilks the old ladies for money. The fat ones he shtupps for fun."

•••

The Boar's Head was modeled after an English pub, with authentic furnishings and a bartender, Adam Tierney, to match. In a thick British accent, he welcomed me back to the pub after my long absence, then cursed me for my repugnant habit of ordering American beer. I hadn't been at the Boar's Head since Carmen died, but it looked the same. Men were gathered around tables drinking dark beer and ale from thick mugs, while the booths in the back were filled with couples who looked as if they were meeting clandestinely. Two college-age men were throwing darts. Pipe and cigar smoke hung in the air like fog over a warm bay.

After he served my beer, I asked Adam if Felicity had been in the pub Monday night.

"She came in that night a mite after eight," Adam said, "and ordered her usual. Waiting for someone, she was, but he never showed up. She left around eight thirty."

"He?"

"Her regular mate. At least once a week they're here, more often most weeks."

"Can you describe him?"

"I could, yes, but his name's Austin Cloud."

"Anything about your customers you don't know?" I asked with a smile.

"I'm not knowing why you're so interested in these two star-crossed lovers, especially since I told all of this to the police. Retired, aren't you?"

I took a sip of my beer, ignoring his question. "Are they always alone?"

"Another man joins them once in a while, or comes in with just Cloud. Sandy hair, wire-rimmed glasses, and wee eyes. Jim's his first name, but I don't know his last."

"When was the last time they were in?"

"Oh, I remember that quite clearly. Last Thursday. A booth near the loo is what they wanted, not their usual spot. Then tore into a mighty tiff."

"What was it about?"

"Busy that night, it was, so all I heard were snippets, but I think Jim was threatening to talk to someone about Austin. He may have said the police, but I can't be sure."

"You mean talk to the police about Cloud?"

"The din was quite thick. I'm just not sure."

"Go on."

"Mrs. Ward threatened Jim, telling him to keep his mouth shut, waving her finger like a lance."

As I mulled over what Adam had told me, he refilled my glass.

"Thanks," I said.

Adam cocked his head toward me and smiled wryly as he wiped a rag across the bar. "Part of the service at the Boar's Head, it is, my friend. Answers to your questions and all the American poison you want to drink."

• • •

It was after ten, approaching my usual bedtime, when I said good night to Adam and left the Boar's Head. Jim, Felicity, and Cloud swirled through my brain as I drove off. Without planning it, I found myself near Edna's apartment. It was way too late to knock at her door, so I parked my car across the street from her building to see if things looked quiet. The night was cool and moonless, but I saw what looked like a sporty red convertible among the cars. Just then, a tall man in a long overcoat came out of the building, walked quickly to the red convertible, backed out of the lot, and drove away. As it passed under the light on the street, I easily made out the plate on Cloud's car.

At home much later, I fought to battle a wave of unfounded jealousy. Was Edna now Cloud's latest victim, or was she involved with him in some other way? Something I'd seen in the photos of the crime scene disturbed me, and my mind kept returning to the grisly images of Jim facedown in a pool of blood. Although I hadn't thought of it for months, the last moments in the hospice with Carmen came hauntingly back.

The next morning questions about the case started up instantly, picking up right where they'd left off when I finally fell asleep. I tried to clear my head by immersing myself in my morning ritual, but thoughts of Edna swirled in the steam from my coffee, images of Cloud and Felicity scrambled along with my eggs, and *Mushrooms* popped out of the toaster.

O'Rourke, using Adam Tierney's information, would know the connection between Jim Hemple, Austin Cloud, and Felicity Ward, but he still didn't know about the tie to the burglaries. I felt guilty for concealing the facts from him, but I had to keep Edna out of this if I could. I called O'Rourke to find out if he had any new evidence.

"Not yet," O'Rourke said, "but we're going to sweat Cloud and Mrs. Ward at ten this morning."

"Mind if I listen in?"

"Fine, as long as you just listen."

"I'll be there," I said.

•••

"I already told the other policemen all of this," Felicity said. "Austin and I met for a drink at the Boar's Head."

O'Rourke was questioning her as I watched through the two-way mirror. She wore a dark, fitted long skirt, slit up the side considerably above her dimpled knee, and a white silk blouse with a few too many buttons undone. Apparently unable to get comfortable, she shifted her weight back and forth in the small wooden chair.

"Did Jim Hemple join you and Mr. Cloud?"

"Yes," Felicity answered, exhaling a long breath and pursing her lips. "How long is this going to take? I have a nail appointment at eleven."

"Why did you threaten Mr. Hemple? Was he going to implicate Cloud in a crime?"

"Austin didn't commit any crime, and I did not threaten that little pipsqueak." Felicity pushed her chair back from the table, pulled up her skirt, and crossed her legs with a flourish.

"We have a witness who will testify to your threats."

Her nails were painted a navy blue that matched her skirt, and she buffed them with a tissue as she replied in a matter-of-fact, controlled tone.

"It was very noisy in the bar that night. I'm sure your witness is confused."

"Family Services says you have a history of abusing your husband, and on more than one occasion, you've threatened him with a firearm."

I wondered if O'Rourke was bluffing, or if he'd checked the domestic complaints more fully. Either way, Felicity wasn't flustered a bit.

"That's a matter of public record. I'm sure you didn't call me down here to discuss all that."

"What is the nature of your relationship with Mr. Cloud?"

"Why, Captain O'Rourke," Felicity said, wagging her eyebrows. "I thought you knew. Austin and I are lovers."

From my vantage point outside the room, I could swear she winked at O'Rourke.

"Is your husband aware of this relationship?" O'Rourke shot back.

"Do you really think it would matter?" Without waiting for a reply, she added, "Now, if you have nothing further, may I go?"

"For now. After we interrogate Mr. Cloud, I'm sure we'll have a few more questions."

"She's a cool customer," I said as O'Rourke joined me outside Interrogation Room Two.

"Like ice," O'Rourke replied. "Way too cool."

"But? I hear that 'but' in your voice, which tells me you've got another theory."

"Based on the bartender's account, Mrs. Ward had time to get back to the shop. She did threaten Hemple, and she certainly has a temper that can get out of control quickly."

"But you don't make her for it?"

"Let's put Cloud in Room Two and see where this goes." O'Rourke picked up the phone to the holding cells, and five minutes later a uniformed officer led Austin Cloud into Interrogation Room Two.

Broad-shouldered, around six feet two, weighing about one hundred and eighty pounds, Cloud wore fashionable, expensive clothes. His sandy blond hair looked as though it had just been styled. He had large, robin's-egg blue eyes with thin brows and the longest lashes I've ever seen on a man. A smallish nose and baby-smooth face with an ingenuous expression gave him the look of a bemused boy in a man's body. It was easy to see why women would find him attractive.

"We'd like to ask you a few questions, Mr. Cloud," O'Rourke began.

"I'll be happy to assist the police in whatever way I can," Cloud replied with a smile that revealed two rows of perfectly white teeth.

O'Rourke stared at him, expressionless, until Cloud's smile faded. Then, in a low, soothing voice, O'Rourke began slowly, asking routine questions about Cloud's place of residence, work history, and how he had come to know Hemple. As O'Rourke's questions became more pointed, Cloud's demeanor remained calm, almost detached. It was clear that Austin Cloud knew the drill.

"Where were you between eight and nine thirty last Monday evening?"

"I'm afraid I can't say."

"Can't or won't?"

"A woman's honor is at stake."

"Honor?" O'Rourke said. "That's a laugh, coming from you. This is a murder investigation. Now, where were you Monday night?"

"I can't say," Cloud replied.

"Is it true you make your living bilking rich widows?"

Cloud's face remained expressionless. "I've already explained I make my living as a sales consultant."

O'Rourke leaned over the table, putting his nose a few inches from Cloud's face. "In her statement, Felicity Ward implicated you in the death of Jim Hemple."

"My, my," Cloud said, flashing his perfect teeth. "Is this where I'm supposed to break down and confess?"

O'Rourke circled the table and came at him from the other side, his mouth almost in Cloud's ear. "Is it true you're attracted to Mrs. Ward because she's so disgustingly fat?"

Cloud arched one eyebrow and smiled again. "And what's your particular weakness, Captain?"

O'Rourke drew back and stood next to the table. He was getting nowhere, and he knew it.

As he walked out of Room Two, Cloud was still smiling.

Austin Cloud was scum who preyed on lonely women, and perhaps was the leader of a successful burglary ring. From there to murder was not a large step. But Felicity's threats to Jim nagged at me. Was she simply a jealous lover trying to protect her partner, or was she involved in the burglaries and the murder?

"What does your gut tell you this adds up to?" I asked O'Rourke.

"Ward's a strange one, but for my money, Cloud's the heavy on this."

"What makes you so sure?"

"Have you seen his sheet?" O'Rourke slid it across his desk.

His record confirmed what Al Goldstein had told me about Cloud's past. It also contained details of more bunko arrests, but no formal charges.

"This guy's a prince," I said.

"Cloud's a longstanding accomplice of Hemple on various drug charges and other shady dealings," O'Rourke said. "He can't account for his whereabouts at the time of the murder, and the argument confirms he had reason to silence Hemple. That's opportunity and motive in my book. He's up to his slimy neck in this murder, but we have no proof."

"Can we arrest him on bunko charges?"

"What charges? We can't get any of his victims to come forward."

"Can we put a tail on him?"

"Jesus Christ, Ira. I know my job. I'm the captain now, remember? Of course we tailed him. Round the clock for a few days, but I don't have the manpower to keep it up. Besides, it was getting us nowhere."

If I gave O'Rourke the connection to the burglaries, he'd quickly grasp the possible tie to Edna's shop as a conduit for the stolen property. I still hoped I could keep her out of it without jeopardizing my friendship with O'Rourke, and without going to jail for withholding evidence in a murder investigation.

"Do you mind if I take a shot at the bunko victims?" I asked. "Maybe they'll talk to a harmless old man."

"Be my guest. But bunko's not what I want to nail this son of a bitch for. I want him for Murder One."

"So do I."

I particularly wanted to question one possible victim, but I worried that pushing Edna too hard would risk upsetting our relationship. Had Jim Hemple hidden the source of the consignment merchandise from her? Had Cloud been her illicit business partner, or was she another victimized widow? Was I being a blind old fool, seeing Edna through the prism of my own need? Even so, how could I protect her from all this? Right then, I had no answers.

• • •

The House of Glass was closed on Mondays, as were most shops in that part of town. When I called her at home, Edna said she was headed to the shop to finish a Tiffany lamp she had been working on. She agreed to meet me there in an hour.

The deserted sidewalks and streets gave me an eerie feeling, like the last person in a ghost town. The air was cold and still, and even the birds were silent. A few security lamps gave off the only light in the shop. An urge to drive away prodded me, but I stepped to the door and pressed the button. The harsh sound of the bell startled me as it swarmed over the quiet street.

"It's good to see you, Ira," Edna said as she opened the door. Her cheeks were rosy, unadorned by makeup, and she had swept her hair back from her face. A blue smock partially covered a red sweater and jeans. Her smile welcomed me, but didn't quite erase the uneasiness I felt.

"How's the Tiffany coming?" I asked as I followed her down the stairs.

"Slowly. I just don't have the time."

Spread on her table among various pieces of glass were her tools: a pair of pointed pliers, a solder iron, a distinctive Fletcher Gold Tip cutter, and a Styrofoam lamp mold. Behind her was another work surface, which contained a diamond-bladed band saw, another pair of pliers, and a slab-glass hammer. Louis Armstrong's voice on "La Vie en Rose" wafted from an unseen source.

"I have a few more questions about Jim's death, and uh, other related matters."

"I thought we covered all of that," Edna said. Her voice fluttered as she tapped a piece of blood-red glass with the slab hammer.

I eyed the hammer, noting its trapezoidal shape. She followed my gaze and started to speak again, then fell silent. She gave me a shy smile. "My knight in shining armor," she said. "Go ahead and ask your questions. I know you're trying to help."

I blushed and spoke quickly. "I'm confused about the sequence of a few things on the night of the murder. What time did you say you left the shop?"

She hesitated a moment. "I had a splitting headache, so I left early, around six thirty."

"Ah, an old man's memory. When I talked to you before, I thought you said seven thirty."

"We were all under a strain. Maybe I was confused."

"Me, more likely."

She applied foil to the edges of a section of glass, then fitted it into place on the lamp mold. One song complete, Armstrong rasped "A Kiss to Build a Dream On."

"Is it possible Jim was using the shop to sell stolen goods?"

She put down the foil and looked out the window, avoiding my eyes. "I didn't want to believe it at first," she answered, so quietly I could barely hear.

Although I'm not sure why, I whispered also. "What made you suspect?"

"The shop was losing money, a little each month. At that rate, I'd have lost everything—the life I've rebuilt from nothing. Jim brought in a few pieces at first, unusual pieces he said were done by people he knew back East. He said if we sold them on consignment, I'd get 10 percent of the sale price, and with the cost of carrying inventory, well, I was willing to allow it. Then I recognized a piece done by a friend who'd told me it had been stolen from her house."

"Was Felicity involved with the consignment merchandise?"

"No," she said with conviction. She'd apparently never considered the possibility.

There was no good way to do this. I was into it now, and there was no stopping. "I have reason to believe Jim was involved in fencing stolen property with a man named Austin Cloud, and they may have been involved in a series of burglaries."

Edna's shoulders slumped and her whole body seemed to deflate. "I—I don't..."

I gave her a moment to compose herself. "Did Jim know about your relationship with Cloud?"

She plopped onto the stool behind the workbench and dropped her chin onto her chest. "Oh, Ira," she sighed. "Please, get me a glass of water."

She hadn't moved when I returned with the water. "Drink this," I said, but couldn't tell if she heard me. "Edna?"

"Do you think less of me?" she asked in a whisper.

I didn't know what I thought, or how to answer, so I ignored her question and went on. "Please tell me what happened."

She looked weary to the bones. Slowly, she sipped the water, then took a deep breath.

"My headache wouldn't let up, even after a hot bath," she said. "I couldn't get the possibility out of my mind that Jim's consignment merchandise was really stolen property. If I was implicated, I might lose the shop. I came back a few minutes after eight, to confront him."

She spoke with almost no inflection in her voice, as if someone else were speaking and she was an unwilling partner, merely moving her lips. Mercifully, the music ended.

"Did he threaten you?"

"Worse. He told me the horrible truth about Austin. And he laughed at me."

I could put it together from there. The trapezoidal surface of the slab-glass hammer fit the coroner's description of the wound. And I remembered her distinctive Fletcher glass-cutter in the crime scene photos. An investigation that resulted from accusations about stolen property would certainly implicate her. Edna had probably confronted Jim, and he'd explained the facts of life to her. He worked at her shop, she had kept the inventory records, and quite possibly she was having an affair with his accomplice. I wondered which part of the truth she had found so horrible she might have killed him for it. Was it Cloud taking advantage of her, as he had done with so many other lonely widows, or had Jim told her about Cloud's affair with Felicity?

At that moment I didn't want to know if she'd killed him, or why. It didn't matter anymore. Edna had awakened in me feelings I thought I'd buried with Carmen. How could I believe she was a murderer? Maybe Jim had threatened her, or maybe she'd lost control. I didn't care.

Carmen had always said I was married to the job more than to her. Right then, more than anything, I wanted to prove to Carmen and myself that feelings could be the most important thing to me.

"That's enough, Edna," I said. "Let me drive you home."

She held my gaze. "I need to finish this piece tonight. Come for me tomorrow, Ira. Please."

When I held out my hands, she cupped them with hers. I hugged her, kissed her on the lips, then went quickly up the stairs and out the door.

•••

The next morning the loud whack of the rolled-up *Gazette* smacking my front door woke me. Stretched out on the couch and stiff from a nearly sleepless night, I was torn between my feelings for Edna and what I knew was right. What had she meant when she said I should come for her today? Did she mean she'd go to O'Rourke with me, or would she go away with me? But I was a cop, I'd always been a cop, and it didn't matter what a cop felt; he just had to do his job. Maybe Carmen was right after all. I'd have to bring Edna in.

Unfolding the *Gazette,* I stared dumbfounded at the front-page story: TWO DIE IN

SUSPICIOUS FIRE.

The bodies of Mrs. Felicity Ward, 44, and Mr. Austin Cloud, 32, were found in the basement of the House of Glass, an antiques shop on Front Street, when firefighters responded to a five-alarm fire. The building was heavily damaged. Firefighters at the scene suspected arson, although no official explanation has been released. A police spokesman quoted the coroner as saying the exact causes of death were not yet known. Last week a murder victim, James Hemple, 31, was discovered in the same location. The spokesman went on to say the owner of the shop, Mrs. Edna Burwick, is wanted for questioning.

•••

So that's it, I thought. Seems this knight won't be saving any fair maidens. And the only person I'll be turning in is myself. There's no fool like an old fool.

Alena Dillon

Dashed

I was going to be a fireman. That was my plan when I was a five-year-old kid, before I knew I had the upper body strength of a jellyfish, before I actually thought about what it means to work with flames and smoke. Back then I figured the job was all about riding big red trucks and petting Dalmatians. Being a fireman just meant being the big burly guy in the mustard yellow jumpsuit who visited our elementary school once and invited me to sit on his knee while he talked to my Kindergarten class about memorizing emergency escape routes out of our houses. It meant rustling the unwashed hair of a lonely boy with an absentee dad, and making him feel special for once in his goddamned life.

I was going to be a wrestler. When the spotlight hit me, people in the arena would jump to their feet and cheer. Girls would love to look at me. Guys would practice being me. My wrestling name would be something catchy like Jason Fear, or maybe Jester Jason, for the alliteration. And as I strutted toward the ring to some metal or punk rock song, the crowd would go nuts.

I was going to be a veterinarian. Maybe because I was embarrassed by Ma's plastic flamingo obsession, and by working with live animals I could prove I was different from her. Better. But I really started wanting it the day Otis broke his leg. I was fifteen, and carrying my dog down the stairs. He was young then and could walk fine on his own, but I held him a lot because I liked to feel his warmth against my chest, and when he gazed up at me with those sweet brown eyes and licked my chin, I was sure we understood each other. He spotted a squirrel out the front window and leapt from my arms. When he landed, something snapped and he let out the most gut-wrenching combination of a bark and a cry. When I think about that sound ten years later, it still sends a chill down my back. His whole body started shaking and he looked up at me like he was begging me to fix him. But I didn't know how. If my dog was ever in pain like that again, I never wanted to feel so helpless, so I decided to become a vet. But that was before I realized we didn't have money for a four-year college, never mind vet school. And before I got a C in high school biology.

I was going to be a husband and a dad. Not the kind who runs away to Florida because he finds a prettier wife and a cushier job. The kind that sticks around because his kid is worth it. That's all I want to say about that.

I was going to be a good son. The kind of son that grows up and buys his mother the first vacation she's ever had, who pays for retirement so she isn't working at Market Basket until she croaks. Not the kind who comes home high right out of rehab and makes her throw a suitcase on the floor and scream, "Get out!" While I packed that day, I saw her tremble, not out of anger, but from nerves, like her skin was quivering from repressing every instinct in her body that told her to protect me. If I was someone other than the skid being dumped on the street, I would have told her not to give in, to be strong. And when she called early the next morning, sniffling into the phone, and told me to come home, I almost said, No, you were right the first time. But I didn't. Because I wanted somewhere with food in the fridge. Somewhere nice to sleep. Somewhere safe to go when I was loaded.

One thing is for sure. I wasn't going to be an addict, popping pills in my childhood bedroom, using in strangers' apartments in Peabody and Lynn Lynn The City of Sin, shooting up in playgrounds, even as I watched kids racing toward me, unbounded by their childhood vitality and all the possible selves that waited in their futures.

Not an addict.

Never an addict.

Jason A. Feingold

Blanden, I

"Do you believe this?" I said to my wife as images of bombings crisscrossed the television screen.

"Believe what," she said. It wasn't a question to which she expected or wanted an answer. Her nose was buried in her iPad, and nothing short of nuclear weaponry was going to dislodge it.

"This war," I said. "This stupid illegal war."

"Hmm."

This was the war I would have protested in my youth by shouting in the streets. But, alas, I was no longer capable of burning flags, marching on Washington, tuning in, turning on, or dropping out. I was in the latter half of my life. I had passed over the event horizon of passion for such things.

My wife didn't care about the war. Her concerns were elsewhere, although I was never exactly sure what they were. I knew enough to know her concerns didn't involve me.

"Where was this war when I needed it?" I asked out loud. That earned me a funny look from my wife. From myself, too.

My life has been a series of missed opportunities. It isn't my fault. I was born too late to be part of the generation that was shaped by the Beatles and too early for the nihilistic angst of Generation X. I always felt I need to create something, do something. I went the safe route instead—wife, family, a job with prospects (largely unfulfilled), precisely because I was unable to harness the creative tension of either generation. Now those demands take everything from me. I have no time or energy for anything more.

Mrs. Blanden was stifling, but she hadn't always been that way. I can remember two or three occasions when we were younger where she was beautifully carefree. It had taken her years to become so constantly unaware of me.

The children were her idea, and I did my duty, conceiving them not just to placate her, but also in the hope that they would provide a bridge between us. Kids are so needy. I didn't realize that children kept married people together because they made their parents too tired to consider anything else.

I didn't know if my life was a tragedy or a farce. I was just a victim of circumstance. It wasn't my fault. My life might have been inconsequential in the grand scheme of things, but I took a certain amount of pride in the fact that I kept plodding along in spite of knowing that there was no reason to expect things to get any better.

I have dreams, though, both at night and in the day. I dream that things will suddenly get better, that my life will burst tangentially from its current orbit by virtue of a piece of mail or a telephone call or because of what I see across a crowded room. I dream my life will change in some eruption of good fortune like spontaneous kisses on V-J Day.

I didn't expect anything to improve. Despite that, or perhaps because of that, I spent a lot of time listening for the first sweet note of total worldwide disaster. Disaster equals freedom. Disaster is the stripping away of all pretense and doubt. Disaster is the reduction of meaning to a raw, brute struggle for survival. My fantasies might be vague, but each day I rose thinking this can be the day, and each night I fell asleep thinking that tomorrow could be it. In the end, all the aspects of my life were sane and regulated and predictable like the cycles of the moon. Citizen Blanden is reliable if nothing else.

"I can't get Excel to work," one of my co-workers said as he entered my cubicle.

"No problem," I told him. Even though it's not my job, I go to his cubicle and fix it for him.

"Where's the Johnson file?" another co-worker asked me on my way back to my cubicle. Once again, it's not my job, but I find it for her. No problem. I was confident and in control in my job. I knew how the computers work. I knew where to find the files we needed and where to return them when we were done. People asked me questions about how to do things, and I was never at a loss for an answer, (provided that they asked me about the computer system and the filing system). At my work I was safe; even valued. There were no surprises, no pitfalls that I didn't see coming from a mile away. I walked the floor with confidence. My co-workers were pleasant to me, and I was pleasant with them. Sometimes, though, they got quiet just as I entered a room, but that didn't happen very often. I was too well-liked to believe that they would make fun of me behind my back.

There was a time in my life when I wholeheartedly believed that I had felt the whole gamut of human emotion from hate to love to indifference. I did not realize that I had never been in love until the moment it happened. In my defense, I loved my wife when I married her. I thought I did, anyway. I genuinely believed that I did. I love my children when they are good, although they can get quite annoying. Starling, however, I loved from the instant I saw her. She alighted on the forefront of my thoughts out of an unremarkable gray sky on an unremarkable day with no more thought than a bird gives to the branch upon which it chooses to rest, indifferent to the indelible imprint her claws make upon the bark.

I first saw Starling across a conference table. She did not see me the same way I saw her. Her eyes slid off me like a shimmer off of hot pavement. She was the most beautiful woman I have ever seen. She is the most beautiful woman I will ever see. Throughout the long, boring presentation that was the reason we were in the room together, I watched her as closely as I dared, cataloging everything she saw, every expression on her face, every movement, every posture. At some point, our eyes met and stuck together for an instant, and it seemed like everything I was poured out of me to her; that my entire self was decoded, compiled, and printed out, and laid at her feet. When she looked away, I knew that she had found me unthreatening, inconsequential, and worst of all, irrelevant.

It was not supposed to be that way. It was supposed to happen like this:

"I love you," I would say.

"I love you," she would reply, simply, casually, as if stating the immutable tautology that water is wet.

After an amorous pause, one of us would say (and it did not matter which), "I never believed this could happen. What do we do now?" Then we would go back out into the world long enough to untangle ourselves from our separate lives so we could mingle them together forever. It would be difficult, and no doubt there would be many trials, but we would endure. We would have each other to look forward to. We would have each other as a reward.

All that, though, was the leading man's role. I was an extra, a walk-on in an epic film whose cast of thousands revolves around her. She was Cleopatra and the Virgin Mary,

Nefertiti and Salome combined and set in a world apart from me, a mere billionth of a man, an indiscriminate fragment of the teeming masses, a Prufrock without a name of his own. My only purpose was to provide a foil of unrelenting mediocrity as a yardstick with which to fathom her otherwise immeasurable excellence.

She would never be mine, never ever. The epiphany hit me so hard I gasped, drawing her eyes for an unwanted second time. I did not dare to look into those eyes. I feared to see what I knew they contained. I knew I would regret not looking into her eyes again, not speaking to her (I knew I wouldn't dare), and most of all I would regret the unconscionable crime of being what I am.

For a year, I watched Starling from afar. For a year, I contrived plausible reasons for walking past her cubicle. Each time I caught her eye I would attempt to find the smallest mote of love for me in them, but her eyes only brushed me casually, like when a cashier accidentally touches a customer's hand while making change. If I were pushed out the window on the thirty-seventh floor, my face and the face of my murderer would fade in her mind into an amorphous blob of contemptible goo. I knew I was on the extreme margin in her life, unable to leave an impression even if I was crucified with pushpins on the OCEA bulletin board in the employee lounge.

Sometimes when I was alone in my windowless, airless, tight-fitting office which I had finally earned with a modicum of realized potential somewhere along the line, in the moments between completing one task and starting another, I would stare at my notepad and wish that I could draw her face. That would be something, a tribute and memento to her made by my own hand, the blue lines serving to accentuate my art *in situ*. Unfortunately, I cannot draw, so I never touched pen to paper for that purpose.

Sometimes I wished that I could write a poem to her beauty or a song that declared my love for her. I wished I could serenade her like King David or David Cassidy. Music is yet another talent that I lack, and the one time I tried to write a poem about her it came out like a memorandum, so I tore it into quarters and stuffed it into the shredder. When I day-dreamed about her, all I could do on that notepad was doodle concentric circles, each one giving some kind of motion to my otherwise idle fantasies.

Twelve months passed. Another seventieth of my allotted threescore years and ten dripped away into a puddle that quickly seeped into the dry and thirsty earth. My hair thinned, and my paunch grew. Fifty-two weeks. Over that time, I slowly transitioned from vaguely unfulfilled to actively dissatisfied. The only thing I could really connect with besides the impossible fact of my unrequited love was the war that dragged on and on and on, the war that did not affect me in the slightest. At least once a week I could not help but launch an anti-war sermon at my wife. I gradually became aware that while she listened to my tirades, she most likely wished that I would go and fight and never come home.

Thoughts beginning with the cruel utterance "if only" began to echo through my head like a catchy TV commercial jingle. If only I hadn't married, if only we didn't have children, if only I had the money to make it on my own, then, I would think, it would be possible, it would be just within the realm of possibility that Starling could love me. If only I were younger, if only I could lose some weight, then she could love me. If only I could talk to her. If only I had anything to say. If only if only—only if.

One afternoon after lunch when I was staring dully at my blank notepad, I thought perhaps she might notice me in the distant future. Perhaps our love must be the work of natural selection; perhaps it must take time for it to evolve naturally. She could be trans- ferred to my department, I imagined. We could attend a conference at the same hotel. I could see her at the bar and say hello or, even better, she could say hello to me first.

This desperate grasp at plausibility enlivened me and enriched my days for many weeks. I would be patient. I would wait. I had been waiting all my life, I told myself, and I pretended it was easier because I finally knew what I was waiting for. Good things come to those who wait.

It was not long after my decision to settle down and wait for things to happen that I learned Starling would be leaving the company. Leaving for good. Leaving forever. I knew that I was unlucky, that the universe was not a Blanden-loving place, so I told myself that this was bound to happen sooner or later. Only the Xerox machine in the supply room was truly eternal.

The news got worse. She was going off to get married, and not just a regular marriage. The rumor was that her fiance was well-off, an up-and-coming peterpeterpumpkineater, but with enough money to keep her on the outside of the eponymous squash. Everyone but me knew about it months before. Why hadn't I been told? Did they know how I secretly pined for her? Did they notice me staring? Did they see me buzzing around her cubicle like some errant gnat? Had someone told her? Did she think it was funny? Or did she think I was some kind of weirdo stalker?

All good things must come to an end. Those words popped into my head like buoyant wreckage from the *Titanic* of my life. I spent the next two weeks *not* walking by her cubicle, *not* looking for her when I entered the lounge or any other public area. I braced myself for the painful process of separation. I would see her no more. In fourteen days she would be gone; then ten, then nine, then eight, then two.

I could not help but notice that the war dragged on. I wished very much that it would end.

I tried to savor each moment she was there, even if I had to be aloof from her. I wanted to reflect upon these last days, capture their essence in mental amber so I could remember them later. I realized, though, that my memories were really intangibles; there was nothing real enough to sustain remembrance. Even though she was close by, there were times when I could not remember her face. Two days remained before she was gone forever, and all I would be left with was a faint fading wisp of a daydream.

Near the end of that next-to-last day, I made my way to the employee lounge, loose change clinking in my pocket, wondering if I should get a Diet Coke or the real thing. I was surprised to find Starling sitting at one of the cheap Formica tables with Allison and Teddy from Accounting. I took my time in front of the vending machine, trying to look like I was unable to make up my mind so I could eavesdrop.

"He used weapons of mass destruction on his own people," Teddy argued.

"So?" replied Starling. "He didn't use them on us."

"He's a killer," said Allison. "He had to go."

"But why war?" Starling asked rhetorically. "Look at how many people have died. Look at the mess. How can you say that this situation is any better?"

"At least they have a chance," Allison said. "At least they're free now."

"You have to admit that things are better than they were," said Teddy.

"Better for who?" Starling demanded.

I turned to face the discussion. Did I dare to talk to them about the war? I tried to summon up the substance of my earlier tirades, but my memory was suddenly woefully deficient.

"She's right," I finally said. "It's a stupid war."

"See?" said Starling. "Even he gets it."

I turned back to the machine and dumped my coins into the slot, then pressed the button for Diet Coke. I popped the tab and turned back to Starling and Allison and Teddy, but they had stopped talking. I waved weakly and went back to my airless office.

I knew I would never see Starling again. If only there could be more time, I thought. More time. My love for Starling would go unrequited, perhaps one day forgotten but never forgiven. It wasn't fair, I told myself, but that was a lie. It was fair.

She will never come to me, not even in daydreams. I never had a chance.

Raima Larter

Motherhood

Julia was up early, as was her way, having her morning Diet Coke and cigarette. She'd moved to the back porch, out of consideration for Brittany's feelings about secondhand smoke, even though Brittany wasn't actually there.

The sun, a blood orange disk, peeked above the nearby black walnut grove. A mist rose from the gulley below, snaking its way toward the treetops. Julia pulled her phone from her pocket and punched out Brittany's number. After four rings, it went to voicemail. Again.

"Hi, Brittany. It's Mom. Where are you?" Julia paused, her hands shaking, and took a long draw on her cigarette. "Call me when you get this message. Okay? Bye."

She sighed, tucking the phone away, and clomped down the porch stairs toward the shed, wishing she could remember how to pray.

•••

Brittany was up early, although not by choice. She'd felt the vomit surging up into her throat as she lay in the lumpy bed and barely made it to the toilet in time. She'd flung the motel room window wide, hoping to air out the smell.

It opened onto a wooded area behind the motel. A soft breeze wafted through, bringing with it the sweet sound of birds. She thought their singing should cheer her up, but all it seemed to do was make her cry again.

She pulled the note from her pocket, a slip of paper Jake had left for her two days before.

"Sorry, babe," it read. "I didn't count on this. You understand, right? xoxo."

She crumpled the paper and tossed it in the waste can, then began slamming clothes into the tattered suitcase. Her stomach rumbled. She ought to eat, but the mere thought of food made her queasy.

She really needed to do laundry, too, but that would cost money. She shouldn't have sprung for this motel room she couldn't afford, but she'd grown so tired of sleeping in her car in rest areas, wandering away from the decrepit town in New York, a place where Jake's parents apparently never lived. Nobody there had ever heard of that family.

•••

Julia sucked at her cigarette one last time, flung it to the dirt at the bottom of the porch steps, and ground the stub beneath her sandal. She clomped across the packed dirt and summer-crisped grass, heading for the shed. It was already getting hot, despite the early hour.

She squeaked open the heavy wooden door, shuffled inside, and placed her sweaty soda can on the side table. A billowy cloud of purple steam from the first vat wafted over her. The dye had a peculiar scent, a smell you don't find anywhere else. Julia was beginning to grow attached to the odor, which smelled to her like freedom and success.

The dye boilers were on timers that switched on at 4:00 a.m., but she liked to check the vats by sunrise, just in case. Once, a power surge in the middle of the night caused the breakers to trip and the timers to fail. She'd lost a full day's work.

It happened when one of their wild Ohio summer thunderstorms spun up a tornado, compete with hail and massive destruction. Julia's yarn-dyeing business, still in its infancy at the time, would have been one of the casualties if it weren't for the flukiest of flukes that sent the tornado hopping over her place to land squarely on the neighbors' home.

Blew it to shreds. There was nothing left but a pile of sticks the size of twigs and a tangle of pink fiberglass insulation wrapped around the lone sumac tree that had escaped the twister's wrath. She felt bad that her own good fortune had been bought at the expense of disaster for her neighbors. Fortunately, Errol and Arlene were out of town at the time, visiting their grandkids up in Ann Arbor, so even though their property was a complete loss, no one had been hurt. Thank God.

Julia had been the one to call them with the bad news. As it turned out, they never came back. Just up and decided to stay in Ann Arbor. "It's a sign, Julia," Errol had said on the phone. "God doesn't want us there no longer."

Julia wasn't much into signs, but she wondered whether the tornado sparing her dyeing shed might have been a sign. She also wondered whether Rosalie, who just happened to show up at the Truck Stop Café the day after Julia got the idea for a yarn-dyeing business, meant something.

•••

Brittany wasn't stupid, although she admitted she did stupid things sometimes. One of the stupider ones was letting Jake talk her into leaving with him. That decision ranked right up there on the stupidity scale with her earlier decision to go off the pill last winter.

She didn't like the way it made her feel, though—all weepy and sad all the time, and for no reason. What did she have to be weepy about? She was months away from high school graduation, had a boyfriend and a job at Walmart. She had a future, even though it wasn't the one Mom thought she should have. Sure, dyeing yarn was fun, but it was just a game—not the sound business idea that Mom insisted it was.

What was there for Brittany to be sad about? Nothing, so she assumed it was the pill causing all the crying. True, she'd never known her dad, and Mom's too-easy explanations that she was interested in Jake, who was nearly thirty, only because she was looking for a father figure sorta made sense.

Sorta, but not really. Mom was too much into pop psychology. Really. She'd do better to focus on her own problems, her addictions, and to lay off Brittany and all the things that were apparently wrong with her.

At least Brittany wasn't an addict. She'd never touch tobacco and was committed to all-natural foods. Non-GMO was the best if you could find it, organic for sure. Mom claimed she never noticed if something was organic or not when she shopped, but how hard could that be? You just had to read labels, for pete's sake.

Mom's home-cooked meals were the worst. Everything was made with processed foods—otherwise known as toxic sludge. Brittany would never feed her kids such things.

She placed both hands on her belly and pressed, trying to tell if it felt different inside, but it was like nothing at all was there. She knew she was wrong about that, though. She knew there was a baby there, very tiny now, but it would be a real baby soon enough.

The reality of her situation bore down and her shoulders sagged. She was nineteen and unmarried and pregnant—technically a teenage mother, but not really. Brittany was an adult, although Mom would not agree. But, then, Mom never wanted Brittany to grow up, so what did she know? Brittany was not some little teenager who got pregnant because she didn't understand where babies come from.

She knew. She took the pills, although maybe stopping them was the wrong thing to do.

Tears sprang, yet again, to Brittany's eyes. She thought it was going to be different for her. She was completely different from her mother. She was. Brittany grabbed her purse and headed downstairs, in search of breakfast and an ATM.

• • •

Julia had finished checking the boilers and gone back to the house. Eggs sizzled on the stove and a couple slices of bacon were already crisped and ready to eat. The toast popped up and she reached for the butter. It was a standard breakfast, a favorite of most of her customers at the café—or would be if she had coffee with it, rather than the diet soda that had become her morning habit.

That and the cigarette. She wanted to quit, and she knew Brittany would be happy if she did. The girl was all about natural foods, healthy living, and all that, and found no end of ways to criticize Julia's cooking.

"Mom, everything you make has Ritz crackers or cream of mushroom soup in it," she said on the last evening she'd been at home. "How can you eat this stuff?"

The memory made Julia's stomach cramp and she reached for the pumpkin butter, slathering it onto the buttered toast. Brittany might have approved of the pumpkin butter, since it was homemade. That last night she was home, Brittany had refused the casserole Julia made and, instead, grabbed a yogurt from the fridge. She'd eaten it standing up, leaning back against the counter, glancing repeatedly at the clock on the wall.

"Jake's picking me up when he gets off," she said.

Julia stood and moved her dirty plate to the sink. "What time is he off?"

A pained look crossed Brittany's face and, later, Julia would wonder whether she should have asked her about it. "He gets off at five," Brittany said. "He said he'd be here by six."

"It's almost seven," Julia said, looking at the clock on the stove, then running hot water over the plate. She swished at it with a soapy brush. "Where you two headed tonight?"

Brittany shrugged. "Some guy's place. I don't know him, but Jake says he needs to pick something up."

Julia put the plate in the drainer and reached for the dish towel to dry her hands. "Speaking of picking something up, Rosalie left some raw yarn at the café the other day for our beet-dye project. It's in my locker. I can bring it home tomorrow if you'd like to try it over the weekend."

Brittany had stood up fast then and tossed the empty yogurt container in the trash. "I really don't have time for that, Mom," she said. "I have to work."

"I thought you were off Saturday. Can't we do it then?"

Brittany refused to meet Julia's eyes. She pulled her phone from her pocket. Her thumbs flew as she sent a text. "Can I borrow your car?"

Julia frowned. "I thought you said Jake was picking you up."

She waved her phone at Julia. "He got held up." She reached for her backpack. "Can I?"

"Can you what?"

"Borrow your car." She huffed. "Like I just said."

"How late will you be?"

"I don't know, Mom. Eleven? Maybe later."

"I need to work tomorrow, you know. I don't want to get up and find my car gone, you—"

"I know, Mom. It'll be here. Don't worry." She looked at her phone again, stuffed it into her jeans pocket, slung the backpack over her shoulder, and pushed at the screen door that led to the back porch. "Be back later," she yelled, as the door snapped shut.

Julia looked up from the piece of toast slathered with pumpkin butter, and glanced at the calendar. That had only been last week. Brittany had returned the car in time for Julia to get to work, but something seemed to shift that night. Julia still wasn't sure what had happened since Brittany wouldn't talk about it, but Julia had her suspicions. For the last several weeks, Brittany had dashed to the bathroom every morning. The sound of retching had told Julia all she needed to know.

She spread pumpkin butter on a second piece of toast. She'd made the pumpkin butter herself, last fall, using the leftover jack o'lantern Brittany had carved. It was the last kid-like thing Julia remembered her doing. Everything had changed over the winter. Dances at school that turned out to not even exist, mere cover for parties in abandoned houses with sketchy people Julia didn't know.

Finally, graduation arrived, only to be followed by the summer from hell. Brittany was always angry it seemed, and Julia just as glad when she stayed out later and later with friends, sometimes even all night. She was no longer a child, as Brittany constantly reminded her. And, yes, nineteen was definitely an adult, and Julia agreed with Brittany that it was, but she still didn't like it, and before she realized what was happening, it was over.

She'd left in the middle of the night, right out the front door, leaving it unlocked behind her. At least she'd scribbled a note, stuck in the frame of the hallway mirror.

"I'm in love with Jake," it said. "We're moving to New York."

That was it. No "I love you," no "I'm sorry." Nothing but those two sentences.

Julia pulled out her phone. First she sent a text and when there was, yet again, no response, she tried calling one more time.

Hi. This is Brittany. Leave me a message and I'll call you back.

And then the beep. Julia didn't even bother to leave a voicemail this time.

"She's grown, Julia," Betty had said to her the other day as they sat in the back of the café on a break. "She's nineteen. Time to let go."

Julia stacked the dishes in the sink and glanced at the clock. She'd wash them up later, but she did have time for a load of laundry before heading to work. She was in Brittany's room, rummaging under the bed for stray socks and tee shirts, when she saw it: Brittany's phone, underneath a dirty towel, still plugged into its charger.

She grabbed the phone and backed out from under the bed. Her hands shook as she touched the button to turn it on. Six texts and a bunch of new voicemails. She clicked the first one and listened to her own voice, her heart plunging into the depths of her belly.

• • •

Brittany glided down the cracker and cookie aisle at the Quik Mart attached to the motel. Somewhere she remembered reading that crackers helped with morning sickness, so she picked out a box of thin wheat crackers and looked at the extensive ingredient list. So much awful stuff in these things, but she needed to eat something and this was the only kind of food you could find out here on I-80.

Or was she on I-70? She knew she was in Pennsylvania, but wasn't sure where, exactly.

She was reaching for her phone to check the map when she remembered. The thought of her missing phone made her stomach flop again.

Mom must be frantic. She was surely trying to reach Brittany. Funny how she hadn't thought of that till that moment. Her hand drifted to her flip-flopping stomach and she wondered: did she have what it took to be a mother? How did one know, anyway?

When she'd discovered her phone was missing, they were already on the interstate, headed east, but had only been driving for about fifteen minutes. "I have to go back, Jake," she'd said. "I'm pretty sure it's plugged in beside my bed."

"You can use my phone," he said, his eyes on the road. "Or, we can buy one of those cheap ones they sell at truck stops."

"It's only fifteen minutes back to my place. I really need my own phone."

But he kept driving and refused to discuss it. She should have realized this was a sign, but had stupidly ignored it. Yet another stupid thing she could add to her rapidly growing list. Funny how most of them lately involved Jake.

•••

The dye-making business had grown out of a game Julia had played with Brittany. The girl had always been into crafts and when Brittany was about ten, she had figured out how to extract a lovely dark brown dye from black walnut hulls. It seemed a miracle that the land itself, inherited from Julia's late parents, had given Julia an idea for a way to get ahead on her bills.

She wouldn't have gotten anywhere with her fledgling idea, though, without Rosalie's knowledge and connections, not to mention her well-timed phone call to the loan officer at the bank when Julia needed a loan for the dye vats. It all seemed destined to happen, at least until Jake made an appearance and ruined everything.

After Julia checked the boilers one more time and locked up the shed, she headed for the truck stop and pulled into a spot in the large parking lot. A half-dozen big rigs were parked along the side, several of them idling, but the rest of the lot held only a handful of cars. The morning mist had turned to a milky haze and it was already getting hot and sticky.

She hurried inside, stashing her purse in an empty locker in the staff room, grabbed an order pad, and rushed to the hostess station by the front door.

Betty was working the early shift that day and had just led a group of customers toward a table. Two silver-haired women and a man with a protruding paunch followed her to the back of the room. Julia tied an apron around her waist and glanced at the seating chart. Only three sets of customers besides this last group, and their orders had already been taken.

Betty came back to the station, but before Julia could say anything to her another set of customers arrived, this time two men, probably truckers.

"Morning," Betty said. "Two for breakfast?"

"Yes, ma'am." The man grinned. "A booth, if you have one."

Betty smiled at Julia. Every booth was empty. She leaned to grab two menus and, as she bent over, she whispered, "Any word from her?"

Julia shook her head. She wanted to tell Betty how she'd found the phone under the bed, but Betty was already hurrying the pair of men toward a booth on the side. Julia headed for the table where the two silver-haired women were seated with their male companion. She flipped open the order pad. "Can I get you some drinks before you get started? Coffee?"

All three ordered coffee and Julia hurried off to get the decanter just as the bell on the door handle tinkled and a half dozen people swarmed in.

A couple of hours later when the morning rush had slowed, Julia and Betty slid into an empty booth. Betty had a cup of coffee and Julia a Diet Coke, which she ignored, twisting the corners of a napkin into tight little points.

"Any idea where she is?" Betty asked.

Julia shrugged. "She claimed they were going to New York to meet his parents, but I don't even know if that meant New York state or the city."

Betty sipped at her coffee. "And you found her phone?"

"It was under the bed. It looked to me like she just forgot it—still plugged into the charger and tangled in a towel."

Betty shook her head. "It's not like that girl to be without her phone."

Julia's stomach cramped and she looked away for a moment, blinking to get the tears back in. When she looked back, Betty's face had softened. Betty reached across the table and squeezed Julia's hand, which finally broke down her defenses. Tears rolled down her cheeks. "I know you said she's grown, and I should let her go, but this just feels so wrong."

"I know. I don't trust that Jake character at all."

"I think she's pregnant."

Betty's eyes widened. "Well, that might explain a few things."

"I'm not sure Brittany's told him, though. I'm not sure *she* even knows."

Betty frowned. "How could she not know? Besides, how do *you* know?"

Julia shrugged. "Mother's intuition, I guess."

The door swung open, tinkling the bell. Betty sighed and twisted in her seat, watching two state troopers step in. They took off their hats and stood by the hostess station.

Betty got up, but turned back to Julia. "You could report her as missing," she said, nodding toward the cops.

"She's not really missing, Betty." Julia stood and pulled her order pad from her apron pocket. "She told me where she was going and who she was with. It's not like she's run away."

Betty pressed her lips together and nodded. "True, she didn't run away, but it still don't feel right to you." She tipped her head toward the officers. "Maybe you could just talk to them?"

Julia shook her head, having no intention of taking Betty's advice. She'd handle this herself. Julia approached the officers and reached for the menus. "Good morning. Would you like a booth or a table?"

•••

Brittany stepped into the motel lobby to check out. There was an ATM inside the front door. She dug in her purse for her wallet, but when she pulled it out, and flipped through all the cards, she found the room card key but no debit card.

Her heart plunged into her stomach. Jake must have swiped it. She remembered him asking for her pin number, which seemed odd, but she trusted him. All the gratitude she'd felt toward him for leaving her the car and the keys to it drained away through her feet. She sagged forward and turned away from the ATM. A flush of heat surged into her face, but she didn't know if she was angry or ashamed.

The motel clerk, an Indian-looking man with thick glasses, gave her a puzzled look.

"Anything wrong, ma'am?"

She placed the key card on the counter. "No. Just checking out."

He nodded, punched at the computer and said, "You're all paid up. Will there be anything else?"

She shook her head, thanked him again, and rolled her battered suitcase to the car. She drove for awhile, first heading back toward New York, but took the first exit and turned around, aiming the car toward Ohio. She glanced at the gas gauge. Over three-quarters full, so maybe enough to make it home.

She didn't want to go back, but what choice did she have? Her stomach rumbled again after an hour and she took an exit with one of those truck stop–convenience store combos. A wave of dizziness hit her as she stepped through the door, so she went straight to the cracker and cookie aisle, past a gigantic TV monitor set up near the registers. A group of people were gathered in a semi-circle in front of it. She pushed past them, grabbed a large box of saltines, and headed for the register.

As the clerk rang up her purchase, Brittany glanced at the TV. A red BREAKING NEWS banner flashed onto the bottom of the screen beneath a weather map splashed with alarming streaks of yellow, orange, and red.

"That'll be a dollar sixty-seven," the clerk said, his eyes flitting to the screen, a look of concern washing over his face.

She dug in her purse and came up with two crumpled dollar bills. Her stomach growling, she took quick looks at the screen as she waited for her change. *Tornadoes Rip Across Midwest,* screamed one bold-faced caption. *Ohio Braces for Storms,* read another.

Brittany received a quarter, a nickel, and three pennies as change. She tucked the coins into her pocket, pretty sure it wasn't enough to buy whatever gas she might need to make it home.

•••

Betty said that Table Four needed their check and the truckers in the booth near the register wanted their coffees refilled. Julia grabbed the steaming decanter on her way to Table Four, slid the bill onto the table with a smile, and headed for the truckers.

They sat hunched over their mugs and dirty plates, three guys with shoulders like football players and a fourth skinny older man who slid his mug toward her as she approached.

"Maybe I will have another," he said, nodding toward the window. Outside, the milky haze that had hung in the air all day had disappeared. The sky had turned to black and the spindly trees along the edge of the parking lot were starting to toss about. "Looks like that storm might hit just as I pull my rig out, don't it?"

The others agreed, grumbling about timetables that wouldn't be met. They thanked her for the coffee that she poured into their cups. They watched her stack the dirty plates and lift them, all four plates balanced in one hand, the decanter in the other. "Will that be all for you gentlemen?"

One man grabbed the menu. "Maybe I will have that cherry pie, after all."

"Anybody else? We have brownies, too. Or cake."

"Nothing for me," the second man said, and the third shook his head.

She nodded and turned toward the kitchen as the bell on the door dinged. Rosalie stumbled in, lugging a heavy bag and tugging at her too-tight skirt. "Julia!" she shouted, smiling and trying to smooth her tangled dark hair into place. "Quite a storm we've got brewing today."

Julia gave her a tight smile and nodded toward the nearly empty room. "Take any seat you'd like. I'll be right with you."

Rosalie clomped in her scuffed pumps toward a booth and sank into it with a heavy sigh. "You and Brittany ready for the farmers market this weekend?"

Julia's stomach clenched as she handed Rosalie a menu.

Rosalie flipped the pages quickly and slammed it shut. "I'll just have coffee." She handed the menu to Julia and peered up at her. "Did you get your registration turned in? Should be lots of folks there interested in your hand-dipped yarns."

"I—I'm not sure we can make it."

Rosalie drew back. "Why not? It's a great market. One of the best in the area."

"It's not that. It—it's just that some other things are going on and—"

Rosalie clucked and shook her head. "You should not miss this event, Julia. I told you that. It's a great networking opportunity for you."

The door swung open again as a young couple blew in through the door, dust and leaves swirling in behind them.

"I understand. I'll try to make it," Julia said, "but I have to get back to work."

She retrieved the pie for the trucker and took the young couple's order. Rosalie pulled out her laptop and started tapping rapidly on the keyboard. Julia brought her some coffee and tried, without success, to stop thinking about Brittany, how she screamed and carried on the night the tornado hopped their house and landed on Errol and Arlene's place. She tried, again without success, to stop the scene from running over and over in her mind: ten-year-old Brittany pressed tightly against Julia's chest as they huddled together in the closet. She wondered, now, if she might have been trying to reabsorb her daughter back into her abdomen, back where she'd be safe again.

Brittany hadn't cried, but Julia kept whispering to her, words she no longer remembered. That night, all she could think about was another night when Julia, barely fifteen years old, had run from the unwed-mothers' home in the middle of the night, during a thunderstorm no less, an infant Brittany clutched to her chest.

Julia had nowhere to go that night but home, so that's where she'd gone—straight back to her own mother, the same woman who'd ordered Julia out of the house and into the unwed-mothers' home in the first place.

Mama and Papa had pre-signed the adoption papers. Funny how they'd had Julia's life all figured out for her. What they hadn't counted on was little Brittany's tenacity. Even as an unborn child, she'd burrowed her way so deep into Julia's heart that as soon as Julia caught sight of her, she knew she'd never let her go.

•••

Brittany got as far as their exit before she ran out of gas. The very exit she'd taken a thousand or a million times driving home from school or from Walmart, knowing that in another few minutes—five, ten tops—she'd be home. It couldn't be far now, but of course she'd never had to walk the whole way.

Rain had started to splatter the windshield and it was dark as tar outside. How far was the house? She tried to calculate distance in her head. If she could drive it in ten minutes doing, say, thirty miles an hour, how far was that? She was sure she must've learned how to figure this in school. In fact, she was sure Mr. Thompson taught them how—not that she ever paid attention.

She opened the door and the wind yanked it from her hand. "Yowee!" She slammed the door shut and reached for her hoodie, zipped it on, and tucked the saltines and her purse into her backpack. She sat, wondering if there was an umbrella in the car somewhere. She pulled the hood over her head and leapt out, popping the trunk open.

Nothing but a tire iron, jumper cables, and an empty plastic bottle that may once have contained motor oil.

The rain was a gentle drizzle, not even really rain at all. She should just go, start walking. It was awfully dark, but how far could it be? Thirty divided by ten was three, so three miles? Or a third of a mile? She had no idea, but hoisted her backpack to her shoulders and headed down the ramp. She tried not to think about what would happen when she got home, all the questions and accusations. She tried not to imagine what Mom would say when she found out Brittany was pregnant and Jake had turned out to be the scum Mom had always said he was.

Maybe Mom wouldn't be there. Maybe she was still at work. Maybe Brittany would slip into the house and back to her bed, claiming she'd been there all along. What was Mom doing making all these wild accusations for anyway? Didn't she trust Brittany?

•••

The storm hit just as Julia pulled into her long gravel driveway. Betty had let her leave early, although Julia knew Betty wanted to leave early herself. The truckers were still there, though, needing to hunker down for the duration, as the skinny older guy had informed them, and Rosalie was still tapping away at her laptop, despite it being past 6:00 p.m., so Betty told Julia, "Go. Go home and be safe. I'll take care of it."

Julia dashed into the house with the stack of mail she'd just plucked from her box at the end of the drive. She held it over her head as a shield against the rain that had started to slash the ground with fury. A clattering sound rose as she scurried up the front steps. She turned to gaze at what appeared for all the world to be little pieces of white popcorn jumping all over the grass and the gravel drive.

Hail. Wasn't hail a sign of a tornado?

She fumbled in her pocket for the key, jiggled it in the lock and kicked at the always-stuck front door, bursting into the house along with a whirl of rain and hail and blowing leaves. She slammed the door behind her, shucked out of her jacket, and managed to get the tea kettle on and whistling before the power went out.

•••

Brittany had made it to the turnoff just past the last cornfield and could see the empty space where Errol and Arlene's house used to be, now just an expanse of rocky dirt. It had become a mud pit in the pouring rain. She was completely soaked, which would be bad enough, but then the rain turned to ice or something. Sharp pieces stung her arms and smacked her in the head. It felt like someone was throwing rocks. Was it hail? Didn't hail come with tornadoes? She dove beneath the puny pine tree next to the ditch, the only one remaining from the time Errol tried to establish a hedge along the road. That and a lone sumac, covered with bright red berries, were the only things left of what used to be a gorgeous garden.

Brittany is ten again. She and Mama are in the closet and the wind is roaring outside. Brittany is screaming, "Mama, Mama, Mama," pressing her face into Mama's warm chest. "Shh, baby, shh," Mama says. "It'll be all right." She says it over and over. "It'll be all right. It'll be all right."

The hail clattered around her, bouncing off the springy pine boughs over her head. Brittany hugged herself and let her arms slide down around her abdomen. *It'll be all right,* she thought with fervor. *I won't let anything hurt you.*

•••

The walnut trees by the shed swayed and creaked. Rain slashed the window in wave after wave as hours passed. The sun set and it went from merely dark to pitch black. There was yet another burst of hail, and the power flickered on for a moment, then went out again. Julia found a flashlight, rummaged in the cupboard for the box of tea bags, then made her way to the rocking chair by the front window to sit and sip at a mug. She rocked and rocked, the flashlight in her lap switched off to save the battery.

Julia is fifteen again. She's hitchhiked for hours, her baby, still unnamed, cuddled into a sling. The storm hit just as she passed Errol and Arlene's place and she's ducked into the old shed. She's nursing the baby, when the shed door creaks open. Mama says, "Julia, is that you?" and then Mama's scooping her and the baby into her arms and all three of them are crying. "I was so worried. The home called, said you was missing. It don't matter, though. Nothin' matters but that you're safe."

The storm surged outside for another half hour as Julia sat in the chair, rocking and rocking, certain that Brittany was dead. Of course, she could be in New York, far from the storm, but Julia knew, somehow, in a way she couldn't fathom that this was not true.

•••

The hail stopped as suddenly as it started, but then the wind picked up. Brittany stayed where she was, huddled beneath Errol and Arlene's abandoned pine tree, eating soggy saltines, shivering and whispering to the tiny being inside her belly. *It'll be all right.*

•••

And so it was that the storm finally slowed and the sky cleared. Stars winked into view over Brittany's head as she walked. The power came back on, Julia stepped out onto the porch, and then there Brittany was, trudging up the gravel drive, her face lit by the flickering lamp near the mailbox. She looked exhausted. She was also completely soaked, her wet hair stuck to her forehead. She twirled a stick dotted with red berries between two fingers.

Brittany spotted her mother on the porch as she crunched her way up the driveway. Mama was leaning against the porch post, hugging herself. She didn't look at all angry. *It'll be all right. I won't let anything hurt you.*

Brittany had found the sumac branch near the pine tree that had sheltered her, maybe something Errol and Arlene had planted before the twister took their house. It had powdery red berries that would certainly produce a gorgeous dye.

She held the twig aloft, her other hand on her belly. "Mama, look," she shouted, resolving to tell her mother the truth. "I brought you something!"

Mama. Brittany hadn't called her that in years. Julia walked down the steps and that was when the tears she'd been holding back finally let go. She opened her arms and her daughter, soaking wet but safe, came home to her.

Vivian Lawry

Lethal Love

Selina and her sisters sit in a circle on yoga mats, eyes closed. Sunshine streams through Judika's skylights, bathing the sisters in golden warmth, nourishing the herbs and medicinal plants covering half the room. They end the session with relaxation and candle breaths. As Selina puffs out the last air from the depths of her lungs, she feels a soft, velvety brush along her throat.

The sisters open their eyes to find Selina surrounded by a sprinkling of lavender rose petals.

Judika, the youngest, murmurs, "Beautiful!"

"What the hell's that?" Freya's tone is annoyance edged with worry. The oldest sister dislikes surprises, especially unexplainable ones.

Selina barricades her chest with crossed arms. "How should I know!"

"I'm sure Freya didn't mean to sound, um, harsh." Judika leans forward. "It's just that this isn't...normal."

Selina scowls and shrugs. "Well, I didn't do anything abnormal! I just sat here taking candle breaths—plain, old candle breaths." She draws a deep belly breath and blows it out in little puffs. With the last few puffs, more lavender rose petals float from her mouth.

All three sisters gape.

Freya recovers first. "I've never seen anything like this. I've never heard of anything like this." She gets to her feet and starts prowling a path before the fireplace. "Has it happened before?"

Selina shakes her head. "I've had a tight feeling in my chest for a few days, but...only that." She inhales deeply again and coughs. Lavender petals spew forth. All color drains from Selina's face. "What's happening to me?"

Judika jumps up. "I'll make a cough syrup for you." She dashes across the apartment, gathering equipment and ingredients. She simmers anise seeds and dried thyme in water for ten minutes, then adds horehound and licorice root. She strains the mixture and dissolves brown sugar in it. She decants the syrup into a bottle with a cork stopper and returns to Selina. "Here. Sip one tablespoon at a time. Anise has been used as an expectorant since ancient times, to make coughs more productive. Licorice soothes the throat and helps quell the urge to cough. You can repeat the dose every hour if need be." Judika puts her arm around Selina. "How do you feel, hon? Does it hurt?"

Selina shrugs off her sister's arm. "The petals just tickle—which makes me want to cough when I take a deep breath."

"Try to relax. That should help. You can stay here if you like."

"No, I'll go down to my place."

Freya says, "Let me give you a hand up." She hauls Selina to her feet, and they roll up their yoga mats.

•••

Sunday is Selina's weekly day of rest. Downstairs, she sits in her recliner, sipping the sweet, herby syrup. Her throat relaxes. She ponders the strange sensations in her body. Is it her imagination, or is she starting to wheeze? Does she feel something snaking through her lungs?

•••

Over the next several days, Judika continues to press remedies on Selina—grapefruit juice sweetened with honey, ten juniper berries to eat before breakfast to enhance blood supply to the lungs—"and it's antiseptic." She brings switchel— honey, water, and apple cider vinegar—by the quart. "I'm just throwing everything at you but the kitchen sink here. All of these are home cough remedies I found in Granny's 'receipt' book." The sisters share a smile at their grandmother's old-timey word for recipes. "We'll try them all and see what works best."

Selina uses all the remedies and continues with her life. First thing in the morning, she soaks in a deep, hot bath, followed by Pilates to strengthen her core. She eats hearty breakfasts, such as a tofu scramble on multigrain toast, plus a fruit or vegetable smoothie with protein powder. Grabbing the first cough remedy that comes to hand, by 9:00 she's at the dance studio.

Except during performances, the ballet company maintains a regular five-day workweek. Selina relaxes and stretches her calf muscles by rolling them out over a foam roller, using a tennis ball, golf ball, or lacrosse ball on muscles needing extra attention. Others do the same —including the new lead dancer Dorios. Selina peeks at him. Wide shoulders and a narrow waist make his upper body almost a triangle. Muscles ripple as he moves. He could lift an elephant, let alone a ballerina. And if that weren't enough, he has turquoise eyes and wavy hair dark as a raven's wing. Looking at him, her chest tightens. She looks away and concen-trates on her warm-up.

After the warm-up, the structured workday begins with a ninety-minute classical ballet class—required. Some dancers sigh, or mutter that it's unnecessary. Dorios says, "Our bodies are our instruments. We have to tune them." He tosses a lock of hair off his forehead and strides into position.

Selina sips her cough remedy and joins the other dancers.

•••

During the fifteen-minute break before six hours of rehearsals, Selina meditates and again downs Judika's cough syrup. Often the corps rehearses five or six ballets a day, bouncing from one style to another, but now they're focused on the upcoming performance. Selina labors to perfect her technique for *Le Spectre de la Rose,* the most challenging ballet she's ever danced. The role Dorios dances is strenuous. Sweat glistens on his bare skin, and loose clothes cling to his body. Even so, he smiles, offering tips and encouragement to the lesser dancers.

They call it a day at 6:30 p.m.

Cough remedies and focus on her moves suppress Selina's cough during work hours. But otherwise, those aren't powerful enough, and she coughs repeatedly. Lavender drifts of satiny petals and the scent of roses fill the apartment. By now Selina sees the petals as more threatening than beautiful.

She closes her day with a home-cooked vegan dinner, an Epsom salt bath, and another rollout of her muscles. While she ices her feet and calves for ten minutes, she suffers a coughing spasm that spews lavender petals into the tub of ice and leaves her breathless.

She coughs so long and hard that she can't inhale. She passes out from lack of oxygen. When she comes to, she thinks, *I've got to get an inhaler or something. It might do nothing to treat the disease, but all I ask is to survive the next bout of this. Or maybe Judika can think of something.*

Judika sighs and shakes her head. "The only thing I can suggest is meditation and breathing steam."

• • •

The three sisters have owned the house since their parents died. Judika has the top floor.

Her herbs and medicinal plants need the light, and some of her ceremonies need access to the night sky. Selina has the second floor, half of it given over to mirrored walls and dance rails. Freya has the first floor, plus a basement biology lab where she works on herbicides. Each floor has a separate entrance, kitchen, bathrooms, etc. The sisters live separate lives, but often share dinner or yoga. A week after the first appearance of the rose petals, they gather for dinner at Selina's. She coughs discreetly into her napkin, but can't conceal the petals.

Freya turns to Judika. "Isn't there something in your Wiccan practice—in your books of spells—about this?"

Judika stands, brows furrowed. "Not there. But in the language of flowers, lavender roses mean love at first sight."

They turn to Selina, who sits wide-eyed, mouth agape, and face crimson. "Tell us!" Freya and Judika cry in unison.

Selina twirls a blond curl around her finger. "What's to tell? A new lead dancer joined the company for the season, starting with *Le Spectre de la Rose.* His name is Dorios. He's magnificent!"

Freya stops pacing, taps her forefinger to her lips. "That's the ballet where a young girl returns from her first prom with a souvenir rose, falls asleep, and dreams the spirit of the rose comes to her—something like that?"

Selina nods. "He comes through her bedroom window. They dance through the night." She sighs, her eyes losing focus. "Dorios dances with unbelievable passion. His performance is so natural, it's like instinct." She coughs, grimacing in pain. The petals now irritate rather than tickle.

Judika tugs Selina to her feet and grips her hand. "So how long has this been going on?"

"There's nothing going on! I wish there were. He joined the *corps de ballet* only last week."

"Last week! And you've not mentioned him?" Judika's face reveals her hurt.

Red splotches mottle Selina's cheeks. Her chin juts out. "What's to mention? He doesn't know I'm alive. Why does it matter?"

"Well, thank the gods and goddesses it's nothing serious. There's no such thing as true love at first sight." Freya drops her napkin onto the table and stands, flat-footed, arms akimbo. "No doubt the lead male dancer is as arrogant and self-centered as that prima ballerina you're always complaining about. He's probably a jerk." She turns toward the door.

Selina scowls. "What do you know about love anyway? You haven't been serious about anyone in a decade." She coughs and gags. A whole blossom drops to the floor, the petals flecked with red.

"Stop it! You're both overlooking what's important! A week ago Selina coughed petals. Now it's a whole flower. This is serious!" Judika eyes the speckled blossom. "You've grown a completely different rose. This one is a dog rose—meaning pleasure and pain." She eyes the bloom more closely. "And these speckles are blood."

"Why is this happening?" Selina sobs.

Freya slowly turns back. "You're right. I've been focused on my grant proposal. I'll see what I can find. I'll consult my biology colleagues and faculty in the medical school." She stalks out, banging the door.

Selina says, "I think she's embarrassed that she hasn't tried to help me already."

"Probably."

Selina coughs again and winces. "I'd do anything to make him look at me."

"I'll see what I can find in my library." Judika turns to leave. "For now, try to rest, hon. Don't think about Dorios."

•••

Selina has finished rolling out her muscles and preparing the ice bath for her feet and calves. There's a knock at the door. No buzz from the outer door means it must be one of her sisters. "It's unlocked."

Judika dashes across the room and dumps her armload on the table. "Here's your next supply of cough syrups. Trade them off, whatever works at the time." She taps a fat volume titled *The Element Encyclopedia of 5000 Spells*. "Love spells won't do anything for your cough, but you might be happier if Dorios takes a liking to you. Are you up for some love magic?"

A lopsided grin appears on Selina's face. "Why not?" Judika picks up the encyclopedia and dons reading glasses. Selina thinks she looks very much like the schoolteacher she almost was.

"Several things generally apply to love magic. First, all things being equal, a Friday coinciding with a new moon is the most auspicious time to perform love spells. Fridays in general are the best days. Friday is associated with Aphrodite and Oshun, powerful spirits of love. Friday's named in honor of Freya, Northern Lady of Love."

Selina giggles. "Really? Freya is the name of the Northern Lady of Love? Now that's ironic!"

Judika frowns her disapproval and pushes a bottle toward Selina. "It isn't a Friday, but why wait? We can try something else at the end of the week. Now, bathe your hands in this rose water. That strengthens anything you handle. We'll try Diana's Petition of Love. It's relatively quick and easy." She places an arrow on the table, brightly feathered and carved with symbols of Venus and Diana. "Diana was the Goddess of the Hunt." Then she slides paper and pen across the table. "First, write down your petition of love. Be sure to include your name and Dorios'."

Selina writes, a half page of love, wishes, hopes, and assertions of his powerlessness against her, ending with "This arrow overcomes your reluctance. You will love me now!"

Judika pushes the arrow toward Selina. "Wrap your petition around the shaft and tie it there with these ribbons." Selina does. Judika says, "Come up to my place."

On Judika's balcony, Selina sets the arrow afire and shoots it toward the moon.

Judika hugs Selina. "Good luck, hon."

When Selina returns to her apartment, Freya awaits. "I've been thinking. While I try to find the root of your problem, we need to contain it. Salt is the classic plant killer. Its effects are enhanced by adding a bit of soap and white vinegar." She pushes a beaker toward Selina. "Don't make that face! There's no soap, just salt, water, and vinegar."

"I'm supposed to drink that?"

"Of course! Changing the salinity of your body might kill—or at least weaken—the roses in you."

Selina inhales deeply, pinches her nose, and drinks.

•••

Over the next days, Selina coughs less. Dorios smiles at her during the classic ballet class. Selina nearly swoons. At the end of the week, she sees her doctor.

The nurse weighs her and checks her height, and takes Selina's blood pressure seven times. Her doctor says, "What's happened to you? A year ago, you were well in the healthy range. Today your blood pressure reached one eighty over one twenty."

"How bad is that?"

"You could stroke out at any time!" The doctor shakes her head and reaches for her prescription pad.

"I don't want drugs! Please. Give me a few days. If I can't get it down with diet and meditation, we'll revisit meds." Selina shudders. *I guess that means I lay off the saltwater and vinegar cure. Freya will be so disappointed.* "Right now, I'm most worried about my cough."

"Let's take a listen." She moves her stethoscope across Selina's chest and back. "I'm not hearing anything. Another deep breath."

Selina inhales deeply and coughs on the exhale. Lavender rose petals spew forth. The doctor gasps. Selina tells her the history of coughing rose petals.

The doctor shakes her head and orders X-rays. They show vining images. She asks permission to send the X-rays and samples of the rose petals to pulmonary experts all across the country, seeking a diagnosis and/or information.

•••

Selina gathers her sisters and recounts the day's events. "I can't deal with this alone. I need more from both of you. Judika, I need another spell. Freya, I need another cure."

Her sisters exchange a look. Judika says, "I thought you might. So I have brought chamomile hydrosol for you to wash your hair. The scent should attract Dorios. Also, here's a dried dandelion head. Blow it toward Dorios, sending loving messages and wishes. Focus on your desire and blow!"

"Okay, then." She reaches for the hair wash and dandelion head. "What do you say, Freya?"

Freya heaves a bottomless breath. "Open your mouth." Selina's eyes grow wide but she does. Freya pulls out a tongue depressor and examines Selina's throat. "I see bits of plant matter at the back of your throat. I suggest a nonselective herbicide. We can use a Q-tip to apply it to the visible petals and leaves. And you can inhale it."

Selina nods.

•••

At the next day's rehearsals, Dorios says, "Hey. You're good." He smiles. Selina's heart thumps. Thank goodness her blood pressure is down! And thank goodness her leotard and tights hide the rash on her trunk. She feels nauseous but keeps dancing, a smile pasted on.

Dorios smiles at her the next day too, setting her heart racing. She smiles back and dances through a headache.

That night she gathers her sisters. "Dorios is being friendly. I'm actually hopeful!" She draws a deep, diaphragmatic breath and coughs lavender rose petals.

Judika grabs her by the shoulders. "Tell us everything."

Selina blushes. "I admit, I care for him more every day. But, Freya, I can't keep up this treatment. I might have to drop out of the ballet." Suddenly her body seizes and she falls, every muscle contracting as she jerks, her heels drumming on the floor. Her eyes roll back. Her sisters hold her down till the convulsion passes.

"Oh, Sis, I knew exposure to pesticides has side effects, but not so violent—or to come on so fast. Are you okay now?" Freya wrings her hands.

Selina shudders. "I'll get there—just stop this treatment."

•••

The next day Freya bursts in while Judika is brewing another cough syrup, clearly agitated. She grips Selina's shoulders. "The cause of this is your love of Dorios! A medical school researcher put me on to it. He says it's hanahaki disease—rare but deadly. It first showed up in Japan a few years ago. The name comes from two Japanese words—*hana*, meaning flower, and *hakimasu*, meaning throw up."

"I'm not sure how naming it changes anything." Selina sighs.

Judika says, "Do you have more than a name?"

Freya shifts impatiently. "I'll tell you as soon as you let me! It's caused by unrequited love. Flowers bloom in the heart or lungs. From your symptoms, it must be lungs."

"But I'm not throwing up. I'm breathing out flowers!"

Scowling, Freya says, "Whatever! It must be the same disease—unrequited love and flowers. Regardless, there are only two cures. Either the loved one loves you in return, or the plant is surgically removed. When the flowers and their roots are surgically removed, so are your feelings for him. You would no longer love Dorios."

While Judika cheers and Selina looks thoughtful, Freya knits her brow and continues. "It might also remove all memories of him. Maybe you couldn't love again."

"I could never forget him!" Selina shudders. "Would never want to." The sisters' shoulders slump.

"Oh hon, how can you say that? You can't die for love."

Freya stands tall. "Absolutely not. But here we are. I can only suggest sword swallowing to cut the plants inside. It's dangerous."

"Just do it." Selina opens her mouth and tries to relax her larynx.

Judika shudders. "Wait! Let's try another spell first. Take this copal. Carry it in a charm bag around your neck."

Selina rubs the smooth gold lump and sniffs. It's slightly citrusy. "What's this? And what's it supposed to do?"

"It's dried tree resin—from trees held sacred in Aztec, Mayan, and Incan traditions. Like those other sacred resins, frankincense and myrrh, it can be used to draw romantic attention."

"It can't hurt." She pockets the copal.

"Also," Judika says, "I advise getting a strand of hair from Dorios. We'll put it under dripping water to wear away his resistance. And there's a Romany belief that fairies tie knots in the limbs of willow trees. They're supposed to be powerful love magic." She pulls a willow knot from her pocket and pushes it toward Selina. "Sleep with this under your pillow."

Freya groans. "But what if he never loves Selina? We need to eliminate these roses. You could try smoking. Flowers absorb nicotine, sulphur dioxide, and nitrogen oxides—leading to shorter but fatter plants, dropping leaves, and downward curving leaves. Long term, there'd be the risk of lung cancer. But you won't be smoking long term. Besides smoking, we should keep you in the dark as much as possible. Plants need sunshine, which is absorbed through the skin."

•••

Selina tracks Dorios. One morning he drops the towel he'd used to dry his head and neck. She snatches it up and takes it to Judika, who retrieves a few hairs that she secures under a drip of water.

Dancers are forbidden to smoke, so Selina does that only at home. There, she practically chain-smokes. She hates the taste and smell, and keeps all the windows open to air her apartment.

She avoids sunlight as much as possible, but it helps little.

Freya says, "Shall I try to remove the roses physically?" She holds a pair of tweezers, shaped like eyebrow tweezers but about a foot long. "It could hurt."

Selina gulps. "I'll try anything. I can hardly control the coughing at work now." She opens her mouth and tries to relax.

Freya eases the tweezers deep into Selina's throat and tugs, pulling out virtually an entire tiny rosebush, splattering blood everywhere. Selina screams and collapses. She's weak. Lack of oxygen? Blood loss? She can barely move.

Freya looks at the bloody tweezers and mutters, "I might never be able to use these tweezers again—in the lab *or* in the kitchen."

The sisters gather for dinner. Selina's still coughing lavender rose petals everywhere, but she feels less congested. Pulling out the rosebush left her throat so raw that she struggles to eat.

That night she can't sleep. Deep purple smudges bruise her eyes.

•••

During rehearsals the next day, the prima ballerina falls, suffering an ankle injury. The choreographer turns to Selina. "Step up. This could be your lucky day." He grins.

Selina feels faint. She will actually dance with Dorios!

Moving through the ballet, Selina's heart swells. She restrains her cough by focusing on the dance, on the touch of Dorios's hands as he lifts her, on the sweat slicking his muscles. They dance as if made for each other. Even the first run-through is virtually flawless.

At home that evening, she sniffs the places on her rehearsal clothes that Dorios touched, breathing his unique blend of clean sweat and talcum powder. She performs her bar workout to Louis Armstrong's "A Kiss to Build a Dream On."

Judika comes in during a particularly virulent coughing spasm, orange petals flying everywhere. "Oh, hon. Orange means passion and energy. What's happened?"

•••

When *Le Spectre de la Rose* opens, Selina dances as never before. Dorios lifts her high in a whirl, and red silk rose petals fall from his costume. His assistant collects them, to sell as souvenirs to fans. The twirling triggers a coughing fit. A cloud of red rose petals floats from Selina's mouth. The audience goes wild. They take six curtain calls.

The director and choreographer are so impressed, they decide to keep Selina in the role.

Dorios is furious—until he realizes that the spotlight on the two of them is brighter than any he's enjoyed before. He says, "You are extraordinary! What a pair we can be!"

When they dance, Selina's soul feels they are the only two in the world—though her brain tells her this isn't so.

Audiences continue to be mesmerized. The director and Dorios plan a tour, including "Waltz of the Roses" from *The Snow Queen*. They consider making "Waltz of the Flowers" from *The Nutcracker* a waltz of roses.

At home, Selina coughs up leaf roses. Judika says, "Your feelings are changing the flowers. Leaf roses are climbers. Their tiny thorns curve down and attach to anything. They symbolize hope."

•••

The more they dance, the more Dorios gazes into Selina's eyes. One night he cups her face in his hands and leans in. His gentle kiss claims every part of her heart, mind, and soul. They kiss again. It's a moment of gold and flashes of light, his arms like iron bands welding them together.

At home that night, Selina works out to Etta James wailing, "At last my love has come along. My lonely days are over, and life is like a song."

Dorios sends a bouquet of yellow tulips. Judika says it is a declaration of love—but love is a risk. Still, Selina's heart swells and her spirits soar. Her laughter turns to a wracking cough, but that does nothing to dim her joy.

Judika hugs Selina. "Red roses! True love! Can it be?"

•••

As Dorios and Selina dance, the petals she spews stay red, signifying deep love.

The more intimate they become, the more Selina sees her soulmate. Whether at his apartment or hers, they are seldom apart. In bed, their bodies dance together as perfectly as on the stage. Crushed rose petals scent their nights together.

Over dinner one evening, Judika turns to Selina and Dorios. "Your one-month anniversary is coming up. And April is the month of Venus (Aphrodite to the Greeks), goddess of love and death, of orchards and sexuality, of the waters of the world. So now that you two have a special relationship—now that you are bonded in love—you should celebrate."

Selina and Dorios exchange a look. He says, "What do you have in mind?"

"A party with family and friends!" Judika's eyes dance. "We'll have a lover's ceremony under April's full moon. I'll take care of everything!"

•••

On the night of the party, Judika's apartment is perfect. She presents a lovely table with fresh flowers, sparkling glasses, and silver. The skylights allow moonbeams to bathe the tables loaded with red and white wines, fresh fruit juices, seafood, dried fruits and nuts, and other feast foods. After the sisters and members of the ballet company have gathered, Judika rises and taps her wineglass. "Dear friends! We have gathered together tonight to celebrate a very special relationship between Selina and Dorios. I am honored to be the one to call the Goddess of Love to our table and offer her the wine from our cups and the bread and seafood from our plates and ask her to bless Selina and Dorios that they may continue in happiness, passion, and fortune.

"It is traditional to bring a branch of myrtle to gatherings such as this to represent the tree and blessings of life. Please now present this myrtle to each other, as we witness and bless it for you." She hands the myrtle to Selina and Dorios. "Now you should say something to each other. Just speak from your hearts."

Selina blushes and hands her myrtle to Dorios. She gazes into his turquoise eyes and says, "I choose you, Dorios, because I love you. You are the blue in my sky and the laughter in my morning."

Handing his myrtle to Selina, Dorios smiles. "I choose you, Selina, because you are the most extraordinary woman I have ever met. You are kind, graceful, and beautiful. I love you."

•••

The more they share, the happier Selina becomes. Her breathing eases. The rose petals come only in brief bursts. Dorios urges Selina—begs her—not to change, to continue breathing rose petals. Tears roll down Selina's cheeks. "I'll try. But I don't know that I can control it."

When there are no more rose petals, Dorios bounces between furious and despondent. "Why are you doing this? Without the rose petals you are ordinary! I can't attach myself to ordinary!" Selina's heart—her very soul—is crushed.

When Dorios won't dance with her, the director relegates Selina to the chorus. The hanahaki disease returns with a vengeance. When she coughs red rose petals at rehearsal, joy flashes across Dorios's face. The prima ballerina tugs him back into position. "You cannot trust that one! You return to her and one night you will turn around and see that at her core, she'll always be ordinary."

Selina cannot sleep for the coughing, cannot eat for the pain. She loses weight and blood.

When her stamina falters, the director lays her off.

•••

Selina curls up on her sofa. In the background, Toni Braxton pleads, "Un-break my heart. Say you love me again. Undo this hurt you caused when you walked out the door..." Selina's still on the sofa when her sisters arrive. Selina sits and is overcome, coughing pink roses.

"Pink roses symbolize remembrance," Judika tells Freya. She hugs Selina. "But you must *forget* Dorios." She dices an apple and douses the pieces with honey and cayenne pepper. "When the apple decays, love decays as well. Surely you will learn to love again but more wisely." She sets it aside to rot.

•••

The emerging romance between Dorios and the prima ballerina is all over the media: dining together, visiting the zoo, botanical gardens, and historic sites. Selina is frozen in a limbo of grief.

Freya and Judika face Selina, who is curled up in bed. Arms akimbo, Freya says, "Get over him! He isn't worth your suffering."

Judika says, "You must have the surgery to remove the roses. You will be well. You won't remember Dorios, but you will live. And maybe you can love again."

Selina shakes her head. In the background Patsy Cline wails, "Sweet dreams of you, every night I go through. Why can't I forget you and start my life anew, instead of having sweet dreams about you…" She coughs black rose petals.

Judika looks at the black petals and gasps. "Yes, it is the end of a relationship. But death? Farewell? Selina, come back to me—to us! Surely you don't want to die!"

Selina's smile is wan. "No. But I don't want to live without his love."

Judika and Freya exchange a look. "We can't cure you but we can treat you. We've *been* treating you. We'll not give up till you see the light." Judika stalks from the room.

"I've been working on an herbicide that kills plants but is harmless for pets, wildlife—and people!" Freya sits on the edge of the bed and grasps Selina's hand. "The early results look promising. I'll live at the lab if necessary to speed this along."

Selina squeezes Freya's hand. "I know you'll do all that you can. Just holding your hand is a comfort." They hold hands in companionable silence until Judika returns.

"Here. Wear this." An intricate silver filigree locket nestles in Judika's palm. "The scent of oregano is supposed to help you forget old lovers." She drapes the chain around Selina's neck.

"I put oil of oregano on the pad in this diffuser. Your body heat will release the scent." She kisses Selina's cheek. "Now I'm going to prepare a broken heart bath for you."

Selina and Freya stare at Judika. Freya arches one eyebrow in silent query.

"I'll add white rose petals, honeysuckle blossoms, and rose attar to a warm bath, along with a lump of rose quartz. You'll soak in the scented water till it cools. When you come back to bed, wear the oregano diffuser and put the rose quartz under your pillow."

•••

Drifting toward sleep, Selina thinks of her sisters—all they have done for her—and feels the depth of their love. She doesn't have the love of Dorios, but she does have the love of her sisters. For them, she will try.

The next morning Judika brings a breakfast tray to Selina's room and finds rose petals scattered on the comforter like confetti. She quickly pens a note and leaves it on the tray at Selina's bedside.

Selina wakes in misery, coughing more—more rose petals, more colors—than ever. Then she reads the note: *purple = lost partner or spouse; white = memorial for a departed loved one, but also honor and peace; pink = gratitude and appreciation; yellow = friendship, warmth, affection, and healing.*

Robert McGuill

Dead Drift

He didn't know the fly box had fallen from his vest pocket, or floated downriver into the small white cup of the woman's hand. He was dressing his line when the loss occurred—fumbling with the blood knot he couldn't seem to tie—and when she waded up behind him to return it, the shock of her touch sent him stumbling backward, nearly knocking them both into the water.

"Oh, God!" she laughed. "I'm sorry. I didn't mean to startle you."

"No, no," he said, embarrassed by the murderous look he'd thrown her way. "You're fine. I thought I was alone." He offered an embarrassed smile. Without thinking, he added, "I haven't had a familiar hand laid on me in a long time."

The woman gave with a fussy little wave, dismissing his bumbling attempt at an apology. "It's my fault. I should have spoken up. It's just that I wanted to get this back into your hands before you disappeared into the canyon." She held out the lost fly box, smiling. "You dropped it at the oxbow back there, near the big rocks that look like cathedral spires."

He looked at the small container. Then up at the big rocks. "Thank you."

The woman told him it was nothing. She turned and studied the drift of the current, and asked him how he was managing. He looked at the pool he'd been fishing, and thumbed up his hat and admitted with a glum half-shrug it wasn't all that good. His stand-by pattern, a bead-head pheasant tail, he told her, had failed him—and along with it, his luck.

She sympathized. They weren't biting as well as she had expected either. She patted her vest then, and produced a thin leather wallet from one of the side pockets. She plucked a hand-tied fly from the wallet's fleece backing and placed it in his palm. "See if you can't do better with one of these," she said. "I've been having luck with them all morning."

The fly was a #22 buckskin. He carried several of his own in one box or another, but accepted the gift with fawning thanks, not wanting her to feel the gesture was unappreciated.

She introduced herself. Eva Saint-*something-or-other*. A beautiful, if preposterous, name for someone you meet on a river. But he shook her hand, and they chatted, amiably, first about the day, then about fishing, then about nothing in particular. The conversation was cordial, politely distant. But when the woman suggested she had better be moving along (She didn't want to take up his entire morning!), Walter felt an intense and unexpected urge to ask her to stay. Only what would he have said? That in addition to the fly box, he had lost his heart, too? He might just as well admit he'd lost his mind! She waded across the channel, and he lowered his eyes to the buckskin fly, examining it with a gentle roll of his fingertip. He wondered after the scent of her cologne, which still lingered in the air, and passed the fly beneath his nose, then put it lightly to his tongue.

•••

That afternoon, on his way down the mountain, Walter saw the woman again. She was on one knee near the river's edge, running her hand through the water. She stood, and he saw she was wearing hip boots. A detail he hadn't noticed earlier. They struck him as absurdly erotic; a cruel reminder, perhaps, of just how long it had been since he had enjoyed a woman's company. She smiled pleasantly as the Jeep rumbled by and, recognizing him behind the wheel, raised her rod and waved. Walter waved in return, but did not stop for fear of making an even bigger fool of himself than he already had. He could only imagine how ridiculous he must have sounded, standing there in the middle of the stream, explaining how long it had been since anyone had laid a familiar hand on him. A familiar hand! My god, what a thing to say! Of course he hadn't pulled over. How much more of a bad first impression did he need to make?

He drove on, muttering. "So this is what you've been reduced to, eh? A skirt-chasing satyr? Well good going, Walter. Bravo! That's a classy thing to admit to, isn't it?" He gripped the wheel and shook it. "She was being nice, for Christ's sake. That was all. She gave you a fly, you idiot, not a blowjob. You're a creaky, leaky, misanthropic old sonofabitch, and you've never been any good with *anyone,* so let it go, why don't you? She doesn't want you, and even if she did you probably wouldn't deserve her."

The self-admonitions, though copious and richly embroidered, proved pointless. The hook had been set. He had fallen for the woman, head over hip boots, and would not be able to make himself leave without seeing her at least one last time. So at the risk of complete and utter humiliation, he wrestled the Jeep into low gear, turned it around, and circled back in the direction from which he had come.

• • •

Dinner was her suggestion, and he accepted the invitation without a second thought. It was as if she knew he would return, and had decided to stroll up the gravel road to meet him, just so she could ask. The moment he pulled over, she walked up to his door, laid her rod across the crook of her arm, and said, "I'm tired of eating alone, Walter. What about you?"

They met later that evening in the lobby of the restaurant. They drove separate cars, allowing one another the unspoken option of a graceful escape. But the precaution proved unnecessary. Before the date was midway to its end, they were enamored of one another, a coming together as sweet and easy and natural as two streams converging in a shady wood.

"Really? His name was Stoney?" Walter said, trying not to smile when she told him about her ex-husband, a car salesman in Winslow. Walter said it was shame enough the man was a hustler of the second order. But "Stoney," really? What mother would do that to her child?

"Don't laugh," Eva said, gently. "It fit the man. He was chiseled from rock. From the neck up, anyway."

An admiring smile lit Walter's face. Her name, Eva Sauveur, fit her as beautifully as the little black dress she wore. It sparkled the same way her diamonds sparkled when she laughed and tossed back her hair and told him what a grand time she was having. The wine was only an excuse. He would have said what he said anyway, even if he hadn't been tipsy. "You, Eva, are a catch," he announced, meaning this in the way they used to mean it, back in the day when people used to say such ridiculous things. "What a fool this Stoney character was to let you slip away! If you were mine, I'd have never allowed it to happen."

Eva smiled. "He didn't let me slip away, Walter. I walked out." She pushed up the sleeve of her sweater, tipping her wineglass to her lips. "It took ten years of going out of his way to ruin whatever made me happy, but he finally did the one thing I could not forgive."

"Which was?"

"You'll think it's silly."

"No, I won't."

She allowed a faint smile to find its way to her lips. "All right then. Here it is. I went off to Phoenix one weekend to visit my sick father, and while I was gone Stoney cleaned the garage. Only, in the course of tossing out all the things he considered 'junk,' he threw away my fishing rod. It was just an old cane pole, but it had sentimental value. My father made it for me out of an old cane pole *his* father had given *him* when he was boy." She picked up her glass. Brought it to balance on her fingertips. "The irony was, Stoney didn't know he'd done anything wrong. He actually believed the rod was a piece of junk, and was going to replace it with a new one. It was one of the few times in our life he managed to piss me off without even trying."

Walter picked up his fork. "Did he ever apologize?"

Eva smiled, but it was tinged with bitterness. "I suppose it sounds awful, but I didn't want his apologies. The only thing I wanted was to hurt him. So I did. I stayed out all night and, the next day, when he demanded to know where I'd been, I told him I'd gone fishing." Her chin rose, a haughty defiance finding its way into her voice. "He asked me how I'd managed—given I had no rod or reel—and I smiled and said, 'I didn't need any gear, darling. I was noodling. You know what *noodling* is, don't you?'"

Walter leaned back in his chair, imagining the murderous rage he would have felt had someone thrown away something as precious to him as the cane pole was to her. What luck old Stoney had been such a idiot!

"What about you?" she said with a whimsical flourish, sweeping a lock of her silver hair behind her ear. "How is it a man as charming as yourself hasn't been lured back to the altar? What's your sad story, I wonder?"

Walter gave with a relaxed shrug. "It's been so long, I can hardly remember."

Eva offered feigned astonishment at this, and gave her head a theatric little turn. "She made that *big* an impression, did she?"

Walter grinned. "Well, she wasn't the feminine version of Stoney, if that's what you're asking. Our breakup had nothing to do with bickering or fighting. What did us in was her hideous laugh. A cackling, witchlike thing. It was absolutely chilling." He pretended to shiver. "If her laugh hadn't been so horrifying, we might still be together."

"Liar."

"It's true," he said with a bashful glance. "I worried I'd be struck blind one day and forced to stumble around the house with no means of escape. It was too much to contemplate. I decided I'd rather stand on a street corner with a tin cup, selling pencils, than subject myself to a torture like that."

She laughed, and gave with an amused shake of her head.

"I'm serious," Walter said. "She was a beautiful woman, yes. No one would argue other-wise, not even me. But her voice was so disagreeable—I swear to you it was so awful—you didn't want to be in the dark with her. Even to make love."

"If it was so horrid, how did you manage to father a child?"

"How do you think? We did it with the lights on."

• • •

Walter proposed to Eva that evening, and they were married within a month. The arrange-ment raised eyebrows among family and friends alike, the affair coming together as suddenly as it had. But the newlyweds carried on as if none of it mattered to them. Because it didn't.

"Roughing it?" Eva's sister, Joan, sighed when she learned the newlyweds intended to spent their honeymoon cavorting in the mountains like savages. "The man has money, doesn't he? You both have money. Why aren't you going to art galleries or spending time at the theater? Why aren't you traveling to Italy to celebrate La Biennale? Why isn't he putting you up in ritzy hotels?"

• • •

Walter's son, Richard—his only child from the lost marriage with the cackling ex-wife—was even more blunt. He accused his father of self-indulgence. Succumbing to a late-life crisis that was at once juvenile and dangerous. "You're not kids," he warned Walter. "You're old, both of you, and you've got no business traipsing off into the wilderness alone."

• • •

"What if you get lost or hurt up there?" Joan pressed Eva, sounding the way she had when they were girls, always looking for the worst, always searching for the fly in the raisin cake. "What then? You know who'll come looking for you? No one, that's who. You'll die up there."

"Dying *here* would somehow be better?" Eva asked pleasantly.

Joan frowned. "You know what I mean."

• • •

Walter and Richard exchanged expressions of great severity. Richard's, sincere, Walter's, gently mocking.

"Living in tents?" he scoffed, trying to look more mature than his forty-year old face was willing to allow. "At your age? Running off to places where there isn't any cell service?" He shook his head. "I don't get it, Dad. I really don't." He gave his father a pleading look. "Could you at least get a satellite phone? I'd feel better if I knew you could be reached."

"But we don't want to be reached," Walter said. "We enjoy being alone. We're living a kind of second Eden."

"Good God, Dad. Listen to yourself. You sound ridiculous."

"Why?"

"Why? Here, let me spell it out for you. Because you're old. O. L. D."

• • •

Eva thanked Joan for her concern, but told her she didn't particularly care about the "risks" they might be taking. "We don't have a lot of time left," she said, making a sincere effort to free the words of drama. "That's the long and short of it, dear. The clock's winding down. We're at a point in life where jumping jacks and deep knee bends don't help. All we want is to enjoy one another, and have a good time on the way out."

• • •

"You ought to be socializing with people," Richard said with a pleading look. "People with similar interests. People your own age."

"But we don't really enjoy other people," Walter countered. "Our age or not."

Richard threw up his hands, defeated. He told his father that he and Eva still had years ahead of them. Decades, even, providing they didn't fall off a cliff or find themselves savaged by a marauding bear. Couldn't they see that?

"Sure we see it," Walter said. "But here's the thing. We're not afraid of dying, son."

When he had said this, Walter had imagined himself living well into his nineties with Eva close by his side. He pictured the two of them having a good ten years together before anything even slowed them down. Ten more after that if their retirement money held out. He wasn't being intentionally naïve or unrealistic. He wasn't even trying to be a smartass. He was just calling it the way he saw it. Even to the point of conceding that if they did make it past eighty, yes, things could get dicey. Particularly depending on what fell apart first, them or the house. But so what? They'd get by! They knew what they were doing. It had all been figured out, down to the last detail. Only the last detail proved to be their undoing. It was the one that Walter had never conceived possible.

Eva was diagnosed with the disease just before their three-year anniversary. *Cancer*. She laughed, mirthlessly, when she broke the news to Walter that afternoon, but as if her utterance of the word had made it real, they knew their second Eden was over. Gone to hell, just like the original.

Eva had a faith Walter didn't share, but the timing and circumstances of her illness did nothing to bring him closer to believing. He was old, he complained, and he was being cheated of the simplest thing anyone ever asked of life—companionship. So what, or who, was there for him to have faith in? All he'd wanted for them was a few measly years together —a decade or two as man and wife, and what they'd gotten instead was a knife to the throat. Eva listened and tried to soothe him, saying it was God's will. That it couldn't be helped. But Walter shot back saying that if God needed to torture innocent souls to make Himself feel superior, well then, he wasn't much of a God, was he?

"It's going to be all right," Eva assured him. "It's all going to turn out exactly as it should."

She was always consoling him when it should have been the other way around. Always trying to prop him up with optimistic words, even though his heartbreak was beyond repair.

"The future is *not* lost," she said. "It isn't even broken. It's still ahead of us—in a different, better place. We've had a great run, Walter. Let's never forget that. It was shorter than we expected, yes. But really, how much time would have been enough?"

Walter held her hand, but his own was cold and lifeless.

"I won't allow us to grieve," Eva warned. "We can't hold onto this mortal life forever, and I refuse to embarrass myself by grasping after something that isn't there." She touched his arm. "I don't want to live if I can't live as I was. I wanted to grow *old* with you, Walter. Not *infirm*."

Her father had been broken by physical difficulties before his death. The poor man suffered from Alzheimer's, and after his passing she came to realize that all her acts of mercy, while well-intended, had only upset the old man. She told Walter to take down the picture from the mantle. It held the portraits of her mother, her sister Joan, and herself. She showed him where the backing on the frame had been torn away. She said she had given the montage to her father after moving him into the memory unit in the senior-living center in Phoenix, thinking it would bring him comfort. But what it did instead, she said, was drive him out of his mind. She told Walter her father tore away the backing one night in the desperate hope of finding the names of the people in the pictures—a clue to his own lost identity—but rather than give him peace, or bring meaning back to his life, it tormented him to his grave. "I never wanted to go that way," she said. "It was the only thing I ever feared, Walter. I got this instead, and even though it's going to kill me, I thank God every day for giving it to me."

•••

Walter grew incensed. Twisted with rage. He couldn't find it in himself to believe Eva when she told him they would be reunited in Heaven. Even if he had been willing to concede the existence of God—which he *wasn't*—he said he could not cozen himself into embracing the idea that the reward for such faith should entitle him to an afterlife. He didn't want to lose her, he said. Wasn't that enough?

"You aren't losing me. You *won't* lose me," she said with a reassuring touch of her hand. "I'll prove it to you. Wait and see. I'll send a sign to let you know it's all true. I'll come to you. I'll find a way to speak to you in a voice you'll understand."

He didn't want to hear it. Any of it. Her quiet, monk-like acceptance of what was to come unnerved and infuriated him. What she referred to as "giving over and letting go" he called surrender, and as he watched her ready herself for death he grew more inward and angry.

"I want a Mass and Catholic burial," she said.

He looked at her. Horrified. "Why would you ask for such a thing? You've been at odds with the Church for as long as I've known you."

"This is a time for reconciliation, Walter. I need to make my peace."

He smiled, bitterly. "I won't have to celebrate your life, will I? You don't expect me to get up and tell stories about our geriatric escapades, do you? Because I won't. I couldn't be a part of anything like that."

She patted his hand. "Don't worry, Walter. Just do as I ask, won't you? Just trust me."

•••

Was it wrong to say the service had no meaning for him? Or the day she was buried he thought about starting the car in the closed garage and following after her? If it was, he didn't care. Things were different now. He was old and alone, and when you were old and alone tomorrow was not the same tomorrow that greeted you when you were twenty. Or thirty. It was smaller, more cautious. Charged with a frightening desperation. It was the final few casts at the end of the day when the dying sun turns the water gold and the light is only a few minutes from falling behind the rocks.

He thought about this now as he raised the rod tip, and cast out his line. Things were different. Different in a way than he had ever expected, or imagined. He mended the line with a flick of his wrist and watched it settle on the water. Eva had found her way into his dreams again last night, coming to him like a ghost through fog, catching him with his arms wrapped around his pillow (in the dream, her tombstone). *If you miss me,* she had whispered, bending her lips to his ear, *come and find me. You know where I'll be.*

Walter didn't believe in ghosts, or dead lovers returning to the world of the living. But he missed his wife desperately, and wanted to feel her near him again. The dream wasn't important in any purposeful way. But it reminded him that her memory was here in the mountains—alive in the rocks and trees, the river—and that the cemetery back in town held only her bones.

Fly-fishing had been their religion. The wilderness their church. But where Walter once joked that each cast of the line was a prayer—always heard, seldom answered—he had never set his faith in God, or petitioned God for comfort the way Eva had. It had taken her failing health to bring him to his knees. And even then, he'd submitted grudgingly. He prayed that she be spared, that the diagnosis be proved wrong, but when his plea for intercession failed he cursed himself for giving in to superstition.

He followed the fly on its slow run downriver, mending the line with gentle little corkscrews of the wrist. The small, hand-tied buckskin was on a perfect float atop the languidly moving current.

He had been desperate, that was the problem. Desperate men could be deceived into doing humiliating things, and he had groveled and begged and made promises he knew he would never honor, all in order to keep her alive. But the true irony came later, when the ordeal and its ritual indignities were behind him. Eva had always wanted him to believe in God, and now he did—but only enough to hate Him.

Raising his eyes to the canyon rim, he observed the sky, jagged and blue and wondrously bright. Clouds drifted across the towering red spires in a slow white procession. It was not the blissful union of Heaven and earth his beloved wife had promised him, but for now it was enough.

Melissa McInerney

"The Birds Don't Care"

The dog, a mongrel in every sense of the word, paced in the bed of the pickup truck parked under the scrubby shade of a live oak. Every so often he stopped and rested his chin on the side, eyes fixed on the cowboy setting up the skeet thrower. Cleo stood in the shade of another live oak with her dad and Mr. and Mrs. Cooper and watched the dog. She came with her dad this weekend out of sheer habit, despite not feeling well. Her mom had little interest in the social side of her dad's job, but Cleo normally took to it. This weekend, though, she didn't feel up to it all and she could not tell her dad why.

"My name's Ray. Y'all ever shoot skeet?"

Cleo, her dad, and Mrs. Cooper all said no. Mr. Cooper started in on a long story about guns and shooting that looped back to WWII. Cleo knew from experience all his stories returned to WWII. Ray interrupted him.

"That's a no," Ray said. He spat. Cleo followed the blob of brown spit to its target, a yellow tuft of dried-out grass. Cleo never could figure out the cowboys in Texas. She had moved from New Orleans to Kingwood her sophomore year. All the drinking fountains at Humble High had slimy brown remnants of chaw, the choice of the Humble rednecks. They wore tight Wrangler jeans with a worn circle in the left back pocket, the mark of a can of Skoal. They had blue corduroy FFA jackets with their names spelled out in gold embroidery.

Her boyfriend Chris was the farthest thing from a cowboy. He played hacky-sack and listened to the Dead. His hair was long and he wore huaraches and baggy shorts. His T-shirts said things like "'I'd rather have a bottle in front of me than a frontal lobotomy." He was an Air Force brat who'd lived all over, and he expected her to open her own doors. But he was sweet and goofy. He listened to her. The night she got pregnant he had surprised her with a picnic on the top of Mt. Bonnell. It was April 1st, so she thought it was an April Fools' trick. She was wound up about a ten-page paper due and the struggles she was having with Calculus.

"This better not be a prank."

"Relax." He held out a joint. "Have some. Enjoy the ride."

She had filled her lungs and did as he said. The road wound upwards through the posh neighborhood, the houses tucked back into the hillsides. He knew she should be studying, not hiking. She trudged up the steps to the top of Mt. Bonnell next to Chris, the spectacular view of the Colorado River and rolling green hills lost to her.

Ray could have been anywhere from thirty to sixty. Colorless white-blonde hair curled from under his wide straw hat. His skin was the mottled red of a very white man who had spent too much time in the harsh Texas sun. One leg was shorter than the other. He was lithe and sinewy. He had an opened shotgun cradled in one hand and talked about gun safety.

"See this end? That's the barrel. It points to the ground when you're not shooting."

Cleo tried to concentrate. Instead, her thoughts stubbornly returned to Chris. She had met Chris between Thanksgiving and Christmas. She had rushed her way through guys those first few months of college with a heady, blind urgency until she stopped to catch her breath.

Chris was calm and steady and she had breathed the even, light breaths of a child asleep with him until a few weeks ago.

Right now, on this bright day in May made for shooting skeet, Chris would be taking his final in History 301, slumped down in his seat with his legs splayed wide, chewing on his pen. Her bed here at the ranch was hard and narrow, like the one in her dorm. She missed Chris. Not for sex, but for the all-enveloping hardness of his male body next to hers, making her feel safe and secure.

"If you wanna be deaf or blind, don't wear these," Ray said as he held up a headset and clear plastic glasses.

She hadn't noticed that he put the gun down. The Vicodin the doctor gave her must have kicked in. A cramp struck her hard, below her belly button. She folded in on herself, her arms reflexively protecting her stomach. She'd done this for years, as if she was practicing for now. She backed up and leaned against the tree.

"You okay?"

Her dad grasped her upper arm and Ray paused mid-spiel.

"My stomach's upset, that's all."

Mr. Cooper brought her a Coke. Mrs. Cooper helped her sit down. Ray was by her side, his hand on her shoulder. She ran the can across her forehead. The dog whined. Ray snapped his fingers. The dog leapt from the truck and scampered over.

Ray said, "This here's Troy. Troy, meet Cleo."

Cleo felt the pressure of his callused palm and it calmed her, she couldn't say why. Up close she could see that he was young, maybe early 30s. The way he spoke and moved made her think he was older. Shaken and embarrassed at the attention, she ran her fingers through Troy's scrubby hair and scratched his ears. Troy's tail thumped in the dirt, sending puffs of dust up. He sniffed her stomach and sneezed. Mrs. Cooper reached to pet Troy and he pushed himself closer to Cleo. He wouldn't put his head on her stomach, though.

Ray rose and picked up his gun.

"That's the gol-darndest thing," Ray said as he started up on gun safety again.

She rested a few moments more. The Coke helped, the icy sweetness energizing her. She stood up and joined Mr. Cooper and her dad, who patted her back. Mrs. Cooper, cool and collected in long green shorts and a pink polo shirt, declined to shoot, saying she preferred the saner option of sitting in the shade. Cleo glanced back to where Mrs. Cooper had settled, studying the way she draped herself elegantly on the dented metal chair, her languid air the opposite of Cleo's brisk, no-nonsense mother.

Ray tugged the skeet thrower to the edge of the large field. He stationed each of them about fifteen feet apart along a white limestone walkway. It reminded her of the driving range at Kingwood Country Club. Troy followed Ray, adjusting his trot to Ray's walk, dropping his haunches to sit when Ray went through the mechanics of the gun with each of them. When Ray got to Cleo, Troy sat next to her and leaned against her leg. Ray handed her the Remington shotgun, the wood polished to a warm brown with a lighter buttpad.

"This beauty has a pretty good kick, so stand like this," he said as he moved her legs in the wide stance skeet shooting demanded, her left leg forward with her left arm.

Ray placed her left hand at the end of the wood before the metal barrel. He showed her how to sight and when to raise the gun. His hand lingered on hers. "You all right to do this, darlin'? Troy'll keep you company if you want to sit in the shade and watch."

"I'm fine," she said. "I want to shoot."

Ray smiled, his eyes crinkling at the corners. Her natural inclination was to smile back, flirt a little. His calm dominance and easy masculinity combined with her present state of mind shut that idea down. He patted her hand and moved on towards the skeet thrower. Troy stayed with her, circling three times and laying down a few feet behind her. She wanted to do well, her competitiveness quelling the intermittent pain in her belly.

They warned her that she would cramp for three to four days after the abortion. They had a whole checklist, two stapled pages that she had to sign to prove she understood every directive. The physical part was clear. No one prepared her for the hollowness that she felt, as if removing the baby had scooped out all her emotions, too.

Maybe part of the reason she came was to put some distance between her and Chris, the "are we still together" after they left the clinic lodged in her consciousness. Her fragile composure would hold up here with her father and Mr. Cooper. Mrs. Cooper was more worri- some. She had known Mrs. Cooper twice in her life already. Once when she was little, in New Orleans, and now, for the four years her dad and Mr. Cooper had worked together in Houston. Mrs. Cooper was like a glamorous, worldly aunt, and Cleo knew she couldn't lie to her. It was her turn. She swiveled forward.

"Pull!"

Cleo raised her gun up to her shoulder and squeezed the trigger. She missed. The clay bird, as Ray called it, fell to the ground. The kick surprised her, the strength of it, but the pain barely registered through the Vicodin.

She missed twice more. Ray came over and talked about "stations" and "rounds" and "doubles." He positioned himself behind her and showed her when to swing the gun up. "In skeet shooting, timing is everything," he said.

When she hit her first bird, a surge of pride rose in her. When she hit the next eight in a row, they all applauded on each one. She was positive the hits had been accidental, or beginner's luck. Her shoulder ached and a blank tiredness settled over her. Mrs. Cooper came over and asked Ray to take Cleo back.

"Is that okay? I thought you might want a lay down with that tummy ache."

She nodded yes. She liked being mothered by Mrs. Cooper.

Ray helped her into his truck when he had gotten things squared away with her dad and Mr. Cooper. Troy rode up front between them, sitting tall and alert. Cleo crossed her arms across her chest and leaned into the door. Ray's self-possession threw her a bit. He didn't act as if he noticed. He twiddled the radio dial and hummed along with Willie Nelson.

The cabin was dusty, with faded dark green cowboy print curtains in the living room. The bedspread in her room had rosy-cheeked cowgirls with pigtails lassoing and riding. She lay curled on her side on top of the bed. The view should have lifted her spirits: a corner of the stable, newly painted barn red, the pen with a few horses switching at flies with their tails, and the mild blue skies of spring. She wanted to call Chris. She wanted to call her mom. It was long distance. Her dad would see the charge and ask her what was so important that she had to call collect, on a weekday, when charges were high. She was listless, unable to do more than watch the breeze stir the air, making the beams of sunlight soupy with dust. The bathroom faucet dripped with maddening irregularity. She got up and fiddled with the rust-stained faucet. She brushed her teeth. The ranch was quiet, except for the occasional clash of pans from the kitchen. What would her baby have been like? Chris' eyes? Her mouth? Would he have been a good father? She lay back down. The pillow was lumpy. She punched it. She punched it again, and again, and again, anger at Chris surging inside. Fuck him. She was through with men.

•••

After tossing and turning for another hour, she had showered and tried to hide the dark circles under her eyes with concealer. Mr. and Mrs. Cooper were with her dad at the bar. She joined them and ordered a Rusty Nail. She wasn't sure if she should drink with Vicodin. What the hell. At least she wouldn't feel a thing.

Her dad leaned forward, a look of concern on his face.

"Feeling better?"

She knew he meant well. He had "meant well" her whole life, even when he knew nothing. He would be puzzled and hurt if she told him that she had gotten herself pregnant and had an abortion. He would beat himself up with guilt if he knew her brother had sexually abused her for three years until she turned thirteen. These secrets left her quiet in his presence.

She nodded and sipped her drink.

That evening, they all got a little drunk. Ray came in, Troy trotting alongside. Ray was gussied up in ostrich boots, a stiff shirt, creased jeans, and a dark felt hat. Her dad invited him over for a drink. He perched on the end of the sofa, not quite joining them. Troy came over and she scratched his ears. Troy sniffed her lap and she pushed his nose away. He did it again. The third time they all laughed.

"Looks like Troy likes pretty gals," Ray said.

"What about you?" Cleo shot back. "You like pretty girls, too?"

Ray chuckled. "Guess I do."

Mr. Cooper whooped at that answer. He was up mixing more drinks, and he turned on the old radio that sat on the bar. Bob Wills playing a Texas waltz spilled into the room. Mr. Cooper lined the drinks up and held out his hand to Mrs. Cooper. She rose and they danced. Ray looked at Cleo and raised his eyebrows. He twirled her around like a straw in the wind across the scarred wooden floor. Afterwards, she asked Ray where he was from. He was from Corsicana, had cowboyed since he was fourteen. He and his cousin Clete were going into town to dance, did she want to go?

Normally, she would have jumped at the chance. She turned him down sweet, though, using her tummy-ache once again. What if it came back? She didn't want to ruin their night off. He smelled like Lifebuoy and sagebrush. He held her like he cradled his gun. Who was she kidding. She wasn't done with men, not by a long shot.

Ray and Clete left, Troy stayed next to her. Ray said Troy would make his way back home when he was ready. The four sat on the back porch and rocked. Mr. Cooper and her dad talked business. Mrs. Cooper patted her leg.

"Look at you, so grown up."

"I don't feel grown up."

"You never do, honey. Then one day you wake up and you're old."

"You're not old!"

"Thanks, but I am. Old enough to be a grandmother now."

Cleo didn't know what to say to that. It never occurred to her that she might have made her own mother a grandma. Mrs. Cooper fell asleep, her legs curled under her. Cleo listened to the crickets. A pack of coyotes yipped and howled, proud they had caught some dinner. She looked at the sky. Clouds had rolled in and the almost full moon lit the edges silver and white, like a negative photograph. The trees were a dense black, but the moonlight reflected off of the bare hillsides, giving the view the same look as an old black and white horror movie.

She was heavy and liquid with food and scotch. She had eaten everything, surprised at her hunger. Mr. Cooper roused Mrs. Cooper and they all went to bed. She must have been drunker than she thought. She missed the bed when she tried to sit and ended up on the floor. She reached around for her pillow and stayed there, her face buried in the pillow. She had made the right choice. A baby at nineteen? She could barely take care of herself.

•••

She read over her instructions the next morning and found none forbidding her to ride a horse. She knew she probably shouldn't, but figured they would be doing little more than walking. Mrs. Cooper invited her to sunbathe by the pool. After last night's conversation, Cleo didn't want to be with her. She had forgotten. Mrs. Cooper couldn't have kids, so she sought them out, as if close proximity would help her get over the sorrow of her infertility.

Mrs. Cooper pulled her aside as they waited for Ray and Clete to lead the horses out of the barn.

"I want to hear everything that's happened at school. Tonight, before dinner? That tummy ache must be better by now."

"Yeah, okay," Cleo said.

She wanted to tell Mrs. Cooper everything. How she thought she might be in love. How they might have broken up. The abortion. The lonely and empty place left inside her.

Getting on the horse was the worst part. Ray's cousin Clete laced his fingers under her left foot and boosted her up into the saddle. Clete was closer to her age, rawboned and shy, not at all like Ray. Troy loped along with them, joyous at the chance to catch lizards. The horses plodded and swayed through the winding dirt trails. Her sanitary napkin had jammed uncomfortably in the cleft between her legs. Clete stationed his horse right behind her and flirted. She wondered who named their kid Clete. Her dad twisted around his saddle and winked, as if she should be pleased with his flirtations.

She would have been, if she'd not been so fragile. She was all tangled up inside with the facts of her sex. The attention from men both sickened and thrilled her, a feeling of power and helplessness that she struggled to control. The unwanted pregnancy humbled her, show-ing her what the female body was made to do, whether you wanted it to or not. She was not conflicted about "terminating the pregnancy." Such a sterile phrase, she thought.

She kept going back to the last argument with Chris. He had wanted the baby, or he didn't want to pay for an abortion, she wasn't sure which.

"Are you sure?"

"Look at the stick."

"Did you do it right?"

"I can pee on a fucking stick, Chris."

"You're sure it's mine?"

"Oh my God."

She paced the floor of his room. He cracked his knuckles, a habit she hated.

"How much is it?"

"Two hundred. I want you to take me."

He shook his hair back, looked up at the ceiling, and inhaled. He squeezed his eyes shut and exhaled.

"If that's what we have to do..."

"That's what we have to do."

She left his room, her hands shaking with disappointment. She had spoken to him once more, telling him when to pick her up. He pulled up in his blue Toyota pickup. He had brought her a chocolate pudding cup and a 7 Up. They drove to the clinic in silence. She went in, the wad of twenties he thrust into her hand damp with his sweat. When she came back out, he drove her back to her dorm. He helped her inside and hugged her awkwardly.

"Call if you need anything."

"Are we still together?"

There was, for lack of a better phrase, a pregnant pause.

She closed the door and leaned against it. If he knocked, sorry that he didn't reply, she wasn't sure she would answer. Being without him seemed a just punishment.

•••

It was Saturday night. One more day. Ray and Clete sat on the porch with Cleo and her dad. She half-heartedly flirted with Clete. Every time she looked at Ray, he was looking at her, his gaze intense. Troy sat next to her. She wondered if he could smell vulnerability. Ray said again that it was the gol-darndest thing the way Troy stayed so close. She coddled and scratched Troy, his happy attentiveness a welcome diversion from Ray's presence.

The Rusty Nail slid down easily, the warm glow from the scotch immediate. Her dad ordered one too, and when it came they'd clinked and he said, "Let's not tell your mother."

This was nearly the same phrase her mom used two weeks ago, when Cleo called her. She wondered if she had made a mistake by telling Chris. She wanted honesty with Chris, but lying would have been easier. Her mom had surprised her. She was brisk and efficient, just as sure as Cleo that this was the right decision.

"Let's not tell your father. Men aren't good at this kind of thing."

She had begun to cry.

Her mother said, "No tears now. What's done is done."

At least her mom hadn't yelled, or accused her of being careless with her body. She had, she knew that, the little pills in their pink plastic case were hard to remember to take. She had missed three days one week, another two days the next. That night on Mt. Bonnell, when Chris popped the cork on a bottle of champagne "because you're the best fucking thing that's ever happened to me," and after he fed her strawberries dipped in chocolate and said, "I love you," she couldn't remember if she'd taken a pill that week or not. His kisses tasted tart and sweet all at the same time. She slid underneath him and forgot everything but the way her body felt next to his.

Mr. and Mrs. Cooper joined them for another round. Mrs. Cooper patted her right knee.

"Feeling alright now?"

She looked across her drink at Mrs. Cooper. She felt the keen-edged knife of her kindness, far crueler than judgment to Cleo. If she knew what Cleo had done—Cleo wasn't sure she could endure the shame.

"Almost good as new."

"Nothing a little scotch can't cure," Mr. Cooper said. "That reminds me of Paris, a night I spent right after the war..."

Mrs. Cooper bent forward, placed her hand on Cleo's shoulder, and pulled her close. Their heads almost touched.

"Have you met anyone? How's Austin? Is school everything you hoped?"

Cleo wanted to confide in Mrs. Cooper. The drinks, the warm, homey room, everything. Something stopped her. Instead, she blurted out the first thing that popped into her head.

"How did you know Mr. Cooper was the one?"

Mrs. Cooper looked over at her husband. He was telling yet another war story, his drink sloshing a tiny bit. He saw her staring and winked at her. She turned back to Cleo.

"Oh, honey, I don't know. Moments like that. He makes me feel like I'm the only woman in the world."

Reckless with the scotch, Cleo asked, "Do you wish you had kids?"

"Every damn day. Course, we didn't get a choice."

Cleo, flustered, took a defiant swig of her drink. Alongside the burn from the scotch was another flare, shame. She would not be ashamed. Abortions had been legal for four years now, since Roe vs. Wade in '73. It wasn't her fault that Mrs. Cooper couldn't have babies.

Troy stuck his nose into her lap, nudging her left hand. She scratched the top of his head and turned her attention to her dad and Ray. She could no more envision her life with a man like Ray than she could imagine her life with a baby. The scotch did its magic, deadening her guilt and shifting her focus to the sinewy muscles of Ray's forearms, visible below his neatly turned up cuffs. Who ironed that shirt? She pictured herself on the ranch with Ray doing... what? Cooking and cleaning? Fucking? She shook her head, distressed that she could think such thoughts so soon.

•••

They shot skeet again on Sunday morning.

"Have y'all forgot everything I told you yesterday?"

He went over the guns again. He lined them up, same as before. Mrs. Cooper sat in a chair in the shade and watched, same as before. Chloe had woken up with a fierce headache. She missed the first round entirely. Her dad frowned, and began to walk over. Ray waved him back. He left the thrower and came near, but not next to her. He looked down at the ground and spoke in a low, soothing voice.

"It's all in the timing." Ray said. "Those birds don't care what's happening with you."

She took a deep breath. *Those birds don't care.* She squinted through the sight. Everything fell away for a while. She shot skeet as if her life depended on it. Bird after bird shattered in the air. Some crashed to the ground whole, the few she missed.

She didn't think about Chris, or her dad, or Ray, or the baby that wasn't. The here and now existed. She let the kick of the gun jolt through her. She felt Troy's warm breath on her leg. She smelled the acrid burnt stench of gun smoke.

•••

That afternoon she put on her swimsuit and sat with Mrs. Cooper in the sunshine. The warmth soaked into her skin. They talked of shoe sales at Neiman's and the lack of good restaurants near Kingwood. Mrs. Cooper was thinking of getting a new dog. Her Chihuahua, Dudi had been dead for nearly two years and she was ready. Not a Chihuahua, though, another breed, maybe a Cocker Spaniel. Mr. Cooper didn't want another dog, but he'd come around. Cleo didn't want to tell Mrs. Cooper about her abortion anymore. She wanted to know how to live with herself. And men. Especially men. They confused and excited, astounded and frustrated. She thinks of men like she thinks about the scotch in her glass, which she seems to be drinking too much of, they are sharp, bitter, woodsy, and foreign, and she craved the taste.

•••

Cleo was ready for dinner early. The pool had relaxed her and the worst of the cramps were over. She flip-flopped her way to the main porch, looking forward to watching the sun turn orange before it slipped below the horizon. She poured herself a club soda, sat in the rocking chair with the best view, and sighed with pleasure. May in the hill country of Texas is as pretty as anywhere, the new buds tippling on the trees and the fresh undercoat of grass pushing through the last of the dead brown matting of winter. Ray rounded the corner, Troy quick on his heels.

"You startled me," she said.

"Sorry. Heading for the kitchen for some leftover steak."

Troy's tail double-timed at the word steak.

"He knows the word 'steak'?"

"Sure does."

She hopped up. "Can I help feed him?"

Ray shrugged. She followed him like Troy, happy and mindless in the present. Ray fed Troy on the porch of a cabin that couldn't be seen from the main house. It had a lived-in look that hers didn't, with boots lined up next to the door, three white rockers, and a table with bright blue glass bottles arranged on top, pots of geraniums lined along the stairs, and baskets of silver ponyfoot.

There were two large feeding bowls on the right side of the porch. Troy trotted over and sat, his eyes never leaving the bag Ray held. She laughed when Troy held his paw out to her before delicately taking the hunk of steak from her hand. She leaned back and Ray was there. His lips brushed her hair and ear lobe. He stiffened and carefully moved his body apart from hers. He stroked her hair like she was Troy, not his future lover.

That she had been firmly, but gently, rebuffed brought tears to her eyes. That she could feel desire so soon after her abortion elicited the same deep shame she felt with her brother. This wasn't a choice she would get to make, either. Ray had made it for her.

She knew what the baby's name would have been. Snow if it had been a girl, and Johnson if it had been a boy. Cleo suspected that Chris' reaction was more fear than real anger. They'd only dated a shade under six months. She wasn't sure she loved him, but he was a good guy. She could do a lot worse. If they were together, she would invite him to her house for a weekend, to meet her parents. It was time.

The last night was quiet. They all sipped scotch half-heartedly and ate barbecue sand-wiches, chips, and potato salad. Ray and Clete joined them, relaxed because tomorrow they would have three days free of guests. Troy sniffed her stomach. She waited for him to sniff again. He didn't. He left her and returned to Ray. He laid down, sighed, and put his head on his paws. Ray winked at her, the kind wink of a decent man.

Mr. Cooper had launched into a bawdy story involving Parisian ladies and men from his unit. Mrs. Cooper rolled her eyes and looked at him in mild exasperation. Clete and Ray laughed in all the right spots of Mr. Cooper's story. Her dad held his glass up to the light and swirled the half-inch of scotch left, a sure sign that he was tight. He tipped his glass towards her. She tipped her glass back.

Cleo looked at Troy through the wavy lines of her glass. The abortion weighed heavy, a choice that would stretch far into the future. She didn't know what she'd do about Chris. The image of that future was as blurry as her vision of other choices, other secrets. She couldn't see herself as a grown woman, a wife like Mrs. Cooper or her mom, quite yet. Troy's brown eyes with their crinkled eyebrows looked up at her, like he knew just what she was thinking. She plunged forward in time for a brief moment. She could see herself sitting with a husband and their friends twenty years from now. She would have that same look Mrs. Cooper had on her face, tired of his stories, but resigned after years together. They would have children, and they would keep their secrets. She didn't know what the secrets would be but she was certain there would be many, melting together like the ice cubes in her glass.

Marlene S. Molinoff

To the Lowlands

It was one of those times in late spring when they left at the crack of dawn—the belly of the car packed full like a low-country shrimper returning to port. The journey would take them twelve hours, if they were lucky. The route followed highway and interstate, from Pennsylvania through six states and the District of Columbia, before resolving itself into South Carolina's rural roads, bridges, and, eventually, a causeway that led to a private island populated by the rich and the very rich. Ordinarily, Jill hated the drive, but this time she was preoccupied.

She and her husband made the trip From Philadelphia annually to open their summer home in the Carolina lowlands. Roger had surprised her by bringing along Pat Conroy's *Prince of Tides* on audio CD. He had selected it in place of the usual James Patterson or Tom Clancy thriller she was used to tolerating to keep him alert. "I thought we could use a change of pace," he said. "It's about Charleston and the lowlands. I thought you might like that." Despite her literary snobbishness—she would never willingly have selected a Conroy novel herself—she was touched that he had tried to please her.

Jill was the mother of their three children now grown up and married. She was sixty and deeply disturbed by the state of mind in which she found herself. Her emotions were muddled. A week ago she had gotten word that someone she cared about deeply—Barry Ostermeyer—was terminally ill, and she had gone to see him. Before that, it had been almost twenty years, though they made it a point of speaking every few months and remained close. They checked in with each other at every important juncture of their lives. He knew about every vacation, every job change, every event with one of her children. Now, as she and her husband drove farther and farther away from this dying man, she felt something akin to panic. She was certain that his death was imminent, and she fixated on how she would receive the news. Roger knew nothing about their relationship. She hadn't talked about Barry in years, and she wasn't about to.

"Can't you leave that thing alone for a minute?" Roger was swatting at her iPhone with his free hand.

"Oh. Only you're allowed to do that?" she said.

They both laughed.

"It's good to hear you laugh," he said. "You've been holding onto your iPhone like it's a loaded gun about to go off. What's going on?"

"You should talk. You're always checking yours."

It was true. Roger loved being connected to the world, and on these long car trips, he was forever tracking sports scores, his favorite stocks, and the constant stream of emails he received. It was tough to defend himself. Usually on these daylong drives, Jill treated him as a captive audience, dissecting the nitty-gritty of family, close friends, and the nuances of their relationship, while complaining that he rarely got what she was trying to say.

"Is one of the kids having a crisis of some kind that you've been sworn to secrecy about?" he asked.

"Nothing like that. Just a work dispute. You can't help me with it."

She was right. He didn't know much about her work. She was a high-powered editor for the government, and a lot of the stuff she worked on was classified. He'd give it up for now. "Let's put the audiobook on again," he said. "Maybe that'll take your mind off it."

She forced herself to concentrate. Tom Wingo had come to New York to save his twin sister Savannah after her recent suicide attempt. He had just met Susan Lowenstein, her psychiatrist—Jill was picturing her as Barbra Streisand—and was telling her about incidents from their childhood. What a luxury it was to be tangled up in the messy details of their lives. Interspersed with Gothic tales of an abusive father and a socially obsessed mother were lyrical passages describing Charleston and the low country surrounding it. Jill loved the Carolina horizon line, especially over the tidal marshes of the sea islands in the lowlands, where stands of tall pines reached toward the rise or fall of celestial bodies, and she was enjoying these lush descriptions in spite of her mood.

"Can I play that passage again?" she asked him, referring to the one about the bright summer night when Tom, Savannah, and Luke were very small and their mother took them down to the dock at sunset. Roger shrugged his assent, and she paused the audiobook and started it again.

It was growing dark on this long Southern evening and suddenly, at the exact point her finger had indicated, the moon lifted a forehead of stunning gold above the horizon, lifted straight out of filigreed, light-intoxicated clouds that lay on the skyline in attendant veils. Behind us, the sun was setting in a simultaneous congruent withdrawal and the river turned to flame in a quiet duel of gold...

She stopped it. "What did you think of that? Gorgeous, right?"

"I don't know. Didn't you find it a bit over the top?" He was puzzled. He'd been trying to get her to talk all morning, and now she wanted his literary opinion?

She didn't answer. She put the CD back on and played the passage again.

•••

By the time the dreaded text box appeared, it was already late afternoon. Roger had just done a long shift, and Jill was in the driver's seat waiting for him to finish pumping gas somewhere near the North Carolina border in rural Virginia, beyond the traffic that had delayed them by more than two hours. She read it quickly. "Our dear friend has left us peacefully after a circus of events including a bedside vigil with a faith healer arranged by Irena, his current. Memorial plans to follow." Jill was one of many on the list of recipients, and Barry's friend Ben had made no attempt to personalize the message in spite of having reached out to her only a week ago. It hit her like a sharp blow to the stomach. She unbuckled her seat belt, opened the car door, and dashed past her husband, calling out, "...restroom," over her shoulder.

Under the bright fluorescence of the convenience store, she hurried through the maze of cereals, boiled peanuts, chips, and packaged candies, afraid she would lose control of her emotions before she found the toilet or be forced to wait in line for its privacy. There was no one there. Closing the door behind her, she leaned heavily against it and sank to the tile floor. Her hands were pressed tight to her mouth to stop the sounds that were welling up, but she was helpless to suppress her grief. It surged through her in waves until, completely spent, she rested her forehead against the cold metal door. A sharp knock startled her. How long had it been? She had no sense of time when she heard the voice through the door.

"You planning to stay in there all day?" Jill picked herself up, splashed water on her face, and emerged, not looking at the woman waiting in the corridor. At the counter she ordered tea sweetened with honey.

•••

It seemed to Roger that he'd been waiting for Jill for quite some time. He had moved the car from the gas pump to one of the diagonal spaces in front of the convenience store and stood there scrolling through the messages on his iPhone. He was anxious for her to drive so he could get a little work done. He paced the length of the storefront. Annoyed. He hated this trip as much as she did, but there was no way around it. They always had so much gear to bring down at the beginning of the season: this time it was the new set of golf clubs he couldn't resist and the tools he happened to discover up north; the fresh stock of water pistols and pool rafts Jill had purchased for their grown kids and their friends, as she did each year; and the spare pots, pans, and serving pieces she anticipated she would need to entertain the endless houseguests who would be visiting them over the coming months. He stopped by the rear window to look in at the carefully arranged items on the rear seat and floor, and then at his watch. It was almost four o'clock. Maybe she wasn't feeling well. He was about to check on her when he saw her approaching.

Jill ignored the fact that her husband was waiting by the driver's side. "I'm fine now," she said, as she brushed past him, got in, and began readjusting the seat, steering wheel, and mirrors, which Roger had changed when he moved the car over from the gas pump.

He slid in on the passenger's side and buckled his seat belt. As she was about to back out, he put a hand on her shoulder and said, "Are you sure you're all right? You're white as a ghost."

"I'm OK now." She knew she should say more than that, but Barry's death was still too raw for her to talk about. Besides, she had no idea what to say to Roger. It had been such a long time since they knew Barry socially in Atlanta, and they hadn't talked about him in years. She knew Roger had had his suspicions at the time, but nothing had been acknowledged. Grudgingly, she said, "You're right. I am upset, but I don't want to talk about it right now. I'm working it out."

"I don't get it, Jill. OK, I guess. Want the audiobook? I've got a few emails to catch up on. Then I can drive again if you need me to."

She nodded. "Sure." And he put the CD on.

Susan Lowenstein was about to become Tom Wingo's lover. He was telling her about the incident that caused him to have a nervous breakdown, lose his job, drive his wife into an affair, and come to New York where he'd met her.

Roger was drifting in and out of the story. He was trying to answer a pressing client inquiry about a potential Pfizer deal to buy a midsize biotech company and gain access to an anti-inflammatory drug. It was a fascinating deal. The drug was currently under FDA review for treatment in a multimillion-dollar category, and they needed him to weigh in quickly. Typically, he would give something like this his full attention, but at the moment he found himself preoccupied by his wife's state of mind. Jill was a difficult woman. Some of her work was top secret, but he could usually tease out at least the category of the problem she was dealing with. Anyway, he had a feeling that wasn't what it was. He glanced over at her. She looked deeply troubled. It had to be something personal. He stopped the CD.

"Could Conroy make the plot any more complicated to follow?" he asked. "I mean the poor guy can't get a break—first his brother, then his wife, and now his sister?"

"It's not so hard to follow. Come on. I'm really into it. Put it back on," she said.

She'd been like this all week—sullen or strident by turn. "Want to tell me what's going on with you? I can't get a word out of you lately."

"Oh for God's sake, Roger. You're the one who never wants to talk."

"Jesus, Jill! Take my head off, why don't you?" He leaned over and restarted the audio-book. Then he grabbed his iPad and started pushing buttons. But he was pissed. He glared out the window.

The truth was Roger hadn't seen this side of Jill in a while. It reminded him of a time years ago, when he'd suspected she was having an affair. It had been during his million-mile period. They'd bickered about all the traveling he was doing while she was stuck home with the kids. He'd thrown it in her face that she liked the money well enough and certainly knew how to spend it. One night in bed, at the height of his pride, she'd refused him when he approached her. "Did you find someone better at it?" he'd challenged her. He'd even named her friend Barry as the guy he suspected. But she'd flatly denied it, and he'd let her off the hook. He was never sure. For a long time, he'd held it against her, indulging his thought that maybe she was different than the person he had assumed she was. What a jerk he'd been, and it had almost cost him his marriage. God knows, he hadn't been so innocent himself back then. But now? It couldn't be happening again. They were way beyond those years. He'd back off and give her some space.

A few minutes later, Roger saw the first of the many unrelentingly corny signs adver-tising South of the Border. On every trip, they joked about these signs, and both of them looked forward to passing the cheesy motel and amusement park they advertised. With its politically incorrect Mexican bandido and acres of neon, it had marked the border between the Carolinas since 1950: Pedro's fireworks! Does yours? Only 150 miles to go. He'd opened his mouth to read it aloud, glanced over at her, and clamped his jaw shut.

•••

Jill was thankful that she'd been spared the details of Barry's illness: when precisely the cancer had been diagnosed, how quickly it had progressed, whether he had days or months left when she had seen him a week ago. They had always managed to get in touch throughout the many moves and changes in their lives, especially when anything important was going on. That was why when he hadn't called for so long, she was alarmed to hear someone else's voice on a call from his cell phone. It was Ben. He immediately reminded her of who he was and of the time they had met many years ago when she and Barry had borrowed his apartment. "Barry's at Mount Sinai," he said. She was relieved for a second; she had thought he was already dead. "I'm afraid it's very serious. He's been diagnosed with pancreatic cancer. It's in his bones. He hasn't got much time." She was barely digesting what Ben was saying, when she heard, "He'd like you to call him, but he wanted me to tell you first."

She'd called immediately. Barry sounded weak and exhausted. Jill tried to keep the tone light, teasing him that he didn't have to go this far to get her to come in to see him. For a long time he hadn't asked, but over the last year he'd been nagging her, whenever they talked, to hop a train into New York. Maybe it was premonition.

"Yeah. Well, maybe not," he said, barely laughing. She could hear labored breathing.

Jill didn't want to see Barry, especially not frail and vulnerable. She needed to think of him as the adversary who had fought her fiercely as she struggled to get free of him. She had made the decision to stay with Roger. She had refused to see Barry, and she had held firmly to it all these years. But now she couldn't refuse. She made excuses to Roger about a client meeting and went the next day. On the train ride into the city, she felt the apprehension building, almost forcing her to call and cancel the visit. She knew what Barry was capable of. Sometimes they argued over the phone, and it reminded her of their vicious battles toward the end of their love affair.

She remembered the last time they had been together. It was almost twenty years ago, when she was attending an editorial conference in New York, and Barry had booked a room across town at The Gramercy. They hadn't seen much of each other since he'd moved to Atlanta and she and Roger had resettled in D.C. It'd been over a year this time. So that when they finally met, the longing was intense. In spite of her better instincts, she had spent the night with him and awakened feeling confused and remorseful. She wanted to leave without waking him, but as soon as she moved, he reached for her.

"Don't run away from me. Please."

"I can't stay. I have to get back to my hotel. You don't understand what it's like. My phone's turned off. I'm sure Roger has been trying to reach me."

He let her go and rolled away from her. She got out of bed and began dressing as quickly as she could. She would shower at her hotel.

Barry got up, reached for his boxers, and began pacing, back and forth, across the room. She was standing at the foot of the bed, about to step into her shoes when he stopped, face-to-face with her, and took her jaw in his hand forcefully. "I can't take this anymore. You understand? You make love to me like that, and then you get up feeling all guilty and go home to him?"

She ripped his hand off her jaw, gouging her chin with her fingernail. "I told you. It's the only way I'll continue to see you. It's non-negotiable." She stepped into her shoes, covered her chin protectively, and wiped away a dab of blood.

"What are you afraid of? Losing all that money? You're a big girl. You'll survive."

She glared back at him. "That's not fair. I've got money of my own. Do I have to say it again? I love Roger. I love my life with him. It's much more complicated for me." She was trembling. "Look. I've got to go. I'll call you later."

"Fuck you! Don't bother." He walked past her and put his fist through the wall beside the door. Then he pulled the door open for her.

She ran past him and he slammed it.

•••

The man Jill visited in the hospital one week ago was no longer Barry. He was pale and feeble, with deep circles under gray-blue eyes that riveted her. He was alert, and it was obvious that he had been waiting for her. "I'm sorry. Did you expect me earlier?" she asked. She was pinned in place, just inside the door. There was a young man standing by the bed. Probably Craig, Ben's son, whom she'd been hearing about since his childhood. An uncomfortable moment of introduction followed: She walked toward him; they shook hands; then Craig said Irena had fallen apart and he was the one delegated to make all the arrangements for Barry's release to home hospice care later that day. Moments later, he left them alone.

As soon as Craig was gone, Barry asked her to come closer. "He's so smart, that kid," he said. Barry always talked about Craig as the son he'd never had. "He managed my meds all morning so I would have some time with you, without too much pain." His eyes bit into her. "Don't be afraid. Come closer. I'm not contagious." She took a few steps toward him. "Do I look that bad?" She shook her head. "Come closer." She stood beside the bed. His hand was shaking as he offered it. When she took it, he shuddered, and she let it go.

Outside in the corridor, nurses in clogs clomped by on their way to other patients. Having little idea what to do beyond the instinct to make Barry more comfortable, Jill swabbed his lips with ice and gave him a drink through a bent straw. "I know you were waiting, but I made really good time. The train, the subway, it all worked perfectly," she said nervously. He put his head back and closed his eyes; he kept pawing at his hair under the baseball cap he wore.

"Why the hat?" she asked. She was struggling with her emotions, so her tone came across as sarcastic. He'd always been vain about his thick, curly hair, and she suspected it was thinning or worse.

He grimaced. "I have a lot of visitors. Sometimes I need to hide. The pain." She covered her mouth with her hand. "It's all right," he said. "Not so easy to die. Much harder than I thought." She kept moving around him, straightening a sheet, propping a pillow, attending to him. He held her with his eyes.

His breathing was shallow. He was almost panting. "It's so ironic. I always believed. Time was on my side."

"I'm sure you'll have the time you need to do what you have to."

He was shaking his head. "Not what I meant. I meant. Roger's older than I am. I thought one day. You and me."

Jill's face reddened. She began backing away.

"Don't run away, Jill. Christ. I've spent half my life. Trying to get you to listen." He patted the side of the bed. "Sit down. I need to talk to you."

She sat beside him. He reached up and traced the contour of her face, his faint touch disappearing as he moved his finger.

"I wanted to tell you. I think you made the right choice. All those years I spent. Going from startup to startup. That would have killed it for us."

He was talking about the decision she'd made not to go to California with him more than twenty years ago as if it were yesterday.

"Did you ever regret it?" he asked.

"I was torn." She looked away when she said it.

"Really, Jill?" He coughed and struggled to regain control. He turned her face back toward him and held it.

There had never been another choice for her than the one she'd made. She was terrified of the risks Barry took and even more terrified of giving up the security of the life she had with Roger and the kids. And now Barry was calling her on it. She shook her head free and then continued shaking it in denial, but she was remembering the relief she'd felt when Barry had given her an ultimatum and left for California. She had counted the days of silence. She had been sure the affair was over.

"You knew. You must have. That I would fail out there without you," he said. They had met in Atlanta when he was an up-and-coming entrepreneur and he had hired her to edit a series of articles he was desperately trying to publish to further his business career. By the time one of them was selected for the *Harvard Business Review,* she'd become his lover as well as his indispensable amanuensis.

Her eyes were filling with tears. "I'm sorry you've carried that with you all these years."

Barry continued talking in his slow, halting syntax. He told her that he'd intended never to call her again when he left for California, but the physical longing had been more than he could bear. He wanted to believe each time he saw her after that, that he could convince her they belonged together. Gradually, he'd come to understand that she would never leave Roger; he had even come to respect her for it.

It was futile for him to be telling her all this now. She eased herself down beside him on the bed, put her head on his shoulder, and breathed with him for the first time since she had entered the room. She was desperate to give him something, even though it could not be what he wanted. As he stroked her hair, she murmured, "I'm sorry. I'm so very sorry…" and listened to his breathing as it slowed.

Then the pain broke through. She could almost feel it. He began breathing heavily again. His face was gray.

"Can you lower the top of my bed a little bit, Jill? I don't want to call a nurse."

She got up to lower it. "Is that good?"

He didn't answer. He was breathing hard to control the pain.

"I should get someone," she said.

He clutched at her. "No. Don't go. Stay a little longer. At least until Craig gets back."

She sat down on the edge of the bed. When she touched his hand, it was clammy.

She watched in horror as he struggled to regain control of his breathing as waves of pain overwhelmed him.

"Please let's get some help," she said. "I can't stand to see you in so much pain."

Without taking his eyes off her, he reached for the call button, pressed it, and waved her away.

The intensity of his eyes under the brim of the Yankee cap when she kissed him and when he looked at her for the last time haunted her as she ran down endless corridors to Madison Avenue and across 96th Street toward the Lexington Avenue subway. She was frantically rubbing her mouth with her knuckles, trying to obliterate the dry, insistent kiss that had sealed it.

• • •

The car flew by another giant billboard for South of the Border.

"Be a Deer! Bring some Doe. Only 50 miles to go," Roger read aloud in a singsong voice, startling Jill out of her reverie. It was almost nine o'clock. An exit sign flared in the head-lights. They both looked at it with relief.

"Can you drive for a while?" She was already pulling the car off 95 and into a space at one of the enormous Pilot Truck Stops that dotted their route through the Carolinas. "Otherwise, I need a cup of coffee."

Soon they were sitting wordlessly, sipping coffee and sharing a bag of chips at a table in the all-night café. They had been on the road for fourteen hours and still had almost three to go.

"I'm starting to think we should have waited for South of the Border," Roger said. He was running a paper napkin over a greasy spot on the table.

"You never Sausage a Place!" Jill said.

He laughed. "Seriously, you think we should stop there one time, just to see what it's like?"

"I kind of think we know."

"You're probably right." They sat quietly for a while. "It's late," he said at last. "Should we get going?"

Jill slouched down into the cushioning of the booth. "Not yet." She saw his concern. She leaned heavily into the vinyl, feeling light-headed and nauseous. The stark, transient atmosphere of mostly empty tables with lone men here and there hunched over coffee and fried food was having a strange effect on her. She shivered in the overly air-conditioned room and shrank further into herself.

Roger came quickly around the table. He sat down next to her, wrapping an arm around her and pulling her close. "Doesn't matter. Forget it. We can talk about it another time. You sure you're all right?" She nodded "yes," her head against his chest. They sat there for a few minutes more.

She reached for his free hand and laced her fingers through his till their palms touched. She let go and sat up to look at him. "I've been upset because I heard last week that Barry Ostermeyer was very sick, and he died today. I got the text this afternoon. Do you remember him? My client from when we lived in Atlanta? He came to the house to review manuscripts. I think we went out to dinner with him a couple of times."

Roger leaned toward her and brushed a few stray strands of hair behind her ear. "That's bad luck. He was pretty young, wasn't he?"

"Fifty-nine," she said.

"Did he ever make anything of himself?"

She didn't answer.

"Look, I'm sorry you're so upset. But you can't take to heart every death you hear about, Jill. We're getting to be that age, you know?"

He didn't say it to be cruel. He wanted to tell her that they should drop the charade, that he knew who Barry was. But she seemed so fragile. She was crying. He put his arm around her again and held her. She leaned into him, and he felt her begin to relax.

"Life can turn savage," he said. He was speaking into her hair, still holding her, "and you have to figure out a way to get through it." She was breathing more easily now. "I know you don't think Pat Conroy's a great writer," he said, "and I agree with you. But I was really struck by what happened in the last part of *The Prince of Tides*. You know, what he has Tom Wingo say when he's trying to get his life back together—something about forcing himself to understand that betrayal can be an act of love. It's when Tom's grappling with the fact that he had thrown his wife out of his heart and someone else had welcomed her in. Remember that part? It really got to me, and I was wondering what you thought about it."

She moved away from him, just enough to look at him. "You're kidding. You want to know what I thought about that?" She had to ask. She was sitting up by now looking at him.

"No. I'm not kidding at all. What did you think?"

"I thought it was nice. A bit corny but nice." She tried to smile.

"I get that it's corny. Powerful thought though, that forgiveness often involves acknowledgment of your own culpability."

So this was it—Roger's way of comforting her. He was telling her that he had suspected the affair was with Barry and now he knew. But he'd grown up. He felt some responsibility for it, and he'd forgiven her. They would never mention it again.

"Let's do it," he said, rising.

As they left, his hand was in the small of her back, guiding her.

• • •

Jill was at the wheel again. Roger hadn't been able to drive for very long. They had whizzed past South of the Border, and he had lasted another forty or fifty miles beyond that. She had taken over about two hours ago, and they were past Charleston on the final leg of their journey when the exhaustion hit with the weight of a heavy sheet thrown over her.

Alone in the darkness, she was tormenting herself. Although she kept reassuring herself she'd done nothing wrong by not telling Roger she had gone to see Barry, only the decent thing—helping a dying man find peace—she was well aware that she'd had the chance to tell her husband about all the years she and Barry had stayed in touch, and she had not said a word. She felt compromised by this lapse and forced to question the hold she and Barry had had on each other and what it meant she might have missed out on or withheld from Roger. She felt part of herself fall invisibly away; instinctively, she reached for her husband.

"Was I sleeping? What time is it?" her husband asked. He sat up and looked around. "Good for you. We're almost there."

"Yes. Almost there. I was thinking how nice it will be to have the house to ourselves for a while this summer before the kids come."

"I like that, when you're cooking just for us, and we can have a quiet drink on the deck before dinner."

"I like it too. We've had a good life together. We've raised three nice kids, who married decent people. Not everyone is as lucky." She was thinking about Barry: how long it had taken him to find financial security and a decent life. How he had never married. She shuddered.

Roger interrupted her thoughts. "You make it sound like it's over. And anyway, do you really think it was luck? Come on!" He was jostling her shoulder. "Don't you think we had anything to do with it?"

"No question. We've always made the right choice."

Jill looked into the rearview mirror at the blackness behind and thought about Barry. Then she looked as far into the distance as the LED headlights would allow, at the vast expanse of pine forest with the sparkle of marsh ponds here and there, the full moon illuminating trails of clouds hanging over the lowland's long horizon line. "And look where it has brought us," she thought aloud, feeling the beauty of the place and the relief at the end of a long journey.

"I can't believe it!" Roger said.

She looked over at him. Surprised by his reaction. He was leaning forward. He'd unbuckled his seat belt.

"Why not?"

"You've passed the turn-in for our road, Jill," he said impatiently. 'We're almost at the beach. Just pull over. I'll drive us in."

Mary Natwick

Last Run on the Colorado

the third day

"Well," Sherri Ann grumbled, catching sight of the green-helmeted kayaker a hundred yards down-rapid, "it was good while it lasted."

It was after tourist season, but still, the Colorado River run through the Grand Canyon rarely was completely without kayakers and whitewater rafters. She'd been lucky to have two days to herself.

She finished out the Class III rapids, mostly standing waves, a little drop and boil. She hung back in an eddy to let the other kayaker gain some distance ahead of her. The last thing she wanted was to spend the entire day leapfrogging another kayaker. It could even be that he—or she, there was always that possibility—could be part of a group, even worse for her peace and quiet.

Late that afternoon she floated around the last bend before Trashy Flats, her takeout point for the day. The next camping spot was ten miles farther. As she expected, Green Helmet was already there. Solo. He'd set up close to the middle of the campsite. Either he wasn't expecting anyone else, or he was just a camp hog. She'd seen this site strung out with six or seven tents, looking as haphazard as cars parked in a dirt lot. The first to arrive got the best spot; everyone else shoved in around them.

Steam rose from a cookstove perched on a flat rock. Past that, he crouched by a sleeping bag spread on a tarp. He was lean and long-muscled, a marathon runner's build, with worn-in but not worn-out quality cargo shorts and T-shirt. She was pretty confident he was harmless. One of those gentle types who craved nature time on the river, she judged, not an adrenaline junkie. Something about the soft, worn-in clothes said that, instead of the flashy, tight-fitting gear the whitewater show-offs wore.

"Hey," she called from the shallows, "room for another?"

He glanced her way, stood up. "Yeah, sure."

"Thanks." She let her kayak scrape gently on the sandy beach. "I'll stay out of your way."

Meaning, she hoped she was making it clear, that she didn't want company.

"No problem," he said easily. He turned his back to her, stirred something in the small aluminum pot. The scent of bacon and onions and...lentils? and bay leaf drifted in a tantalizing cloud past her nose.

She pulled her kayak out of the river and set up camp as far as she could from him, which was only about fifteen yards down the small sandbar. The smell of his soup rode above the sharp hint of the coming chilly night.

She let her kayak serve as a symbolic barrier between their sites, like a pillow between feuding siblings.

Sherri Ann set up her tent—there was something too personal about sleeping in the open in front of a stranger, even if the tent was no real protection. She filtered muddy Colorado water and soon had clear water bubbling in her quick-boil stove. She poured the water into a bag of dehydrated, vacuum-packed lasagna and started heating a second cup for tea.

The sun, which had long since left the narrow canyon, slipped off the tops of the high bluffs. The night peepers chorused their pulsating love song. Sherri Ann parked herself in front of a log someone dragged over for a bench, preferring it as a back rest after a long day's paddle. Sipping her tea, she admired the long, turquoise snake of twilight sky visible from the canyon floor. *Most beautiful place on earth. I could die right now and be happy.*

The crunch of boots on sand came from behind her. She sighed. Boots stepped easily over the log.

"Hey. I'm Tremble." He sat down beside her and plucked a blade of tough, late-summer river grass. "I figure we're going to be running into each other for the next while, might as well do intros and all."

"Sherri Ann," she said a bit shortly. "Good to meetcha."

"Sherri Ann." He gave her a lazy grin. "What kinda name is Sherri Ann? Why not one or the other?"

She blinked. "You're giving me grief? With Tremble? Is that the name your parents gave you?"

"Yep."

"Why would your parents do that? Tremble, really?"

He was silent a moment, stripping veins off the blade of grass like peeling off pieces of string cheese. "I guess they thought when I announced myself to the aliens, like," he lowered his voice to a booming bass, "'I'm Tremble,' their knees would quake."

She laughed. "Well, Tremble, since I'm not an alien and all, I hope you don't mind I'm not shaking in my boots."

"Don't mind," he said. "You doin' one last run on the Colorado too, hunh?"

"One last?" She looked at him directly for the first time. A shock of sandy hair, neither long nor short, ends stiff and clumped from sticking out below the helmet. A long, skinny face with sharp cheekbones and dark shadows under eyes whose color she couldn't determine in the deepening night.

"Oh, for the season?" She turned back to her original view, westerly to line up with the snake-y length of dark-blue canyon sky. "I've run the Colorado even in January. You just gotta bring a little more gear, good pogies to keep your hands warm. But this year...yeah, it's probably the last time I'll get out here."

"Yeah," he said quietly. "This year."

She went on, "I was expecting more people, for sure. It's not usually this empty."

"Usually." He huffed a brief, surprised laugh. "Yeah, well, times aren't exactly *usual.*"

"Mmm," she said noncommittally. She had his number now. Chronic depression, just like her dad. If you were to believe her dad, the world was always on the brink of disaster. And it was best not to ask for details because you'd get a litany of why everything was going to hell.

A lull settled. She sipped her tea, wishing the night hadn't been ruined by thoughts of her dad, wishing Tremble would go away. Fighting against the guilt of not asking him more, drawing out his story, because clearly he wanted to talk about it.

A cool, moisture-laden breeze brought the complex mineral smell of wet sand and rock. Water rippled against the shore with a soft hush of fluttering silk. She waited him out.

He tossed the blade of grass aside. "Well, long day. Gonna get some shut-eye."

She turned her head to toss him a quick, unfocused glance. Enough to be polite.

"All right. Sleep well."

He stepped back over the log, the crunch of his boots receding toward his campsite.

"You too," came floating down to her, riding a current of melancholy.

the sixth day

Sherri Ann was following Tremble through the thundering Class IV-plus Muddy Grumble. Ever since his comment about this being a last trip and how these weren't "usual times," she had fought triggered memories. Through the bigger rapids she stayed closer behind him than she would have preferred.

Having run the Colorado through the Grand Canyon close to a dozen times, guided and solo, she hadn't bothered scouting the Muddy Grumble. He hadn't either. They were straight-forward as long as you stayed away from the wicked sieve between the large rocks on the left.

He was a good kayaker, good enough to run the Grand Canyon solo. Maybe, she corrected herself as she watched him take the wrong channel, maybe not experienced specifically on the Colorado, because now he was headed toward the sieve.

His kayak disappeared under foam. She caught sight of his green helmet bobbing briefly up before the kayak spun around. He was hitting the chute backward. The kayak slammed against the boulders of the sieve. The roar of water intensified as it surged around and over his kayak, which couldn't fit through the narrow opening.

He was pinned sideways against the sieve.

She stroked furiously left, a fortunate takeout point just above him. She flung her paddle to the rocks at the same time as she cleared her kayak skirt, ripped it open, and grabbed the rope she stashed in the hull for emergencies. Heaved her kayak onto land.

She raced across rocks and scrambled up the boulder he was pinned against, pitching an end of the rope around—thank God—an easy anchor point. She could see flashes of bright green under the roil of water. It was possible he was holding an air pocket between his face and the rock. Letting the line out, she tossed the other end smartly at the top of his boat where, if he had any luck, he'd feel it and grab for it.

No. And she could see there was no air pocket. She had one shot, without risking her own life. Without hesitation she dropped off the boulder on the upstream side, grabbed the rope herself, eased backward into the water as if she was rappelling down a cliff. She let her feet float up in the swift current. Head skewed to look over her downstream shoulder, she kicked the stern of the boat as powerfully as she could to shove it off the rock. One kick, two, and she heard a long, agonized scrape. She kicked furiously. The Kevlar deck ground off the rock and was instantly whisked downstream in the tumult around the rock. She hoped he'd be able to right himself.

Now she had to concentrate on her own dilemma. Her hands clenching the rope, she walked her boots above waterline, dragged hand over hand to work her way out of the current to the ribbon of still water at shoreline. Staggered out, panting. Not done yet. Gathered up lengths of rope as she ran, dashed back to her kayak, studied the current as she wrapped the line in sloppy loops, spinning the last few feet of rope around the middle on autopilot.

What a nightmare. She didn't see a way to ferry past the deathtrap of a chute back to the safe side of the river. She needed to get to Tremble quickly, make sure he wasn't facedown in the pool below the rapids, but she wasn't stupid enough to throw herself into the rapids without scouting the flow. She was pretty sure there was no one upstream to save *her* ass if she got in trouble.

She checked the narrow shoreline upstream and downstream. Upstream looked like a possibility. She left the kayak where it was, scrambled over a boulder heap and scoped the lay of the rapids. Her heart eased. If she put in above the boulder pile, she could ferry over to the good side, no problem. She only had to schlepp her kayak over the top.

Four minutes later she plunged into the stillwater pool below the thunder of the Muddy Grumble. It glowed with the peculiar light-blue water that flowed from many of the side canyons before mixing with the murky Colorado. On a gravel bar at the bottom of the calm pool, Tremble's kayak bobbed in the shallow water. His gaudy, green helmet was flung on the shore, his paddle a few feet farther inland from that.

And there, with dramatic drag marks leading away from his gear, he lay face down in the grit, looking like a beached sea lion sunning itself on a blustery day.

Sherri Ann marched up to him and kicked him middling hard in the thigh. "How *dare* you make that run without paying attention! How could you have let yourself get *pulled!*" [kick] "*into!*" [kick] "*the left!*" He rolled over; she kicked anyway. "*CHUTE!*"

He shoved himself stiffly into a sitting position. "Ouch. Uh...hey, Sherri Ann."

He ran his fingers through his dripping, chin-length hair, rubbed his face hard with both hands. "It wasn't, uh, wasn't supposed to go like that. I stopped for an hour, thought for sure you'd gotten ahead of me, and—"

"Oh my God. Oh my *God!* You did that on purpose, I *knew* it! And what, I was supposed to watch your body float past my campsite tonight? I found my dad after he blew his brains out, you asshole, and I'm not going to let you ruin my perfectly good trip with your self-centered, self-absorbed *suicide!*"

Water streamed down her face, off her hair, perhaps, because it was getting in her eyes and on her cheeks. Angrily, she wiped them dry. "You can just go kill yourself somewhere else, mister, because you're not going to do it on my watch."

He looked at her gravely. "I tried to keep you out of it, Sherri Ann. I'm sorry. I thought you'd gone ahead when I stopped."

He hesitated, patted the sand beside him. "Take a load off?" he offered. "I need to tell you something."

"No," she said but she sat anyway. "I don't want you to tell me how a love went wrong, or your best friend died, or you saw a baby get beaten by a gorilla at the zoo."

His lips quirked at the last one, then he sighed. "Okay, then. I want to ask you something."

Her dad had a dramatic sigh as well. "Yeah, what?"

"Where have you been since the middle of June? What have you been doing?"

"This summer? That's easy." She could see that he needed to get out of his headspace. She was good at that. Did it for her father for years, even made him laugh sometimes.

She unclipped her PFD, unzipped her wetsuit a little. "I'm a farmer and an engineer. I live in Georgia but I work on a lot of inventions, farming equipment mostly, and when I do that, when my head's really in invention mode, I go to a cabin my family has near Page, Arizona."

"Mmm-hmm." He picked up a short, squat stick and tapped it idly against the dirt.

"Okay, go on."

"Okay, so, I had this idea for a new gear shaft for a combine, and I won't go into *those* details, but I holed up in my family's cabin and just cranked—" she leaned toward him and poked his chest with a finger, "hah-hah, gear shaft? cranked? on figuring out the design for that and a couple other things. End of June, beginning of July, something like that. So, three months."

"And...you didn't see anyone the whole time? No radio, no TV? Newspaper?"

"Nah, I was in the middle of nowhere, and everyone knows to stay away when I'm inventing. I don't charge my cell phone, I don't have internet, I don't have a TV. Just me and my drawing table and about five thousand cans of soup and beans."

He scratched idly in the dirt with his stick, then smoothed the marks out. "No trips to the grocery store."

"Nope. And then I finished, got it all backed up on an external drive, packed the truck, and hit the river. I *always* go kayaking when I finish a project, it's my reward, you know? There's a put-in point a few miles from the cabin. I have a deal with a guy at the far end, he drives me and my gear back to my truck after, and then I get on with life."

Abruptly, he dropped the stick and stood up. "Yeah. All right. Okay. I'm good to go now."

He scooped up his paddle and helmet, stuffed the latter on his head, and shoved his boat off the beach before crawling over the deck and wedging himself into the cockpit. Without a backward glance, he paddled into the rippled water below the pool.

He didn't thank her for saving his life, but her dad never had either.

the sixth night

That night they shared a campfire, some quick burning shrubby sticks of willow and mesquite she'd collected from a flood-height jumble toward the end of the day. She was determined to keep a close eye on Tremble until he gave up on the suicide-by-rapids notion. Maybe she could do a better job with him than she had with her dad. She'd had a fair amount of practice.

"Look." She held up a plastic bag containing four marshmallows and jiggled it. "Treat time!"

He managed a small grin that didn't reach his eyes. "What are you planning to roast them with? A kayak paddle? Not much on this sandbar to whittle into a pointy stick."

"Maybe I'll dangle them over the fire on a rope," she said.

His eyes widened.

"Kidding." She groped through a pocket in the outside of her bag. "In desperate times, desperate measures. You stab the blade of your pocketknife through the middle. Just don't put it too close to the fire or the handle will melt. If it's plastic like mine, anyway. Takes a while to get toasted, but hey, what's time to a turtle?"

Despite her talk of stabbing, she eased the point of her blade carefully through the middle of a marshmallow, held it eight or nine inches from the coals, and supported her arm with the other, which was propped on a knee.

"Looks complicated," he said, but went through the motions of stabbing a marshmallow and roasting it anyway.

It turned out that toasted marshmallows are hard to pull off a knife blade. She mimed sticking it in her mouth and pulling it off that way. Tremble almost chuckled when she hammed it up.

He approached the back side of the blade, lipped the marshmallow, and pulled, so the sharp edge sliced through the crispy mallow and away from his mouth.

"Oo, that's smart," she said, but she had already used her fingers to pull off and eat the mallow. She made a big deal out of having fingers stuck together. "Can you pull the other one out of the bag for me?"

He dangled the empty bag in front of her face. "This bag?"

"Oh, *you*."

He handed her the last marshmallow, which he had tucked in his palm. They roasted their treats side by side, ate them with relish, washed up in the river. Without discussion they spread their tarps one on either side of the dwindling fire. She slithered into her sleeping bag, lay back, and put her arms behind her head.

The stars looked *more* tonight, richer, brighter. She felt the droopy contentment of a tired, healthy body. She had saved Tremble for another day. She admitted to herself that she was enjoying the baby-step end of her self-imposed isolation. Jumping right into airports, city noise, cross-country travel was a shock to her system. This was nice. A little exercise after weeks of inactivity, a tiny bit of conversation, a trip into her favorite wilderness. Nice? It was paradise.

Even with the suicidal Tremble. Or maybe especially. She felt useful. Necessary, even, like she, in particular, mattered.

They were on a high bank, ten feet above the water, sandwiched between two falls. The roar in the distance entered her conscious mind and receded, following the drift and return of her thoughts. The canyon broadened here, revealing a myriad of stars fallen like dew across a wide stretch of black sky. If she focused solely on the sky, she felt a sensation of falling, as if she might do a belly-flop into the starry night.

She sighed dreamily. "We could be the last people in the world."

A short, hacking laugh shot out of Tremble. "Yeah. I guess we could."

"Isn't it beautiful? So many stars, it's hard to find the constellations." Inside her sleeping bag, she used her heels to spin on her bottom forty-five degrees. "That's gotta be the Big Dipper. So...there's the North Star."

"Mmm-hmm," he responded. "Lode star. Guide star."

"Yeah. They're so beautiful. That red one, in Orion's shoulder? I think that's Betelgeuse."

"Betelgeuse. Isn't that the red one that's supposed to go nova soon? Not that we'll have to worry."

"Long after we're gone," she agreed easily. She changed the subject, as she had so often with her dad. "Crickets sound sweet against the river noise."

"Background music for the end of the world."

"The end of their world, anyway. How long do crickets live?"

"Not long. Probably this group won't be around long enough."

Her husky laugh rode the slow gurgle of the river. "Yeah. Probably not. Are we supposed to feel sad for them?"

"Nah. Not even for ourselves."

She sat up. "You're being all angst-y again! Do you know any campfire songs?"

the tenth day

"Name your favorite color."

They were playing a naming game, and Tremble had chosen the subject.

They were exploring a side canyon. Sherri Ann was determined to deliver Tremble safely to his takeout point. Ever since the near-disaster at the Muddy Grumble, she stayed behind him, camped at his campsite, and left at the same time in the morning.

"Favorite color. Hmm. Emerald! I just saw it on a skink's tail on the bank." Sherri Ann pointed.

"I saw it too. Except it was a snake, not a skink."

"Nope. It had legs."

He looked at her in a way she couldn't interpret. "Snakes have legs."

"Snakes have legs?!" She splashed him with her paddle. "Name one snake that has legs, silly."

One side of his mouth quirked. "Around here or in general?"

"Ooh. Aren't you the biologist? Around here, if you're so smart."

Promptly he said, "Rattlesnakes, cottonmouths, sidewinders, gopher snakes, garters, ring-neck." He paused dramatically. "Vestigial legs, but legs nonetheless."

"Oh, *you*." She giggled and dug her paddle in for a burst of speed. "Race you to the pointy rock, left side of the bend."

"Head start! No fair!"

the thirteenth day

It was Tremble's turn again. "Name one fear you have, one silly fear."

He stretched back on his kayak and flopped his legs over the side. They were drifting down the Fricassee Float, a seven-mile stretch of flat water where the canyon walls were shorter, farther apart, and sunburns abounded for unwary rafters.

"Ummm." Sherri Ann chewed on her lower lip. "Okay, well, sometimes I get this fear when I'm stopped at a light and there's a car in the lane next to me?"

"Yeah?" He smirked. "Is that the fear?"

"*You.*" Her lovely double-pulsed laugh floated across the water, hah-*hah*. "No, the fear part is sometimes, I'm *aware* of the driver, like maybe I get a feeling they're looking at me?"

She glanced over to make sure he was following her story.

"Go on." He back-paddled without sitting up to keep his boat from slipping ahead of her.

"Sometimes I just get this creepy feeling that I'll look over and—don't laugh, swear you won't—"

"Never," he assured her, dragging the paddle.

"I just wonder if I'll look over and—" she leaned toward him, nearly swamping her boat, "*he won't have a head!*"

He paused. "The aliens don't have heads," he pointed out carefully. "I'd just be grateful to be in a car with doors that lock and windows that roll up."

"Oh, great. I tell you my most neurotic fear and you laugh at it? Paybacks, when you least expect it!" She charged ahead, laughing, and he couldn't bring himself to call her back, tell her what needed to be told.

At the end of the next rapids, when he'd rested his paddle on the bow of the kayak and begun to relax, she came up behind and deftly dumped him.

When he rolled back up, sputtering and irritated, she crowed, "Payback!" and laughed so hard he looked simultaneously shocked and bemused, like maybe an angel was hugging him.

the fourteenth day

"Okay, your turn," she said. They were heating water for their dehydrated dinners, kneeling side by side on a long, flat rock. "Name an image, something that pops into your head."

He swallowed hard. "An empty city swimming pool."

"Whoa. That came fast. Why that?"

He turned his face farther away than he had to to see the river, hiding his expression. "I guess...I've been thinking about it a lot...I saw one recently, and I mean, I looked at it and thought, what happened to all the kids?"

He looked back at her. Tears brimmed his eyes. "What happened to all the kids, Sherri Ann?"

"Don't," she said softly. "Stay in the moment, Tremble. I don't know what happened to you, but just pay attention to now. Your breath. Your body, touching this rock, touching the air, warm inside your jacket and pants and wool toque. The water gurgling around our rock. The little frogs. The breeze. The scent of the river. Right now. You're here. That's all that matters."

He exhaled. "Yeah. You're right. You're right."

"Just listen to the river, okay?"

They sat in silence. Tremble's breathing came ragged and fast.

"I know you want to keep this in the moment, Sherri Ann. But there's something I have to tell you. I *have* to, okay? I've been putting it off, pretending everything's okay—" his next breath in shuddered and his voice shook, "but it's not. I can't let you not know. It's not fair to you."

"Okay," she said slowly. "But remember, Tremble, I'm not a therapist or anything."

"God. God, no, that's not going to help."

"I think you should see someone when you get back. My dad—"

"It's not like that, Sherri Ann. God." He huffed a breath that held no laughter. "I can guarantee you, your dad did not go through this."

"Okay, yeah. I'm sorry. You're right. I didn't need to bring up my dad."

"Whoa, okay, let me slow down. I get that was highly traumatic. Not to disrespect that at all, yeah? This is just a whole different thing."

"Okay, Tremble. Lay it on me."

"Yeah, okay." He exhaled noisily. "Yeah, whew. Shoot."

He turned off the flame on his camp stove, reached over without asking permission and turned off hers.

Tremble cleared his throat. "About three months ago, which must have been days after you went incommunicado, the Earth was invaded by aliens."

Wow. He was worse off than she'd thought.

She tried to keep judgement out of her voice. "Mmm-hmm. Go on."

His ragged laugh cut off as he put a hand down and spun from kneeling to sitting.

He gestured for her to do the same. "When I pictured telling you, it never occurred to me you wouldn't believe me. The rest of the world's been living this, this nightmare for three months, and you're holed up in your cabin or floating down a damn river."

She sat next to him, their backs to the river. "It's...pretty farfetched. You can understand that, right, Tremble?"

"Yeah. But just hear me out, okay?" He cleared his throat, stared at their sleeping bags already set out. "June twenty-second. They came in all at once, hundreds of thousands of spaceships, hit the biggest cities, New York, Chicago, Los Angeles, all over the world, London, Paris, Tokyo, Shanghai, Delhi, Moscow, God, hundreds of cities hit. They have bombs that turn concrete to dust. Took out malls, banks, government centers, churches, hospitals. The world's in chaos. No governments left. Everybody's grabbing food, whatever. Stupid-ass looters hitting jewelry stores, electronics, like that's going to be worth anything.

"They want the natural resources. They're strip-mining the Appalachians, they've built a crap-ton of oil rigs on both shores. They're dredging the oceans and taking all the fish. Alaska's full of oil wells, they're pounding the shit out of Arizona and Nevada for plutonium or uranium or God knows what. I could go on and on. Hundreds of thousands of spaceships, Sherri Ann."

He stopped talking, sucked in through clenched teeth, held his breath. The peepers filled in the silence, pulsing.

"But that's not the worst part. The whole world's, like, their private hunting ground. Millions of them, *millions,* Sherri Ann, they ride out in hordes, thousands of 'em riding these air bikes, like snowmobiles except fifteen, twenty feet up? You can hear the buggers squeaking at each other, this whole storm of clicks and screeches and squeals, fingernails on chalkboard. It's a game, they ride out in huge groups, let's stampede the humans, and they come around a building or across a town, thousands of 'em at a time, and spot a group of people, and they all start up that screeching, they're so excited, let's chase people and watch 'em run til they drop from exhaustion, so much fun. They friggin' *eat* people, or just leave 'em, it's all sport. They must have gone for the children first because there aren't any left, children are maybe these delectable little morsels, *God,* I can't even describe it, all the children disappeared within *days.* That first month...I lost my mom, my sisters, my friends. Everyone I worked with. Second month I happened across a basement with cases of energy bars and bottled water. Five of us down there. The food ran out, we all came out at different times. By then the aliens had moved into the suburbs, but they'd circle back every once in a while. Like hunters wanting a challenge. I guess blasting into crowds was getting boring for some."

He looked across the river, wiped his eyes.

"You ever read about passenger pigeons, how they used to fly so thick they'd blot out the sun? Or bison, a hundred thousand in a herd, so many it sounded like thunder when they ran?"

She shook her head. She wanted to scoot back—he was too close—but she stayed where she was.

"We're the bison, Sherri Ann. We're the passenger pigeons. On our way to extinction. Not a hundred years from now, not twenty years. More like this *month.* Maybe we *are* the last two people on Earth. Bodies piled everywhere. Can't bury the dead. They've got heat-sensing equipment. Doesn't matter where you hide. People chased down in the streets, gunned down in amphitheaters, in casinos, nightclubs, shopping centers, apartment buildings, and their damned screeching, they ride those air bikes through buildings, so excited to find someone to kill. It's not even *fair*. Not a weapon we have works against their shields."

He shifted, bent his knee, faced her.

"Look, it should prove to you I'm telling the truth because I don't care if you believe me or not. I mean, not for me. I had to say something. I had to tell you before you walked into it.

"So now I've told you. Just—please be ready. Imagine the worst and multiply it by a thousand."

She waited. This time the gurgle of the stream awoke to take over the silence.

Apparently he was done because he jerked away from her suddenly, went to his sleeping bag. He scooched down into his bag and rolled onto his side so his back was to her.

She watched the constellations twirl on their nightly journey through the sky.

What he said was overly dramatic. She reminded herself to consider the possibility that he was telling her a metaphorical story about his own schizophrenic hallucinations and paranoia. Yes, they'd seen no other river-goers, which was surprising, but she could think of a couple explanations. The government ran out of money again and closed all national parks. Or...the forest service knew a paranoid schizophrenic was in the area and restricted access for public safety.

But she wasn't getting a twitchy vibe. He had been sad, maybe suicidal. After spending so many days together, she thought he'd given up on the idea of ending his life. She looked with fondness at the back of his head, barely a silhouette now in starlight. She treasured the frequently lighthearted, fun days they'd spent together. She was amazed to realize she greatly enjoyed his company.

What did the aliens look like? Did it matter to her if tomorrow, when she reached civilization, she was going to die? Would she want to choose her own end, as Tremble tried to do, or would she take her chances?

She fell asleep pondering the questions.

the last morning

Tremble was gone. On the seat of her kayak, tucked under a scruffy, heart-shaped chunk of sandstone, was a note.

> *Sherri Ann,*
>
> *I never meant to finish this run. I can't face it. I'm sorry I'm not stronger for you. I want to go by my own choice. I meant to do it days ago, on the Muddy Grumble, but.... And later, you were so fine, sunshine under the stars, talking about us being the last in the world and still, you were laughing.*
>
> *Thanks for making the end so sweet. Please don't look for me; pretty please if you see a body at the end of the rapids, pass me by.* —*Tremble*

The morning was crisp, desert clear, with a sharp blue sky. She thought she wouldn't eat breakfast. She thought she would. She couldn't decide whether to hurry or to slow down, but her hands knew the motions of packing so well, they decided for her. Everything was in the kayak, and she was pushing off, and the river swept her up and carried her along.

She knew what he was going to do. He was going to skip the takeout above the Class VI, unrunnable Pearce Ferry Rapids. That's what she would do, if she was determined to commit suicide. Charge right into that unrunnable hole. It would suck him in, thrash him around, and not let him go until he decomposed and shredded into tiny bits.

Her heart was sick. She wished she had talked more. He wasn't her dad. He wasn't clinically depressed. She loved their games, and teasing, and companionship. She could have told him that even a few more minutes with him, a few hours, would have been worth all the world-endingness to her. And that whatever happened, could happen to them together.

If he was schizophrenic...

If he was, he had a beautiful personality for someone with paranoid hallucinations.

The river gave her easy rapids all morning. She tried to slow down, to enjoy her last day, but she found herself impatient with the current. She wasn't sure why she was hurrying. She wouldn't be able to catch up. She looked at her watch, calculated times, guessed at when he left this morning. Which rapids was he running at this moment, and the next? Which moment was life and which was death?

She felt adrenalized, hyper-aware of the river and blue sky and the splash of her paddle in the water and even her worry. She wished he was here, that they shared the ozone-rich air, the bounce of kayak on waves, the fun pit-drop in the stomach as the kayak boofed a four-foot waterfall, the feel of being water, being wave and curl of current. *Say the world ends five minutes from now,* she would say, *why would you want to lose this moment?*

The morning evolved into a wild, ecstatic Sufi dance. She was crazier than the river, she could pick it up and shake it, she could stomp across cliffs in seven-league boots, and she whooped and yelled down the last wiggly roller-coaster slide, shaking her paddle high overhead, rocking side to side for the delight of it, swooping around the last bend, howling a wolf call to hear the echo rebounding from the bluffs.

She was alive. Right now, it was a fine thing to be.

•••

On the wide, muddy bank of the takeout lay a green helmet. A kayak beached above waterline. A paddle rested across a cockpit.

And there was Tremble, laughing, wading into the water as, with a shriek of joy, she stroked toward him. He took hold of her kayak's grab handle, he slid the bow past his body so he could lean to her, he kissed her full on the mouth, their first touch. Her kayak slowed as he kissed the side of her mouth, her cheek, her ear, the back of her neck. He beached her canoe, waded out and found her hand, held it steady as she stepped out, held both her hands. Held her eyes, held a goofy grin on his face.

"You," she said, which held the story of her worry, her anger, her happiness, her hope.

"I'm here," he said, which held the story of a transformation. A story of holding on.

The Earth toiled around the sun, chock-full of species living and dying, those parasitical and those contributory. Destruction and birth, despair and hope. A few spins of Earth around its axis, recorded in no great universal tome, a few days more ephemeral than dragonfly wings, were nonetheless memorable to two beings on the shore of the Colorado River, who may as well have been the last two humans on earth.

Elaine Fowler Palencia

Save Yourself

The screen door banged behind her as Emily charged into the house. In the living room, as he always did on Sundays, her father sat in the flowered armchair, glorying in the Sunday newspaper.

Emily said, "Guess what? Revered Otto visited our Sunday school class and said we're going to have catechism class on Wednesday afternoons after school."

Her message delivered, she spread her arms wide, turned in a circle, and gave herself up to the Sunday dinner odors saturating the house: chuck roast, cheese scalloped potatoes, green beans cooked with bacon, apple cobbler. Her mother had made the meal before they left for Sunday school and church.

Lowering the newspaper, her father gave her a straight look. "Do you know what 'catechism' means?"

Jumping up and down, Emily said, "It's something we have to learn so we can join the church."

Her mother came in, patting her hair back into place. "Mercy, it's windy out there."

"What's this about Emily joining the church?" her father asked.

"Oh, well," said her mother. "It's—"

"You do it when you're nine," Emily broke in. "It's our whole class. We get sprinkled with water from a rose in front of the congregation." She continued hopping around the room, burning off the energy trapped while she sat still through church. "When can we eat?"

"Are you in favor of this, Martha?" asked her father.

Emily's mother set her purse on the piecrust table. "Well, I guess. She'll learn something."

He shook his head. "Emily, you don't know what you're doing. You're not old enough to know. They shouldn't even ask you. When you're old enough to make up your own mind, that's the time to consider joining the church. You're going to have to promise to believe things you don't understand. Martha, I wash my hands of it."

On a whining note, Emily said, "Everybody's joining. And we get this little catechism book for our very own." She hadn't expected her father to object. The only reason he didn't go to church, her mother said, was because he wanted to rest on the seventh day, like God.

"It won't hurt anything," said Martha, as she started for the kitchen.

"Won't hurt anything," said Emily's father, mimicking her higher voice. "By the way, what was the sermon about?"

Martha turned. "Did you hear that the Johnsons bought Del Collins' house?"

"You don't remember, do you? Why go if you can't even remember the subject when you get home?"

Emily stopped bouncing. Her mother's lips were pressed in a straight line. Behind her back, she crossed her fingers and hoped her parents wouldn't get into one of their wrangles.

"It...the sermon...was about sin," Martha fumbled.

"What about sin?" His voice sharp now.

"Why don't you go yourself if you're so interested?" Martha flung out, and stomped off to the kitchen.

Norton laughed into his newspaper.

Emily laughed, too. Her father knew everything; while her mother only knew what ordinary people knew. Antidisestablishmentarianism. That was the longest word in English; he'd told her so and taught her to spell it. She'd forgotten what it meant.

On Wednesday afternoon, Emily and her friends Mary Ella and Sandra walked the short distance from Tolliver School down Main Street to the church. Reverend Otto was waiting for them in their Sunday school classroom. He sat at Mrs. Charles' desk with his puffy hands folded on the desktop, looking hot and unhappy in his dark suit.

Emily took her seat meekly, anxious about what kind of teacher Reverend Otto would be. No one knew much about him. He and his family had been with the congregation less than a year. His two daughters, as stringy and pale as two wax beans, were ahead of Emily in school. Cathy, the older girl, was said to have a heart condition.

When the ten of them had taken their seats, Reverend Otto scraped back his chair, stood up, and cleared his throat. Looking out the window he said, "Who made you?"

They looked sidelong at one another.

"Anybody have an idea?"

Somebody giggled.

Reverend Otto held up a blue booklet. "The answer is in here. We will be studying 112 questions and answers about our faith. One hundred and twelve. They make up the catechism. You will take your books home and learn the answer to each question. When you have learned them, you will be ready to present yourself for baptism. The baptismal ceremony will be performed before the congregation during regular Sunday church services. On that occasion, you will formally accept Jesus as your Lord and Savior and in turn be accepted into the Body of Christ."

He walked among them, placing a booklet on each desk.

Emily kept her head down as he passed. The robin's egg blue cover of the thin booklet was beautiful, crisp and new and serious. But how did you get accepted into a body? She'd seen the inside of a chicken: wet, ropy intestines and half-formed eggs of different colors, like a clutch of planets, terrible in their vividness.

"Turn to the first page of questions," said Reverend Otto, sitting back down. "Glen, read the first one."

Glen mumbled into his shirt collar.

"Speak up, so everyone can hear you."

Glen read loudly, "'Who made you?'"

"Mary Ella, what is the answer?"

"'God,'" said Mary Ella, quoting from the booklet.

"Question number two. Susie?"

"'Who is God?'" read Susie.

"Emily, the answer."

"'The Creator of all things,'" read Emily.

"Sandra, number three."

"'What is God?'"

"Jimmy?"

"'An uncreated Spirit,'" read Jimmy, and accidentally on purpose dropped his book on the floor. The boys snickered.

Emily raised her hand.

"What is it?" said Reverend Otto.

"What's an uncreated Spirit?"

"That's the definition of God," said the minister. "Larry, read number four."

As the round-robin reading wore on, Emily's eyelids grew heavy. Down the street a jack-hammer rattled. She wished Saturday would hurry up; she and Sally were going to the movies.

"'What are the miseries of this condition?'" intoned Reverend Otto. "Emily, are you keeping up?"

With a shiver of guilt Emily read, "'All mankind being born in sin, are by nature under the wrath of God.'" She had heard Aunt Dreama say, "Without lipstick, I look like the wrath of God. I druther go downtown barefoot as to not paint my lips." But what did lipstick have to do with religion?

"Larry! Pay attention!" cried Reverend Otto.

Before going to sleep that night, Emily knelt on the throw rug beside her bed and opened the catechism. Wanting so much to understand, for she was an excellent and competitive student, she read aloud, sounding out the words she didn't know.

She could understand most of the individual words, but when she tried to put a whole sentence together, it turned to a block of stone with no way inside. From the part she did comprehend, she was getting a sickening feeling about dying and being reborn as a new person. She didn't want to die and she didn't want to be someone else. Who would she be? Would the person she was now just evaporate?

The next Wednesday they continued reading aloud, with Reverend Otto asking the questions to speed things up.

"'What does God require of man?' Craig?"

"O—," said Craig, and bent his head closer to the book. "O-bed—"

"Obedience."

"'Obedience to his revealed will.'"

Emily looked at the page and read the truth about herself. In school she understood every reading assignment. Now, faced with the most important assignment of all, the one that would save her from damnation, she couldn't puzzle it out. She was no better than Denzil Lewis at school, who only pretended to read.

Sniffing back tears, she raised her hand. "What's 'revealed will'?"

Reverend Otto smoothed the few hairs he had combed across his shiny scalp. His jowls lengthened. "Are you working on these at home?"

"Yes."

"Just learn them. Don't interrupt. We have a lot of ground to cover."

At death, sinners would be thrown into a lake of fire. She tasted upchuck at the back of her throat.

Every night, after her father read a story to her, she knelt on the rug with the booklet and tried to memorize a page of questions and answers. She didn't want to ask her father anything about the catechism, because he didn't want her to be in the class. Maybe if she had all the words, it wouldn't matter how much she understood. When she was in the first grade,

Miss Del Sarto, their language teacher, had taught her to say the Christmas story from the Book of Luke in French, for the school Christmas program. She had learned it by rote, memorizing the foreign sounds as if they were a song by listening to the rhythms of Miss Del Sarto's voice. Slowly, through tedious repetition, the sounds of the catechism began to stick in her head. She so wanted to be saved. Otherwise you would go to hell.

The next Wednesday, Susie asked Reverend Otto how they could be "under the wrath of God" if God loved them.

"Who put you up to this?" snapped Reverend Otto.

"Nobody," said Susie.

"Oh, yes," hissed Reverend Otto. "Mr. Nobody. Are you listening to him instead of the word of God? Are you doubting these lessons? Trying to find fault with them?"

"No."

"Then learn them as they are. Show some faith."

Susie started to cry.

"Go sit at the back of the room until you can behave," said Reverend Otto. "Get hold of yourself."

As she passed Emily, Susie leaned down and whispered, "God damn Reverend Otto."

In the late afternoons, while Emily's mother fixed supper, Emily sat at the kitchen table and read the catechism to her.

One day she asked, "Is Daddy going to be thrown in a lake of fire?"

"Why would you think that?"

"He doesn't go to church. Doesn't that mean he's a sinner?"

"Your daddy does plenty of good in the world. Don't worry about him. Who told you about a lake of fire?"

"Reverend Otto."

"Well," said her mother, sliding the skillet of cornbread batter in the oven, "the poor man's got a lot on his mind. They say that oldest daughter of his won't live long. But he shouldn't be scaring kids."

On the last Wednesday of confirmation class, Emily outran her friends to the classroom in the church annex.

Seated at Mrs. Charles' desk with his head bowed, Reverend Otto looked up when she entered the room. The long, sad lines of his face made him look like the Jacksons' coonhound.

"Reverend Otto!" she panted. "Guess what, I memorized the answers to all the questions."

"Is that so."

"Want to hear me?" Emily rattled off the first twelve questions and answers, stopping when she heard the others enter the building. They would think she was showing off, which she was. "I can do the rest," she assured him, and took her seat, where she examined her hands, turning them palms up, then palms down. Was she becoming someone else yet, or would it happen in a flash when she was baptized? Had her palms always been so pink?

That night she dreamed she was flying like a rocket at an upward angle through gray fog, her arms clamped to her sides by a mysterious force, her legs bound at the ankles, her body moving faster than light, unable to stop, a coal car rushing up a tipple, speeding towards the highest point in the universe from whence she would be flung outward into nothingness. A roaring noise filled her ears: the sound of the raging lake of fire waiting below the edge of outer space.

"Emily!" hissed her mother. She was sitting on Emily's bed, jostling her shoulder. "You're having a bad dream."

Emily flung her arms around her mother and began to sob. "I don't want to die."

"It's just a nightmare. There, now," said her mother, kissing the top of her head.

When the big Sunday arrived, Emily took extra care dressing in her pink-and-blue-flowered Easter dress, her black patent leather shoes, and her new white anklets. When she got sprinkled, would she See The Light, like Grandpa Wilson had, and it made him stop going to honky-tonks? Would a change come upon her like the mice changing into coach horses in Cinderella? Her stomach quivered like jelly.

As they were leaving the house, her mother said to her father, who was reading in his pajamas, "We might be a little late getting back because of the ceremony. Could you put some foil over the chocolate pie after it cools?"

Norton looked up from the newspaper and said mildly to Emily, "You're going to regret this, honey."

Turning away, Emily prayed, *Please bless Daddy,* and added a phrase she'd heard her mother use about him: *He means well.*

As they left the house, her mother muttered, "He always has to be different."

Would it never be time? The clock on the Sunday school room wall seemed to stand still. Sandra was wearing a new plaid dress. Craig and Billy wore ties. When Mrs. Charles finally let them go, Emily and her classmates burst out of the room like fireworks.

She was hurrying down the hall that led from the annex to the sanctuary when Reverend Otto stepped out of his office and held up a hand to stop her.

"Emily," he said with a stiff smile, "I'd like to talk with you for a minute."

Taking her by the shoulder, he turned her, so that they were walking back into the annex, against the flow of children and parents.

When they reached the lobby, he turned her to face him. Emily found it obscurely disturbing that his black suit was furred with white animal hair.

"You said that you've memorized all the answers in the catechism. Is that true?"

"Yes. Mama listened to me practice."

"That's a lot of questions and answers. I've never had a child memorize the entire catechism. Not in all my years as a minister. That's a remarkable thing."

Emily felt herself blush.

Although no one else was around, he leaned down and lowered his voice. "How about we show the congregation how much you've learned? I'll ask you several of the questions and you give the answers. We'll do it right before the sprinkling. Watch for me to motion you to the front. All right. Good." He steered her back towards the main building.

Her hands felt cold. Something was wrong. Something. Something. Her legs began to shake.

She was the last to take her seat with her classmates at the front of the sanctuary. On each chair lay a printed program of the service. Her mother sat in the second row among the other parents who were presenting children for membership in the church. She gave Emily an encouraging wink.

The service dragged through hymns and responsive readings. Emily's heart thudded in her chest. Sweat trickled through her hair. Her stomach hurt. Phrases from the catechism whirled in her head. Why did Christ suffer and die?...He humbled himself, and became obedient unto death...There it was again: "obedience." She bit the inside of her cheek, the way she did when she was getting a vaccination to take her mind off the needle, and tasted blood.

Then Reverend Otto was saying something about how hard the catechism class had worked, but that one child had worked harder than all the rest. Like car headlights in the night, his bespectacled eyes swung around and enveloped her in a deathly stare. He nodded slowly and held out his hand to her.

Mrs. Webber stopped playing the organ and the sanctuary stilled.

In that moment, Emily realized what was wrong: he was going to show her off but he hadn't helped her learn. He didn't care if she understood what she was saying or not. He wanted her to promise to believe things she didn't understand. Just like Daddy warned.

She looked away. To her left, a tall stained glass window portrayed Abraham, Isaac, and the burning bush. The flames glowed red and yellow, brilliant with late morning sun. Emily thought of their fireplace at home, its cheery flames dancing blue, cherry, orange, gold, and green. At the same time, another part of her brain imagined standing in front of the congregation, saying the words of the catechism. Of course she could do it. Behind her teeth the answers were lined up, row upon row, pressing forward like soldiers ready to overrun an enemy position.

In the congregation, someone coughed. In the vestibule, a baby gave a sharp cry. Sandra elbowed her in the ribs and she sensed Glen leaning in to stare at her.

"Emily?" said Reverend Otto.

No. she wouldn't do it. Not if the ground opened beneath her feet. It was wrong.

She kept looking at the window and thought about books. Not the catechism, but books that her parents read to her. Books that made her feel safe, even if bad things sometimes happened in them. *Little House on the Prairie. A Child's Garden of Verses. Heidi. Black Beauty.*

As if she were underwater, at the bottom of a swimming pool, she heard a muffled version of Reverend Otto's voice make a sharp, joking remark that included her name. He said something to Mrs. Webber and the sound of the organ resumed.

Then Emily and her class were in a line, walking forward one at a time to be sprinkled by Reverend Otto and welcomed by him into the church. As the droplets of water fell from the rose onto her forehead, Emily crossed the fingers of both hands and hoped this would be enough of a spell to save her from going to hell.

Then she was back in her seat, the same person she had always been. As the congregation picked up their hymnals, her eyes filled with tears of relief.

A hand touched her shoulder. Jimmy's grandmother was leaning forward from the pew behind.

"Bless your little heart," she croaked in a whisper. "Just go on and cry your tears of joy. You're saved now."

Chris Pellizzari

What Lorca Saw

I was still shaking inside the taxi. The anxiety I endured inside the plane had only slightly subsided.

"Please, I have to get off. I'm very sick," I begged the stewardess.

I stood pleading for ten minutes. She offered me free drinks and she told me to breathe in and out, a lot of people had these episodes, she saw it a hundred times before. She used the word "episode," as if she was watching a show. It *was* kind of a show, I'll admit it. Everyone on the plane was watching.

"But we're about to leave the gate," she said in a calm and professional Andalusian voice, something that is quite rare.

I tried to speak softly too because I could feel the eyes on me. Two other stewardesses were standing next to us now. They apparently had not seen this episode a hundred times before and appeared genuinely worried.

"I'm so sorry," I said. "But I have to get off. I can't breathe. I think I'm going to pass out."

"Okay. Wait here, Chris," she said.

She walked towards the cockpit. The two other stewardesses followed.

I sat back down. The old Spanish woman sitting next to me stared at the back of the seat in front of her. There was no doubt she hated me. I was responsible for this delay. She wouldn't give me the satisfaction of a dirty look. But I couldn't spend another minute aboard that plane. I had never felt so sick before, so near death before. There was nothing I could do to calm my heart except get off the damn plane.

I suffered from anxiety ever since I was twenty-two. I'm thirty now, but I never had any problems flying before. Everything was fine until I heard the door shut. I was sitting there reading a magazine on La Liga soccer thinking about how blessed I was to have visited Granada again, and then I heard the plane door shut and it was as if someone had injected panic and anxiety into my vein with a syringe. It was an irrational fear, but it was the most powerful fear I had ever known. I kept saying to myself, "Please God, let me die, I don't want to feel this fear anymore. Please let me die."

The stewardess came back less than three minute later. She tried to wear a smile for me.

"Everything is going to be okay, Chris," she said. "We are going to let you out."

I could feel my heart slow down a little. My stupid, fucking heart. It was responsible for all of this, more than my troubled mind.

"Thank you so much. I'm so sorry," I said.

I still pleaded for God to kill me, despite the good news. I knew it was only temporary good news.

In a matter of minutes, I was off the goddamn plane and back inside Granada's tiny, sleepy airport. This was it. This was it. I was stuck in Granada forever. I could never board a plane again. There was no way in hell I could be trapped inside a plane for a ten-hour flight back to Chicago. There was no drug in the world, except for death, that would keep me trapped inside that metal and those false windows for ten hours.

And now I found myself inside a taxi riding back to Granada. I told the driver to take me to Federico Garcia Lorca Park. It was the first place that came to my mind. I was breathing very heavy now, trying to calm myself. Yes, I would live here in Granada for the rest of my life. I would never see Chicago again. I would never see my mother or brothers again. Relax, calm down. You'll think of something. No, no. This was it. You were destined to live the rest of your life in the city that murdered one of the world's greatest poets.

The taxi dropped me off at the entrance of Lorca's park on the street called the Camino de Ronda. I paid the taxi driver a handsome tip, even though we didn't say a word to each other the entire ride and there was no luggage for him to help with because I travelled with a backpack and nothing else. But I had plenty of money. I was only a teacher in the poor Mexican town of Cicero. I didn't make much, but my father was a wealthy accountant and he was generous with his money, especially to his sons. I have travelled to Spain once every two years since I was twenty-one and he has always paid for it. He thought I was some kind of writer. I *had* published a few short stories in some decent magazines, and he must have thought the trips to Spain were inspiring me to write. It was somewhat true—many of my stories *were* about Spain—but he was simply a wonderful human being.

In that respect, I was like Lorca. His father constantly gave him money to travel; whether it was traveling through Spain as a teenager or visiting New York as a man, the father always indulged the son. It broke my heart knowing I would never see my father again, unless, of course, he flew out to Spain to see *me*.

When I was twenty-one and a junior at the University of Illinois, my father encouraged me to travel abroad. He was a well-traveled man himself and had seen the likes of Rome, Sao Paulo, Buenos Aires, Mexico City, Tokyo, Shanghai, and Copenhagen on business trips. He said I would learn more in the four months I studied in Spain than I would in the four years in Champaign. He was quite right. Maybe he knew I would fall in love with a girl in Granada. He had visited Granada in his youth, he knew what this city was capable of.

Her name was Vera, the girl I fell in love with in Granada. She was in my study abroad group. She was a sophomore at the University of Illinois. I think she was only nineteen at the time. She was an environmental science major, that I'm sure of. She would go jogging in Lorca's park. I joined her a few times, even though I wasn't crazy about jogging. We would meet in the park before heading off to the Center to catch a movie or flamenco show or meet with friends to *tapear* in the only city left in Spain where tapas were still free. My host family's apartment was across the street from the park.

I wanted our first kiss to be in the park, preferably on a bench in front of a water foun-tain, but it wasn't to be. Our first kiss took place outside the elevator of her host mother's apartment, which was ten minutes from the park. We had returned from a night of *tapear* after watching a subpar movie about Lorca called *La Luz Prodigiosa,* which had just come out and was receiving some buzz in Granada. It told the story of an old man in the 1980s who is really Garcia Lorca. Lorca wasn't killed in the olive grove in Viznar after all. Pure crap. Vera liked it, I saw tears in her green eyes inside the movie theater that night. I tried to convince her it wasn't good, but I couldn't change her mind. She was Serbian, born in Kosovo. Her family didn't emigrate to the States until she was eight. She had Serbian stubbornness. If you succeeded in changing her mind, you always paid a heavy price for it.

She was a sexy girl. Her five-foot-two body held firm breasts, a muscular stomach, and a tight ass. She had the face of a gypsy, a Slavic gypsy. If her skin was not so white, she could have passed for a gitana. She had a gypsy's nose and hair as long and full and black as any gypsy. When I was angry with her I told myself she was just a lot of hair.

The sun would soon set in Lorca's park. I had to find a place to stay for the night. I had to start living day by day and night by night. I found a bench near a lonely fountain that was talking about me to a rosebush before I arrived. I stared at the Huerta de San Vicente, the Lorca family home. He wrote many great works here. Can I spend the night in Lorca's house?

"Mr. Lorca, I am trapped here in the city that murdered you. I can never return home. May I spend just one night inside your home?"

He would say yes, I was sure. He would invite me to stay as long as I needed. I would tell him I might need forever. He would say that forever in Granada was not that long.

I remembered the photo of Lorca lying on the ground in Cadaques in 1927, pretending to be dead. The picture was published in Ian Gibson's biography on Lorca.

His house was now shaking. Leaves and oranges were falling off trees. Roses scattered and fell through cracks. The water in the fountain overflowed and surrounded my feet. The whispers of death that engulfed me inside the plane were talking to me again. My heart had its own mind now, and it was running fast, it was being chased by someone. I can't breathe, I can't breathe. I'm trapped, I'm trapped, I'm trapped. I got up from the bench and walked around the fountain. I tried to talk myself out of it. But the fountain water continued to over-flow, to flood the oranges. I felt worse now than I did on the plane. This wouldn't end. This would go on forever, forever in Granada. I felt like dying again. How lucky you were, Lorca, to be dead, to never feel *this* part of life ever again.

I would never see my father again. I would never see my mother again. I would never see my brothers again. I would never see Vera again. I was never going to see Vera again anyway. This was death without death, this was dying over and over again. I wanted to cease to exist. I wanted to cease to exist. I said this a few times, but all I heard was my heart bleeding, mor-tally wounded. Jesus, please. Jesus, please. Mr. Lorca, please help me. Please take me inside. Please offer me some water or, better yet, dry sherry!

The sun was vibrating! It was dancing in the sky, like it did for those young Portuguese shepherds in 1917. It was dancing across the vega in the distance, the vega that spread as far as the eye could see and as far as the ear could hear the Cante Jondo. This was the place, this was the place.

I walked towards another fountain. I had to walk and talk. The sun danced, Lorca could see this sun dance a thousand times from his balcony during his life, and yet he questioned the existence of God. He was no shepherd.

No, this must not be. This was not a stage, this was not Lorca's stage upon which I stumbled around like a maniac, mumbling words that signified nothing. No, No, No! This sun was not invincible. It would fall behind the vega soon and be replaced by a far more compassionate moon. But while it danced in the sky, I would have to hide. I would have to find shelter soon, shelter for the night. I could find far better shelter than Lorca found in August of 1936. They would not have found me in the upstairs of a friend's house.

Only two months before Lorca went into hiding, the great Dutch artist MC Escher was visiting the Alhambra, copying its mosaic patterns. This was a turning point in Escher's art. The designs inside the Alhambra gave the artist a new perspective, a new purpose in life. One artist's life was truly beginning while the other's was coming to an end, two artists who leaned heavily upon the Alhambra for perspective. But study Escher's masterpiece *Relativity*. I was afraid this was how the Rosales house appeared to Lorca in August of 1936. It was the way the inside of many places appeared to me when the anxiety rose in the early sky.

So many different perspectives, different stairs running in different directions. This was punishment. Granada was punishing me. She was jealous. She knew I did not return to see *her,* but to see Vera, to see the places Vera and I visited back in 2003. I had come all this way again to see Vera, not Granada. Things were truly not as they appeared, and Granada was punishing me for it. She was going to keep me for herself forever, like she did with Lorca. God knows how jealous she was of Lorca. If *his* love for her was not enough, how could mine be?

I stopped walking around in circles and walked towards the exit of the park, towards the taxis. I looked up at the apartment across the street, up, up, up until I found my window from 2003.

No, I had to eat something. I hadn't eaten anything all day. I was going to take a taxi to the Bodegas Castaneda, just off the Plaza Nueva. Sure, it was an old Vera haunt, but they also had the best tapas in Granada. Just some small plates of pleasure in the midst of this endless sad song.

I chose a taxi with a young driver, one with a baby face. He could not have been much older than nineteen.

"Bodegas Castaneda," I told him.

He seemed cheerful. He was blasting reggae music and he looked at me through his rearview mirror. He smiled.

"You like reggae?" he asked in Spanish, bobbing his head with the music, his impression of a Jamaican.

"Yes, I do. Who is this?" I asked in Spanish.

"Eric Donaldson. He is not as famous as Bob Marley, but I think he's the best," the driver said.

"This song sounds familiar. I think it's a cover of a Sam Cooke song," I said.

My head was still spinning. The music's volume did not help. I tried to look out the window at all the plazas and little shops and banks off the Calle de Recogidas, places I walked past a hundred times in 2003, holding Vera's hand. But the driver's speed and the volume of his reggae made me nauseous as I tried to focus on a particular building that was behind me before I could properly process it.

He became excited.

"Yes, that's right. It *is* a Sam Cooke song, *Bring it on Home.* I like Sam Cooke too," he said.

"So do I," I said. "He is from Chicago. I'm also from Chicago." Chicago, the city I will never see again. My mistress has murdered my wife.

The driver put away his smile and nodded seriously. "Ah, Chicago! Great music city. I also like the blues very much. Muddy Waters, Howlin' Wolf," he said.

"Yeah, well, Granada is a great music city too, a lot of great guitarists," I said.

He was impressed with my Spanish. "I am from Granada, obviously," he said. The smile returned.

The next song was also from Eric Donaldson. It was *Miserable Woman.*

"Is this your first time in Granada?" he asked.

I was trying to absorb Donaldson's voice. I really liked this song. I watched the granadinos strolling the sidewalks outside my window, the paseo. How can one be trapped in Granada? Listen to the sound of bubbling water inside the Generalife. There are stairs inside the Generalife where water flows down the banisters. Everything here is space and ancient air. How can one be trapped in Granada?

"No, I studied here in 2003. I was here for four months in 2003," I said.

"Yes, we have many students from around the world here. Did you study at the University of Granada?" he asked.

The truth was, I did not study at the University of Granada. I studied in a small school hidden behind a church that specialized in teaching students studying abroad, but I didn't want to get into all that so I said yes, I studied at the University of Granada. I hoped he hadn't studied at the University of Granada because I wouldn't be able to answer any follow-up questions regarding the college. Then again, I could say that 2003 was a long time ago and I had forgotten.

"I would have gone to the University of Granada if I wasn't so stupid," he said with a laugh. He turned around and looked at me as he laughed, so I laughed too. But I didn't mind, I liked him.

"Yeah, well, I'm pretty stupid too," I said.

He *really* liked this answer. He turned around and laughed and nodded in approval.

It was then I realized what I had to do to survive in Granada. I would have to marry a granadina. I was handsome enough, I thought. I could find a Spanish woman who was desperate to get married, just as long as she had some money and wasn't too ugly. I would start tonight, at the Castaneda. I would make it my mission in life, to find a woman of Granada to marry.

What else could I do? I couldn't look for a regular job, I wasn't a Spanish citizen. I couldn't play the guitar in plazas for euros, I didn't play the guitar. I didn't play any instrument. Damn, I wished I played the guitar, that would have been fine, playing it in Granada plazas all day, the granadinos placing euros inside my guitar case. This city was filled with plaza-dwelling guitar players, there had to be some money in it.

Maybe I could write some poems and read them out loud in a plaza, maybe use a microphone so I could be heard over the crowds, the way blues guitarists in Chicago switched to electric guitars so they could be heard over the bustle of Maxwell Street. I would place an upside-down White Sox cap at my feet. They could place the euros inside the cap, but would they? This was the city that murdered its poet—how much did they love poetry, enough to throw a few euros at a stranded American reading his original work in English? Who knew? Maybe?

And there were caves above the Sacromonte occupied by hippies. If all else failed, I could squat there for as long as it took to come up with a better plan, or to overcome this goddam anxiety and fly home.

There were options though, at least there were options. And I still had plenty of money, and I was sure my parents would send me more once I explained the situation. God, I had to call them. But it would have to be tomorrow. Tonight I was getting drunk at the Castaneda.

The taxi driver stopped at the narrow road behind the Plaza Nueva that led to the bodega. He turned around and smiled at me.

"Here we are, a few steps up this street," he said.

I fumbled through my wallet as I stared at the meter for the price. As I fumbled, I asked him if he liked any other musicians besides Eric Donaldson.

"I like Elvis a lot, but I like a lot of his lesser known songs. I like his hits, but I especially like the ones not too many people know," he said.

"Elvis, huh? Yeah, Elvis is cool," I said, handing him the money.

He reached into his pocket and handed me a business card. His name was Francisco Rodrigo Sanchez and below his name was a phone number I've long forgotten.

"When you are done drinking, call me and I will pick you up. I usually do not stray too far from this area. I just happened to be at Lorca's park earlier, but it was unusual. I usually stay around here, you know, close to the Alhambra and Albaicin. This is where the tourists are," he said.

I shook his hand. "Yes, yes, I am definitely a tourist. I will call you when I'm done. But I'm telling you now, I don't know how long that will take," I said.

"Take your time. The night is young," he said in English, English with a heavy Andalu-sian accent.

"The night is a lot younger than me," I said in English as I exited the taxi.

I heard him slowly back away as I walked towards the Bodega. I did not turn around to wave goodbye. I wasn't *that* happy yet.

Ah, the old Bodega in the yellow, orange, and purple light of the setting Granada sun. I saw bottles of wine displayed in the windows and behind them, ham hocks hanging from the ceiling. I knew when I left this place, in an unknown amount of hours, I would be drunk and the moon's brother hand would be on my shoulder, guiding me along.

Ah yes, everything was like it was in 2003, when I came here with Vera. The bull's head, the wine barrels stacked on top of each other behind the bar, a pyramid of wine barrels. There was the painting of the pretty young Gypsy woman near the entrance, a Gypsy Carlotta Valdes whose eyes followed me.

There were beautiful women in the corners of the bar, but they were in large groups. The beautiful women were well protected here. The granadinos looked at me when I entered, including the beautiful women, but they looked because I was tall and blonde. At six-foot-five, I was a giant to the granadinos. They knew I was American, and I was alone. I was some-one worth a three-second glance.

I was the only lonely person in Granada that night. It was a Friday night and the place had a Friday night feel. I realized that Friday nights were mostly the same, Chicago Friday nights and Granada Friday nights.

There was an empty stool in the middle of the bar. I took it without asking the old man to my right if the seat was taken. I assumed the stool was broken, which was why nobody wanted it. I expected it to crash under my weight, but it seemed sturdy. Why hadn't anyone wanted *this* stool, in the perfect middle of the bar? It wasn't wet, either. Nobody threw up on it or spilled vermouth on it. It was a dry, sturdy stool, and yet no one wanted it.

I let my backpack slide off my left shoulder until it was resting on the floor, resting against the left hind leg of the stool. It looked like a tired old backpack, a pitiful, slumping thing. I looked around the bar, nobody was looking at me anymore. The novelty had worn off.

I looked at two couples sitting on opposite sides of a wine barrel. They were using the flat top of the barrel as a makeshift table. That is where Vera and I sat back in 2003. She was intrigued with the idea of eating tapas off an authentic Andalusian wine barrel.

The waiter, not much taller than a twelve-year old boy, but at least forty years older, asked me what I wanted to drink in English. God, I felt like King Kong in this place. I didn't remember the people being this small here in 2003. He spoke quickly to convey to me he was very busy, and he *was* very busy. I could see a young man trying to get his attention from the corner of my eye. Still, I was offended he addressed me in English. It was rare for a granadino to do this, but he wanted me to know how obvious I was and that, perhaps, not all Friday nights were as similar as I originally thought.

I should have answered him in Spanish, but I was too drained for defiance.

"Give me a menu," I said.

He pulled a menu from somewhere under the bar and slapped it on the surface. It wasn't an angry slap, just one that demonstrated decisiveness amidst the chaos. He dashed away and I observed the four other bartenders, short men in constant motion, scooping mystery tapas from under the bar and placing them on the bar surface without even looking, the plates spinning and rattling a little, but the food staying in one place and the customers not batting an eye. Then a spin from the waiter and a wineglass magically in a hand and the glass under the tap of a barrel and the vermouth pouring into the glass, and another spin and the glass, filled to the rim, in front of the customer without a drop spilled. Yes, these seats were too dry for this kind of all directions in one direction madness.

I examined the menu, a single, tall card of a menu, very elegant, with Bodegas Castaneda written in 18th-century blue cursive on top and drawings of wine barrels along the borders. The wine list was on the front, the selection of tapas and raciones filled the back. I wasn't very hungry—anxiety kills hunger—but I was very thirsty. This was the place to be. Even though I felt like a Vietnam vet dressed in marine uniform, pinned with medals, surrounded by flower children, this was the best place to be. The stewardess recommended I drink. I was going to take her advice. I didn't have to call for a waiter, a different midget read my mind.

"I'll have a glass of this sherry," I said in Spanish, pointing to the menu.

I decided to order some food. I was going to be here for a while, and to hold on to this once-in-a-lifetime seat for the remainder of the night, I would have to show the crowd I was eating too.

I didn't need to flip the menu over, I knew what was good here. "Also, one order of jamon serrano and one order of manchego cheese," I said.

He nodded without saying anything, without moving his eyes from the menu, with the straightest mouth I had ever seen.

The granadinos were really smoking, they were going to burn the place up, the wine barrels would explode. I breathed in cigarette smoke and told myself this was the smoke from the guns in the jungles near the Cambodian border or perhaps the smoke rising from fallen Madrid in 1939. There could be a veteran from 1937 inside these walls tonight, he would understand me, I convinced myself.

A glass of pale yellow sherry appeared before me. This was followed by a small white plate containing eight circles of perfectly sliced chorizo and a piece of French bread. This was the free tapa, this was the tradition of great Granada. I wasn't hungry, but I could appreciate good chorizo. Even though I was being held against my will, my jailers were kind, they had good taste, and they held high culture. I finished the sherry in one gulp. Very, very fine sherry, as smooth as the tabletop.

"I'll have another," I told the bartender, a different bartender, an inch taller than the last one.

I took my time with the manchego and the serrano, which arrived ten seconds after I asked for another sherry. But I did not take my time with Sherry Number Two. I lifted the glass to my lips with the sherry spilling over the rim and, five seconds later, lowered an empty glass to the surface. My head was shaking now, but not the shaking of anxiety like inside the plane and the taxi from the airport to Lorca's house. This was a loosening, a release, some machine shaking and nuts and bolts flying in all directions, a joyous collapse. I examined the tortilla espanola, which had appeared without my noticing it and now sat motionless next to the empty glass. I wanted to examine it, perform an autopsy upon it, not eat it. Free Tapa Number Two. I poked at it with my fork and ordered my third glass of sherry.

I looked around the bar again. There was no woman here for me. There was no woman anywhere in this city for me. No woman would take me in, make me a granadino for the rest of my life. I was not the gigolo type. The truth was, there had been only one woman for me, and her name was Vera. She had once been with me here in this city, four months in this city, but that was a long time ago. How many years ago? I don't know, I was in no mood to count. I could hardly count past seven now. I was in the mood for a beer, though. I called over some anonymous short man, some unknown soldier of a waiter.

"I'll have a beer and I don't need another tapa, I'm still working on these," I said, nodding at four mostly filled little plates.

Man, my Spanish was slurring.

"What kind of beer?" the man asked, none too pleased with the American slurring a dialect of Spanish that was clearly not from this region, or even country, or even planet.

"Alhambra," I said.

He nodded like a soldier that understood his order, and marched out of my view. I did not move my head or eyes to follow him.

Alhambra, the name of the local brew was Alhambra. But it was also the name of the grand old Moorish palace that watched over Granada, prayed for Granada, the way the statue of Jesus prayed over Rio de Janeiro, but the palace offered far more inspiration. Vera and I had our second date at the Alhambra. What a place for a second date. The guy that she was with now in Chicago, which was thousands of miles from this place, could he offer her the Alhambra on a second date?

I thought about the Alhambra, empty in the darkness, the tourists long gone. This was when the ghosts came out, a 13th-century ball of ghosts mingling in the Courtyard of the Lions. Lorca was there of course, a special guest, and so was the ghost of nineteen-year-old Vera. She was there, waiting to dance with me. What was she wearing? It was a dress, but I couldn't even see the color of the dress. A thought like that on a day like today would have started my heart racing again, but it was calm. Alcohol might have been what I needed all along, what I *would* need to board that plane.

There was a beer in front of me.

Is this a dagger I see before me, I asked myself.

Beer in a wineglass. It didn't stand a chance. In ten seconds the glass was as empty as the Alhambra, minus the dancing ghosts.

I tried to remember the Eric Donaldson songs from the taxi. But I could not recall them. There was one song, though, that kept playing in my head over and over again, a song I hadn't heard in years. It was *Hello Vietnam* by Johnny Wright. I was a vet who had returned to a home that wasn't my home, to a bar that I had once visited in another world with a girl who loved me before a war. I was surrounded by short people who didn't understand my madness. And I was alone. Good-bye my darling, good-bye my darling.

Two more beers and two more sweet sherries later, a demon over my shoulder, they call him Duende here, told me to leave. I had one of the small men wrap up the food for me, food to go. I didn't want any of them to think I was the kind of American who wasted food when there were so many people in this world that were starving. Even in my own little world, people were starving. There were plenty of homeless wanderers in this city, in this little world of a city, and if I came across one tonight, I would hand him what the small men wrapped up for me.

I removed my smartphone from my left pocket and Francisco Rodrigo Sanchez's business card from my right pocket and, with the backpack slung over my left shoulder, walked over to a barrel where two pretty young women and two well-dressed, well-groomed young men were sitting. I walked over to the prettier of the two women and interrupted her mid conversation and told her I needed a taxi but that I was too drunk to dial the number on my phone. She laughed and said she would do it for me. She must have met many a drunken American in this city in her lifetime. I couldn't tell if the two men were smiling at me or scowling, but I was certain I could handle the two of them physically if the situation called for it, so I scowled too, at least I tried. The way I felt, I didn't know if I had a scowl on my face or a look that said I needed to take a shit.

The pretty woman was talking to Francisco Rodrigo Sanchez on the phone and she was laughing. Then she handed me the phone and the business card and told me the driver would be here in five minutes.

"Thank you for being so beautiful," I said to her. Then I attempted another scowl at the two men and walked out the door.

I paced around the front of the bar in a calculated stumble, never straying too far from the entrance door. Then something funny happened. I wasn't missing Vera anymore. It stopped suddenly, like a headache. Ulysses S. Grant was bothered by a terrible headache during the days leading up to Appomattox. When he was informed that Lee was ready to surrender, the headache disappeared. This was something very similar, I thought, staring at my feet as I moved, or at least thought I moved. *She wasn't here anymore,* I said to myself. She may as well have been a Moor. She was long, long gone. They should name a street after her, she was *that* gone. MataVera Street. This was a *new* Granada. There were many new Granadas in Granada's history, and this was another new Granada. Quite frankly, I wasn't welcome in New Granada.

"No man. Fuck her, fuck this new place!" I said out loud.

I saw the taxi appear at the end of the street. I waved at it but I did not walk towards it. Francisco got out of the taxi and jogged towards me, laughing.

"Hello, my friend. Let me help you," he said in English.

He removed the backpack from my left shoulder and slung it around his right shoulder. Then he put his arm around my free shoulder and guided me to the taxi.

Were these the same people that murdered Garcia Lorca, I asked myself as we moved towards the taxi. The truth is, the granadinos were wonderful people, even if the city was a new new.

He helped me into the back seat.

"Where to?" he asked, smiling like a crazy man, crazier than me. He looked as if he was expecting me to say, "The nearest whorehouse."

I would have on another night, but tonight I wanted to lay my head down on a pillow and sleep until tomorrow night.

"Do you know of any good hostals in the Albaicin? Take me to a good hostal in the Albaicin," I said in English, holding on to my spinning head so it wouldn't pop off.

I didn't know why I chose a hostal in the Albaicin, the old Moorish district, the medieval hill of the Moors, with its ancient rising and winding roads. Maybe because there was a rebellion there in 1499 by Muslims who didn't want to convert to Christianity. Maybe because there was a rebellion there in 1936 by workers and farmers who didn't want to convert to Fascism. Two desperate, failed rebellions against the inevitable. A perfect place, perhaps, to spend the night.

"There is the Hostal Moni Albaicin. Shall we try that one?" Francisco asked in English.

"Yes, try that one," I said.

A song by Elvis Presley called *Judy* filled the taxi as the moving machine wound and rose past crumbling white brick walls. This was the Albaicin, the Albaicin at night, a world within a world, a past within a past.

"Have you ever heard *this* one before?" Francisco asked, his head turned around like Linda Blair's, his eyes studying mine, his eyes far from the road ahead, his smile suicidal.

"*I* have, but many haven't," I said.

I didn't care if he didn't look at the road again. This was a ride, and a crash was fine with me. He stared at me for a century and smiled and nodded his head. When he finally turned around to embrace the slithering road, I reached into my backpack and removed two airplane-size bottles of Jim Beam. The stewardess gave me five bottles as she tried to calm me down. I felt sorry for her. I hoped she was happy now, she was happy tonight and had forgotten all about me. And so I sang.

"Oh Judy, don't let our sweet love wither and die like flowers in the fall, oh Judy, don't you know it's you I love most of all!" I sang.

Francisco laughed like a hyena shot with a tranquilizer gun and slapped the steering wheel twice.

I offered him a tiny bottle of Jim Beam. I just held it over his shoulder, my outstretched arm rested on his shoulder and I was dangling the bottle like bait. He took it without turning around.

"Thank you, my friend. I don't even know your name, but you are my friend!" he shouted as he opened the bottle near his lap with two hands, no hands on the steering wheel, which turned to the right on its own.

After I told him my name, I opened my bottle and took two sips. I sang again. "There will never be anyone else here but you!"

Francisco hummed the tune. He wasn't confident enough in his English to sing.

He took a swig of Jim Beam, half the bottle, the miniature bottle, pressed a button, and released Elvis's *Western Union.*

When Elvis sang the words "Western Union," I joined in and sang the words "Western Union" in my best Elvis voice, which was, despite my condition, pretty damn good.

Francisco almost died laughing and he found the confidence to sing the words "Western Union" in his best Elvis voice, which was, for an Andalusian, not too fucking bad. He finished the bottle and threw it against the passenger door. I removed another bottle from my back-pack and dangled it over his shoulder again.

He accepted.

I knew that ten hours inside a plane was manageable if I felt like *this.* I had it all planned out now. I would have as many drinks as I could at the airport bar before boarding. I would drink until my walk was a stumble. Once inside the plane, once I was strapped to my chair, I would orders drinks until I passed out. When I'd wake, I would be in Chicago. I wouldn't feel a thing. I wouldn't know where I was or who I was.

And I would never return to Granada again. I would never return to Vera again. I wouldn't think about the bitch ever again. She got me into enough trouble already. I wouldn't be here right now if it wasn't for her. As far as I was concerned, Vera died that night. Francisco ran her over somewhere along the road up the Albaicin.

"This is my last night in Granada," I said to Francisco. "I'm going home to Chicago tomorrow, and I'm never coming back. Never," I said.

"That is sad, my friend," Francisco said. "We will miss you. Granada will miss you."

Andrew Peters

An Assistant Salesman's Notebook

1.

The correct way to fold a sweatshirt is as follows: place the item face down on one of the glass display cabinets and spread it evenly with the tips of your fingers; bring the left sleeve over so that it lies parallel to the diagonal of the right sleeve; fold the left sleeve back to lie parallel with the side of the garment; repeat the process with the right sleeve; fold the garment from the bottom into a neat rectangle; return to shelf. Carry out this operation correctly, neatly, swiftly, and Bastard Crean won't threaten violence. Bastard Crean who suffers terribly with hangovers and will lash out, lose his rag completely if you balls it up.

What the fuck is this? *Do yous think it is your fuckin bedroom drawer yous are dealing with?*

Bastard Crean, Senior Salesman at Hennessy and McCaid, the gentlemen's outfitters on Nassau Street. Who has never smiled, whose touch is death, who was once seen punching a member of the Garda Síochána in the face, in the middle of Grafton Street. All are dismayed to see the approach of his long white face, glossed black hair, wild eyes (salty, marine, not land-mammal eyes).

You'll get a fuckin kick.

Worked here for years. Even Mr. Hennessy is scared of him. Mr. Hennessy thinks he makes the rules, but it is really Crean who sets them. Watch him. Follow his rules exactly. No room for error. That's what rules is, says Crean. Rules.

Better is portly bearded Neville, Second Senior Salesman. In the backroom Neville sings:
How can you mend this broken man?
Hur ahh ah hoohah ever win?
Please help me mend my broken heart
ah hin ah hin a hin.

The sweatshirts and pullovers in neat piles on the low display tables, always. The packaged shirts in pigeonholes up the rear walls, rising in bands of hue and pattern. Complex rubric, dark to light but interpolations of texture also. Many, many years to learn, best not bother. Ask Noel. Do not ask Crean (under any circumstances, but especially if you look in the cheval glass that we have angled in such a way as to be able to see a corner of the back room, that one there with the missing wheel, see?, and you observe him slumped over the table, his head resting on his arm, in alcoholic agonies, terrific booze fugues).

Later, perhaps a week, sure enough: slick tails of oiled hair coming down to the table, low groans, sat in there like a monster all day, all a-whimper.

2.

Junior salesmen must give way to senior salesmen in the vending of anything more valuable than a tie or pair of cufflinks. For example, a junior salesman is showing off an expensive tie of candy-striped silk to an eager customer, cradling the thing like holy rope between his two arms and in his head doing the necessary arithmetic (ten percent commission for one of the best ties), and the customer's eye rolls up to the wall of shirts above him.

A shirt, to go with the tie, Sir?

Mmmmm.

The range goes from dark to light, floor to ceiling, you see?

[Taking a step towards] Ah, yes. Mmmmmmmmmmmmmm.

Then Crean's long back slides in to block you. That is the rule. Or Neville shuffles around one of the cabinets as if running up to bowl. He'll take it from here, portly kind Neville. Ten years Neville has been here, not as long as Crean but the rule is the rule. Twenty percent commission on the silk shirts, you see.

In the back room there is a jar of Nescafe, a box of Barry's Tea, may as well go and dig into that. A console table and two chairs to perch on, looking sidewise onto Crean's *Evening Herald,* not to be touched. Or go and stand at the front of the shop and look out the window at the fine, old commercial street (double-decker buses, shuffled greens of the university trees opposite, submerged blocks of buildings behind). You see pedestrians on commercial business, marketing tourists also. All business, yes, but Jimmy Joyce grabbed Nora Barnacle here as she came from changing linen at Wynn's Hotel. So you never know. Think on that until Crean is done, his commission bagged.

3.

No smoking in front of the shop. You must go miles and miles and miles if you wish to light a cigarette while wearing Hennessy and McCaid black trousers and white shirt. An unobstructed display window is of paramount importance, polished daily. Suits, jackets, ties, shirts, cufflinks, hip flasks, sticks for walking, sitting and shooting, Mr. Hennessy has won an award for their window configuration (in partnership with Mr. McCaid, deceased). At Christmas he shakes synthetic snow dust on the shoulders of the winter jackets, buries the wellington boots in authentic holly. Does he want you lighting a Marlboro in front of that? Cupping a fag in your hand like a carnival person?

No, Mr. Hennessy.

Crean returns midway through an illicit cigarette—drop the thing to the ground and pray. Coming past the Molly Malone statue, the white face, the oily hair, from here his eyes are piebald marbles, swirling. Bursting through the quiet coherence of elderly tourists, the grey-wooled heads turn in alarm at the violence.

Step on the butt subtly, smother slowly its fire. Crean approaches.

Smoking, I saw you. *You're a dead fuck now.*

Crean smoking himself but not caring, tidying his hair in the display window reflection. But then Hennessy over his shoulder, returning from lunch.

I hope that is not a cigarette in your hand, Mr. Crean!

No, Mr. Hennessy. I mean, I only came out to put it out. I lit it in the back room, forgetting.

Follow me please, Crean.

To the till, Hennessy purse-lipped. Over the till the large glasses flashing atop the thumb of nose and the mound of expensively silked body beneath, quaquaversal. Big in the trousers, Neville calls him Hennerseat. Hahaha.

Mr. Crean, is there anything we have forgotten today?

I don't think so Mr. Hennessy.

I think, Mr. Crean, we have forgotten to take the alterations to Mr. Kane. Haven't we?

I think we forgot to take them with us when we went out earlier, just like we forgot them yesterday. And now we'll need to get them over there in a rush, won't we?

Sorry, Mr. Hennessy.

And Mr. Kane will be angry.

He will that, Mr. Hennessy. Sorry.

Well, you can drop the alterations over to him now. Take thoughtful Johnny here with you.

Oh, I can manage them, Mr. Hennessy.

Take John, Crean. I want nothing dropped.

And in comes a customer and, Fine afternoon, says Mr. Hennessy, his fingers playing the notes of his tie, Now that the rain has stopped.

4.

Do not stand within four feet of Crean or you can expect a lunge from him, instant punishment.

Get out of it!

Around Crean are invisible hemispheres of forbidden space. With special glasses you could see them pressed together, a two-lobed fruit, Crean existing at the center, buried seed. Enter that surrounding zone and there will be a lightning crack, a thunderous punch.

Get the fuck out of my way!

Crean has full range of the shop, from display window to rear staff room, from the shirt wall to the till console and glass cabinets full of shoehorns, tins of polish, brushes of horse-hair bristle. He travels the deep carpet as he pleases. Only Mr. Hennessy has equal sovereignty over that territory. Senior Salesman Noel can move about easily, but he understands that Crean's corner is not open to him. Watch him skirt the area as he quick-shuffles to a customer. Humming madly. With fear, perhaps.

The Junior Salesmen have a single rear corner only, where the glass-topped cabinets show the cufflinks and tie pins. Do not leave it unless strictly necessary (such as for the folding of sweatshirts and pullovers, see Rule 1).

Crean's corner is a Bermuda Triangle. To be caught there is to be sent to the bottom, traceless, all hands lost. Mr. Hennessy only can cross that boundary, and even then you might observe the fine bristle at the back of his neck stir and twitch, a tucking in of his wide gait.

One day there was a new boy. A Junior Salesman Probationary. He had the urchin look, scraggy necked, in the shirt he arrived in he swam about like some white fish. Hardly more than a child he had already dark slings of concern under his eyes, grave world-worry. Mr. Hennessy, bighearted, fussing loudly, fixed him up with a better fit. A Sea Island cotton double-cuff for you laddie, there you are now.

"There," said Mr. Hennessy, "much better. We can take a little bit off your wages every month." He wished only for success, a long career for him. Mr. Hennessy had a concern for the disadvantaged. He liked to train them up, give them a life. Portly bearded Noel, for example, was once a punk on Grafton Street (in his wallet a faded picture of himself crouching at the mouth of an alley, a rainbow coxcomb running over shaved skull). Mr. Hennessy would lift this Junior Salesman Probationary from bad circumstances, Noel said he recognized a special case when he saw one. But then Mr. Hennessy went for lunch and the boy stood in Crean's corner and Crean came out of the back room quick like a spider and got him by the ear and twisted him to the ground.

Bye-bye new boy.

Crean said that he wouldn't have turned out any good.

Noel said later the boy had had a look of Crean about him, when Crean was younger, and that didn't help him at all.

But rules are rules. When you stand in the backroom to be loaded up with the alterations for Mr. Kane, stay well back. Let Crean approach and lay the suit carriers over your arms. Take the weight of them without complaint.

5.

The ratio of suit carriers to be carried by a senior salesman and a junior salesman should always be approximately three to one. In the dark storeroom, Crean piles them high over the forearms, four, five, six. Two for himself. He'll need a free hand to open the doors, you see. The suit carriers of Hennessy & McCaid are superior to all others in the trade, expensively cross-weaved, reminiscent of velvet to the touch. On the right breast a transparent plastic window and the golden letters: HENNESSY & McCAID. In the valley of cardboard boxes, broken display trees, disused plastic, Crean threatens violence.

I am going to fuck you out of here so fast.

Why?

No smoking outside the shop.

But you were smoking.

Shut up. And always looking out the window. Seeing just about half of everything.

What am I missing?

Shut up. And scribbling in that notebook.

I am only writing down the rules.

Sure you are. Shut up. What for?

There are so many rules that if I don't write them down I'll fuck everything up.

Shut the fuck up.

Across the shop floor then and Mr. Hennessy nodding, glasses flashing. Out the door and taking Nassau Street in single file, Crean leading. Around to Grafton Street, up its shallow grade in the young sun and the dying rain flashing on the litter bins, all over the glossy shopfronts. Birds strung in clear air above, noisy gulls complaining. Past the busker and his crowd, past Hayes Cunningham Roberts to the Weir's corner, into the narrow shade of Wicklow Street.

Now, you leave Mr. Kane to me, you hear?

I sure will (only Crean deals with Mr. Kane, that's the rule).

He's been on the sauce for the last couple of weeks. He's wild, so he is, out of control.

Drinking more than usual?

He's spooked about the operation.

What kind of operation?

Heart. They'll break him open like a crab.

That sounds bad.

Of course it's bad, you fuck. Leave him to me. Don't look him in the eye, even.

6.

Never ask Crean how he came into the world, or where he grew up, or what his father does, or does he like to have a cooked breakfast on a Saturday (if he has been on the lash, which is what he is on every Friday). Punishments will follow. Noel said one day: Crean's old man was a right one, did something terrible to his mother, it was in the papers. And so Crean grew up without his family for a while. When Noel said that you saw the pressure build behind his eyes and his color go up. He said it and stared about and then went to the back room and would say no more.

Another version: Crean's mother died giving birth to him, in his fetal garrulousness he played havoc with her insides as he came out. His father turned to drink, blaming the son for the death of his wife. Mrs. Walsh, the accountant, gave that to us. The rest you can guess, as long as it is unuttered, never comes to Crean's large white ear. His father beat him senseless every day. Maybe. Each night he went to bed with blood trickling from his nose or mouth, the calluses of the soul thickening with every blow. One day the boy Crean snapped and grabbed a bread knife from the table and plunged it into his old man, over and over. When the police came, the blood-soaked crumbs fallen from the blade were on the floor, across the boards of the table. Like someone had died eating tomato soup. Angry soup spilled all over the front of the dead father, pooling in the folds of his soaked shirt. Crean did five years, as a minor. All possible.

Another version: Crean took a Honda Civic belonging to a neighbor for a spin without permission. He left the vehicle in the Grand Canal. But the detritus in the canal, the old prams, bicycles, traffic cones, kept the car afloat and the Garda Siochana Technical Bureau lifted his prints. He did a year, on account of his previous convictions. Mr. Hennessy found him begging on Grafton Street, and lifted him out of the gutter. Not far from where he found Noel. A life, was what he intended to give him.

Don't ask Crean about any of this as you walk along Wicklow Street, the suit carriers laid out across your arms, the valley of the street sonorous with clicking heels of shoppers and the boom and tinkle escaping the door of Tower Records like a sublime beckoning, a call from another world.

7.

Don't ever look Mr. Kane in the eye when he has been drinking. Only Crean can wrangle him. Crean and Mr. Kane once had a fight on the street. Two big men, like bears their bodies slapped and shook each other. When the Garda Síochána arrived to separate them, Crean punched one of them in the face. In the middle of Grafton Street. Apart from Crean, Mr. Kane is the most frightening man in the South City Centre. On the drink. Otherwise a good sort. He is an orphan, forced into tailoring. The head of the orphanage went down the line of children and tapped them on the shoulder in turn, carpenter, plumber, tailor, carpenter, plumber, tailor, carpenter, plumber… and tailor for young Mr. Kane. Horrible adoubement, these things really happened in those days, he says. His hands too big for tailoring, clumsy, his fingertips martyred to his work—scar-smoothed as doll pads, all the whorls chased flat. He makes the best suits in Dublin, despite the drinking and gambling and being very old. Private clients, racing types. From him Crean gets horse tips, Crean returns to the shop with money fanned in hand and grins: *Gee gees.* Mr. Kane works in the light of his small window, bent close to flashing needle. The other window repaired with cardboard, yellowed newspaper. Sometimes he sleeps on his cutting table. Around his room are sleepy volcanos of ashtrays, drifts of cloth cuttings, and high ranges of newspapers: The *Herald* and *Daily Star,* the *Indo* and the *Times,* the regionals left by his connections, the *Leinster Leader* and the *Kilkenny People,* the *Leitrim Observer* and the *Meath Chronicle.* Also, slings of smoke from his Benson & Hedges, less permanent.

Up and down the narrow staircase to Mr.Kane's top floor workroom run once a day the salesmen from Louis Copeland, Switzers, Brown Thomas, alterations folded over their arms in inferior suit carriers. Passing through the vegetable damp from the ground floor veggie restaurant. Crean carves through the lentil cloud and takes the stairs two at a time, leather soles screwing the worn lino. Pauses on the landings.

You keep your eyes on me, you hear?

I hear.

Have them alterations ready for me when I give the signal.

Gotcha.

On me. Your eyes.

Then up again through the narrow stew, the damp squeeze of the walls. On the final landing, Mr. Kane's toilet, finely veined pottery visible through the open door. Disinfectant and cigarettes, the sigh of the cistern. Out of bounds, most certainly.

8.

Whoever you are, even if you are Bastard Crean, you do not enter Mr. Kane's workroom without knocking at least three times. Almighty consequences for those who don't. If Mr. Kane has drink on him. Otherwise, a friendly smile, but altogether not worth the risk.

Crean knocks. Once, twice, thrice. Long pauses in between, but no answer. Raps once more and steps into the room, motioning to follow.

Mr. Kane asleep in the corner, on his wooden chair in front of the sewing machine. His head resting on the glass of the workroom window. The room is tidy, all the surfaces cleared, the ashtrays gone. The cutting table clean also, the scraps tidied to show scarred wood and giant scissors resting. Suits hung everywhere, along the buckled racks and high up the walls. With the suits so arranged the room is crowded (with pretend people, scarecrows, not real people, obvs.). Mr. Kane sleeps on. A bottle of Powers on the windowsill next to his elbow, Crean clocks it and, bending arm and leg, makes a drinking gesture. Clears his throat.

Mr. Kane!

A! Ah! Wass? Wassy? Ah lads. Lads, lads, lads.

Mr. Kane stands, sleep-blunted, witches jaw working drily. Drunk, but old drunk, no bite left. Whorl of hair atop undone, coiling from the crown, he pats it down.

There's some stuff done for you, lads, over here on the rack.

No crushed cans on the mantelpiece, no torn envelopes, crumpled cigarette packs, all swept clean.

I've labelled all the suits for you (shaking hand raised). So there'll be no bother seeing whose is whose, if it comes to it.

Thanks, but we have more here for you, Mr. Kane (two suit carriers proffered by Crean).

I'll not be in for a while lads (the big head shaking, dropping, mouth coming loose, a string cut somewhere. Coughing also, lung soup slapping and cracking.).

But Mr. Hennessey wants them done in a hurry, Mr. Kane. He says he'll need them by…

I'm heading in tomorrow, you see. To the hospital.

Oh (suit carriers lowered).

They called me yesterday. I'm to go in tomorrow morning. James's Street. They said to bring pajamas and a toothbrush and all that.

Oh.

And nothing is to pass my lips after midnight. That's the rule.

So you'll be off for a bit?

That's right. Maybe a month the doctor said. Maybe more.

Oh.

To tell you the truth…

Oh, Mr. Kane…

To tell you the truth I'm not sure I'll be back at all (big, unsuitable tailor's hand comes over mouth, eyes shutter unevenly. Sob.).

Tell you what Mr. Kane, we'll tell Mr. Hennessy that you'll be off for a bit, and then there's no need to worry about the alterations, and that'll be one less thing on your mind, like.

Rain restarts, spits on window.

They're all labelled, you know, all the names is there, I spent the whole day yesterday at it, so if there's any trouble at all, if there's you know what, Oh Jesus…

That's all right Mr. Kane, there's no need to worry about anything like that (hand behind back signals exit).

So everything is in order (knuckling deeply his eye, breathing wetly), everything is ship shape. I'll leave a key in the restaurant downstairs, with the skinny one that does be doing the till.

Mr. Kane moves towards us.

Ah, there'll be no need for that Mr. Kane, we'll see you when they've fixed you up. And I'll tell Mr. Hennessy that you'll be out of action for a while, and Mr. Hennessy won't mind a bit once he knows you're in hospital. He's a decent old lad, is Hennessy. And then we'll be back to business in a month or so, or however long you need.

Mr. Kane advances.

The doctor, he says that they can't be certain of anything. That there's always a chance of (hand over mouth again).

Lookit, Mr. Kane, he has to say that. He can hardly say it's one hundred percent, can he? They're probably not allowed to say that, even, I bet that's the rule.

Ah, thanks lads, thanks (cheeks varnished under the naked bulb).

Not a bother Mr. Kane. We'll let you get back to it, so.

Okay, lads, thanks. Thanks for coming by.

But moving forwards still, head weaving.

Not a bother, Mr. Kane. So we'll be seeing you. Adios amigo (hand held out).

Mr. Kane takes the hand, shakes it weakly once, twice, head nodding, then pulls Crean in, Crean's head going quietly into his shoulder, Mr. Kane's lips coming to Crean's cheek, kissing him there.

Quiet. Somewhere below a door opening and closing. Car horn. Distantly dismayed sea-gulls. Mr. Kane's wet breathing, big head depending over Crean's shoulder, eyes scrunched shut. Close your eyes in case he opens his eyes (Rule 5). Soft kind murmuring from Crean, as soothing a horse.

Open your eyes. Your eyes on him, like he said. Then close them (Rule 5, remember). Then open them again, like he said.

And close.

And open.

And close.

And the sound of suit carriers sliding to floor, and Mr. Kane whispering: Crean, Crean, Crean, Crean. And open. And Bastard Crean's arms brought up, then brought around him, Mr. Kane.

And close.

Haley Quinton

The Soul of a Spider

Georgia Ashworth watched from her grandmother's bedroom window as the flames licked the old barn. The dry wood crackled and blazed as the fire climbed the structure. The roof collapsed with a crash, and smoke poured from the hole in thick, dark clouds. It smelled like burning leaves, but with more smoke. Georgia pressed her face against the window and could feel heat seep through the glass. Grammy would get onto her later for leaving a face smudge all over the clean window, but Georgia would worry about that when the time came. Now, there was a barn on fire.

Georgia was seven years old and had a fascination with fire. When her grandfather burned trash in the burn pile in the yard, Georgia liked to go along. Georgia would stand close to the fire, feeling the heat of the flames on her face. She liked how the air shimmered from the rising heat, and the way little sparks would shoot up into the air. When Grandaddy turned his back, Georgia would find things to burn. Her favorite was styrofoam cups. When she dropped those in, they'd start to melt, then collapse in on themselves and shrivel to nothingness. Once, Grandaddy had caught her and told her to stop. He said burning styrofoam would release toxins into the air that would hurt her to breathe in. Now, she waited until she was sure he wasn't looking, and tried not to breathe in too much.

Beside Georgia was her cousin, Cole, and beside Cole was Wyatt, Cole's younger half-brother. Wyatt was only four years old, and he had to stand on a Lincoln Logs box in order to see out the window. The barn was completely ablaze. Some of the dry grass near the barn had caught fire, beginning to smolder. There was a wail of sirens somewhere in the distance.

"The fire trucks are coming!" said Wyatt, bouncing on his box.

"Don't fall," Cole said.

Earlier that day, the kids had been playing in the living room when Grammy's neighbor, Lucille, had come to the door.

"Ida, you keep those kids away from the barn today," Lucille had said. "I donated it to the fire department. They're going to burn it today so the firemen can practice putting it out."

"Will they bring their fire trucks?" Wyatt asked.

"Oh, Lord," said Grammy. "You shouldn't have said that where they could hear you."

•••

Georgia watched the grass by the barn smolder. The fire trucks still weren't in sight. What would happen if the grass caught all the way on fire? The barn belonged to Lucille, but it still wasn't very far away from their house. If the flames spread, would the house look like the Styrofoam cup, melting and shriveling and finally collapsing to nothingness?

Once, Georgia had dropped a live wolf spider into Grandaddy's burn pile. Its body had twisted in agony for a few seconds, then was consumed. Georgia had never told anyone she'd done this, and now thought back on it with some shame at having tortured and killed the creature; but she also remembered it with fascination. If the house caught on fire, would Georgia be like the spider? At church, Georgia's Sunday School teacher taught them that if they were good, their souls got to go to heaven when they died. But Georgia wasn't always good, like when she murdered the spider.

Did spiders have souls?

There was a flash of red light coming up the drive. The fire trucks were here.

"See the fire truck, Wyatt?" said Cole.

"I see it! I see it!" Wyatt said. He clapped his hands and toppled off his box. Cole helped him back up.

The firefighters piled out of the truck. They soon had their hose hooked up, and a long arc of water burst from it and landed on the barn. Another hose joined it. In no time at all, the fire was out, leaving only the black-charred wooden skeleton of the barn's frame. Georgia felt a stinging sense of disappointment with the fire gone, an emptiness inside, and a cold feeling where the fire's heat had been.

"That was awesome!" said Wyatt. "Did you see how fast they put it out? Did you see their red helmets? I want one of those helmets for Christmas. I wish I had my fire truck here. It's at my house."

"All right," said Grammy, coming into the room. "Show's over. It's lunchtime. Come on, now."

"I want to watch them drive away," said Wyatt. "Grammy, see their helmets? I want one of those for Christmas."

"You still have a ways to go before Christmas," said Grammy. "It's only July. Come on, now. Time to eat."

"I want to watch them drive away."

"Okay, okay," said Grammy. "Watch them drive away, and then it's lunchtime."

Grammy went back into the kitchen. Wyatt was watching the fire trucks, but Georgia looked at what used to be the barn.

"I want to play in it," said Cole.

"Me, too," said Georgia.

"Did you see how fast they put it out?"

"Yeah," said Georgia, frowning. "I wish they'd taken a bit longer."

"Why?"

"I don't know," she said. "The fire was kind of pretty."

"Do you think there were any animals in there?" asked Cole. "You know, those old cats that used to hang around?"

"No," said Georgia. "Well, I don't think so. That guy that started the fire, he would've made sure there weren't any there, right?"

"Yeah, probably," said Cole.

The fire trucks were beginning to pull away.

"I want lunch," said Georgia. "Let's eat."

"No," said Wyatt. "I'm still watching."

"Bye, then," Georgia said.

She sat down at the table, where her bologna and cheese sandwich sat on a plate.

"Don't you want to wait for your cousins?" asked Grammy.

"No," said Georgia. "I'm hungry, and they're taking forever."

Georgia took a bite of her sandwich. She crunched down on a sour cream and onion potato chip. In a few minutes, Cole and Wyatt joined her. They chattered to each other about the fire trucks and the firefighters, but Georgia couldn't stop thinking about the way the barn looked when it was ablaze. It looked like life and death at the same time.

Georgia lay on a pile of blankets on the floor watching television when Cole crawled over on his hands and knees, stopping when his mouth was an inch from Georgia's ear.

"She's asleep," he whispered.

Georgia sat up and looked back. Sure enough, Grammy was sound asleep on the couch, her head tilted back and her mouth gaping.

"We can go see the barn," said Cole.

Georgia nodded. She turned to look back towards the bedroom, where Wyatt was playing.

"We shouldn't take Wyatt," she said. "We can't get him out of the house without him waking her up."

Cole shook his head. "He'll wake her up when he sees we're not here."

Georgia sighed. "True. He'll start hollering."

"I'll go get him," said Cole.

"Fine, but keep him quiet," said Georgia.

Cole crept back towards the bedroom, and Georgia stood up and eased towards the door. Cole came out of the bedroom with Wyatt's hand firmly in his. Georgia put her finger on her lips and directed her fiercest glare at Wyatt—the one that she'd learned from Grammy. She'd kill him if he woke Grammy.

They tiptoed through the house towards the barn. Once they'd crept halfway across the yard, they finally spoke.

"Race you to the barn!" said Georgia, taking off at a sprint.

"No fair!" said Wyatt, racing after her.

Georgia got there first and slammed her hand against the wood. It was still warm, and her fingers came away black. The smoke and ash smell was much stronger here. The frame-work of the barn still stood, but everything else was reduced to nothing but piles of ash.

"I won," she said, panting.

Wyatt picked up a stick and pointed it toward the barn.

"Shh," he said, mimicking the sound of running water. "I'm putting out the fire! This is my hose."

Cole jumped up on a stump next to the barn. Georgia filled her palm with a pile of ash. She spit in it, mixing her saliva with the ash.

"Come here, Cole," she said. When Cole came over, she dipped her finger into the mixture in her palm. She traced her finger along his cheekbones, leaving streaks. "War paint."

"Me next!" said Wyatt, running up.

"I'm not done yet," Georgia said.

"My turn, my turn, my turn," said Wyatt.

"Fine, hold still," Georgia said.

She didn't do as good of a job with Wyatt, just giving him a few streaks on his cheeks.

"Cole, do me," said Georgia.

"I want to," Wyatt said.

"No, Cole has to. He'll do a better job."

Cole frowned in concentration as he dipped his finger in the ash.

"You have to spit in it," Georgia said. "Or else it won't stick."

"Ew!" Wyatt said. "Your spit's on my face?"

Cole spit in his palm and stepped closer to Georgia. She could see the lines of sweat on his face drip and drop through the ashes, smearing them wetly. He traced his finger along her cheeks and forehead.

"Done!" said Cole, grinning.

"I wish I could see what it looks like," said Georgia.

"We can look in the mirror when we get back," said Cole.

Georgia put her whole hand in the ash, sifting it around. Clouds of it rose in the air in front of her like vapor. She clapped her hands, sending the puffs of ash off her skin. Cole whipped off his shirt.

"Draw something on my chest," he said.

Georgia traced lines down Cole's chest.

"Your turn," he said.

Georgia paused. A few years ago, she would've stripped off her shirt without even thinking. But they'd gone to the lake earlier this summer, and Grammy made her wear a T-shirt in the water since she'd outgrown her swimsuit. She'd taken it off when Grammy wasn't looking, but then an older lady she didn't even know had gotten onto her about it, so she'd put it back on.

But the designs on Cole's chest did look cool, and there was no one here to see her. She yanked her shirt off. The sun felt strange on her bare skin, and she felt exposed. Cole's finger traced along her chest, which felt funny. She shivered. His tongue poked out of the corner of his mouth in concentration.

"Done!" Cole announced.

Georgia felt a peculiar sense of shame from the way Cole was staring at the intricate triangles he'd traced on her chest. After a sudden thought, she looked towards Lucille's house. No sign of her. Was her car still in the garage? Georgia couldn't tell. What would Lucille tell Grammy if she saw Georgia shirtless? Georgia reached down and grabbed a handful of ash and plopped it on Wyatt's head. It coated his red hair in gray dust.

"Hey!" said Wyatt. "No fair!"

He got his own handful of ash and smeared it on Georgia. She did the same to Cole.

"Ash fight!" said Georgia. "Whoever has less on them at the end wins!"

By the time they were finished, it was impossible for them to tell who had more ash on them, because they were all covered from head-to-toe in a fine layer of grit.

"Let's go in the barn," said Georgia.

"Do you think it's safe?" asked Cole.

"Of course," said Georgia. She wasn't sure, but she wanted to see it anyway.

They stepped inside. They'd been in there lots of times, but it looked really different now. There had been a few stalls and small rooms, but the fire had consumed them, leaving only the outside walls standing. Georgia felt a pang of sadness, remembering all the times they'd played cowboys and Indians in here. What would it feel like to be in a fire? Georgia stood in the center of the barn and imagined the swirling flames engulfing her. Three years ago, when Georgia was only four years old, she'd seen the news right after the Oklahoma City bombing. A lot of kids had died. The last image she remembered seeing before the screen went black was a fireman carrying a small child with blood in her hair.

Georgia looked up at the corner of the barn, and she could see a tiny spider started to spin its web. Each of their footsteps sent up a cloud of ash. Georgia looked for the cats that used to hang around, hoping she didn't find a burned-up corpse. She went to the back wall and rested her forehead on it. There'd be a spot of ash in the center of her forehead.

"Ow!" yelled Cole from behind her.

Georgia spun around. "What's wrong?"

Cole was sitting on the ground by the barn, clutching his ankle.

"What happened?" Georgia asked, crouching down beside him.

"I stepped on something," said Cole. "A nail, I think."

The nail was lying beside them. Georgia picked it up. It was rusty. She swallowed. She knew what happened with rusty nails.

"How bad is it?" she asked.

"Not that bad," said Cole. "It didn't go that deep, I don't think."

"Let's go back and clean it out," said Georgia. "Can you walk?"

She helped Cole stand up. He took a few steps, but he couldn't put much weight on that foot. She put her arm around his shoulders to let him lean on her. His bare skin was warm against hers.

"Wyatt, get our shirts," said Georgia, conscious that no matter what happened, she didn't want Grammy to see her shirtless.

They set out again across the yard, leaving a trail of ash behind them. Wyatt carried their T-shirts in a little bundle.

"Let's go to the back door," said Georgia. "We'll have to leave our clothes outside."

They stopped by the back door. Georgia stripped off her shorts, and shoes. Her socks and panties were also gray with ash, so she took those off, too. She looked at Wyatt and Cole, and then down at herself. The three of them stood there naked, their hair and skin coated in ash. Only the parts that were covered with their underwear was white, like tan lines after swimming.

"We'll have to take a bath," said Georgia. "I'll go first. Be. Quiet."

The back door opened to the pantry, which led to the kitchen and then to the hallway, where the bathroom was. Georgia stepped inside, tiptoeing to the kitchen. The door closed behind her, and she turned to glare at Wyatt, who had let it close too loudly. She put her fingers to her lips.

They crept through the kitchen, then to the hallway. Georgia closed the bathroom door behind them. Grammy and Grandaddy didn't have a shower. Georgia put the stopper in the drain and filled the tub with warm water.

Cole helped Wyatt get in first, then Georgia and Cole climbed in. The tub was a bit too tight for the three of them. It had been about a year since they'd all three taken a bath together, and they were bigger now. Their knees knocked, and water sloshed over the edge of the tub. They helped each other scrub up, and rinse the soap out of each others' hair.

There were footsteps outside the bathroom door. They froze, staring wide-eyed at one another.

"Kids? What are you doing in there?"

There was a long pause.

"Taking a bath, Grammy," Georgia said.

"Why?"

"We wanted to," she said. "We're pretending like we're at the pool."

"Well, come on out of there. You're too old for that. You're too big to all fit in that tub. I'm sure you're soaking the floor," Grammy said.

"Okay," said Georgia. "We'll be out in a minute."

They all sighed as Grammy's retreating footsteps. Georgia stood up and turned around.

"Am I all clean?"

"Yeah," said Cole.

"Stand up, I'll check you," said Georgia.

Water streamed off of Cole's body, but she didn't see any more ash. Wyatt was clean, too.

Georgia stepped out onto the floor. Grammy was right. It was soaked. She got some towels from the bathroom closet.

"Ow!" said Cole as his foot hit the floor. Georgia winced. She'd forgotten about the nail.

"Let me look at it," she said. They sat down on the floor, and Cole put his foot in Georgia's lap. There was a small, red hole where the nail had been. It hadn't gone deep, but it was rusty. Georgia had heard about lockjaw, which could happen when you step on a rusty nail and your jaw would lock up and you could die because of the bacteria from the nail. Georgia had to figure out what to do to help Cole but keep them from getting in trouble.

A few weeks ago, Georgia had been playing with one of the stray cats. The cat had scratched her, and Grammy had poured hydrogen peroxide on the cut to clean it. The hydrogen peroxide was in the kitchen cabinet.

"I'm going to get something to clean it," said Georgia. "But first, let's get our clothes."

They wrapped themselves in the towels and crept out of the bathroom, then sprinted to the bedroom where they slept when they spent the night at Grammy and Grandaddy's as fast as they could with Cole hopping. Their spare clothes were in the drawers.

"You two stay here," said Georgia after they were dressed. "I'm going to get the hydrogen peroxide."

Grammy was in the kitchen.

"Hi, Grammy," said Georgia. "What are you doing?"

"I'm starting on your supper," she said. "What does it look like I'm doing?"

Grammy was fixing meatloaf, her hands deep in a bowl of raw meat. Her hands glistened with the slimy egg.

"That looks good," said Georgia. Seeing Grammy work on dinner made Georgia feel a little bit guilty. Grammy was more of a mom to Georgia than her real mother, whom Georgia hadn't seen all summer. Grammy had explained to her that there was something wrong in her mother's brain, a sickness in her head. She just wasn't ready for the responsibility of having a child, Grammy had said. She liked to travel around, and didn't want to settle down anywhere. Cole's mother was the same—she was Georgia's mother's twin sister, and they had the same sickness in their brains. But Cole lived with his father and stepmother. Georgia lived with Grammy and Grandaddy, and Georgia was suddenly acutely aware of the strain Georgia must put on them.

But now was not the time for repentance, not with Cole sitting in the back room with a hole in his foot.

"Well, it will be good when it's finished," said Grammy.

Georgia nodded. The hydrogen peroxide was in the cabinet. She sidled over to it.

"What are you doing, Georgia?"

"Nothing," said Georgia. The bacteria was invading Cole's body through the wound on his foot at this very minute. She opened the cabinet. "Can I help you set the table, Grammy?"

Grammy frowned at her. "Sure you can, in an hour when it's almost time to eat."

"Why don't I just go on and get the plates down?" said Georgia.

Grammy just shook her head. "You are a strange child sometimes, Georgie."

Georgia started piling the plates on the counter. She glanced at Grammy through the side of her eye. Grammy was looking down at the meatloaf in the dish. Georgia put her hand on the bottle up there. She yanked it down.

"Okay, Grammy, I'll set the table in an hour. Bye!"

She ran back to the bedroom, where Cole was sitting on the floor holding his foot.

"It's hurting more now," he said. "I think it's swelling."

Georgia sat down beside him. The wound was in the middle of his foot, and sure enough, it was looking a little bit puffy.

"This will help clean it," said Georgia. She opened the cap and started to squirt it on Cole's foot.

"Ow," he said. "That burns. Ow! Ow!"

"Shh!" said Georgia. "Do you want us to get caught?"

"It really hurts!" said Cole.

"I'm getting Grammy," said Wyatt. "Grammy!"

"No, Wyatt, get back here!"

But Wyatt was running out of the room.

"Grammy, Cole's hurt really bad and Georgia's making it worse!"

"Why couldn't you just keep quiet?" Georgia said.

But Cole was just holding his foot.

"What's wrong?" asked Grammy.

"Cole hurt his foot, but it's okay because I'm helping," said Georgia. "I just got the hydrogen peroxide from the kitchen."

"Oh, that's what you were doing," said Grammy. "Cole, let me look."

She grabbed Cole's foot. She saw the bottle sitting beside him.

"Georgia, this isn't hydrogen peroxide. It's rubbing alcohol. No wonder it burns so much," said Grammy.

"Oh," said Georgia. "Sorry."

Tears were streaming down Cole's face, and he ignored her.

"What happened, Cole?" asked Grammy. "Cole? How did this happen to your foot?"

"I stepped on a nail," said Cole.

"Where? In the house?" Grammy asked.

No one answered.

"Where did you step on the nail?" she asked again.

Wyatt looked like he was about to burst. Georgia narrowed her eyes at him, willing him to keep quiet.

"We were playing outside," said Georgia.

"Where outside?"

They didn't answer.

"Where outside? If there are nails out there, I need to pick them up so that you don't get hurt again. Plus, they could hurt the mower next time Grandaddy mows."

"We were playing in the old burned barn," said Wyatt.

Georgia groaned.

"You were playing *where?* That's so dangerous. You know that, right? The barn could collapse on you and you could *die!*" said Grammy.

Wyatt started to cry.

"Well, we're fine. We didn't die," said Georgia.

"Well, Cole's hurt," said Grammy. "And we're going to have to take him to the doctor to get a shot."

"A shot?" said Cole. Then, he started to cry harder.

"But I cleaned it!" said Georgia. "I killed the bacteria so it can't hurt him or give him lockjaw."

"That's not how that works, Georgia," said Grammy. "We'll talk about your punishment later. For now, we're just going to have to work on getting Cole to the hospital."

"Hospital?" he said through his tears.

Georgia stood up and went to the living room, sitting down on the couch. Tears were starting to leak out her eyes, too. She clenched her teeth. It wasn't fair. She hadn't meant for Cole to get hurt. She'd just wanted to see the barn to see what the fire had done to it.

"Georgia, you'll have to help me get Wyatt in his booster seat," said Grammy. Grammy held Cole's hand.

Georgia snatched Wyatt's hand so hard he whined.

"Shh," she said, yanking his arm. "You're the one that told."

She pulled Wyatt after her and into the garage. Grammy helped Cole into the front seat. Georgia grabbed Wyatt under the arms and put him in the booster seat. Grammy buckled him in, and Georgia sat on the other side.

As they pulled down the gravel driveway, Georgia looked out the window at the barn. It stood gray and ashy against the sky, and the surrounding grass was charred and blackened. She felt shame at letting Cole get hurt. It was almost the same feeling as when she'd taken her shirt off, and when she'd killed the spider. The car kicked up gray dust on the gravel driveway, and it mingled with the darker ash still pouring from the barn. Her shame was like the light and the dark boiling inside her.

Ron Riekki

le chien

It's a known medical call. We get those rarely. Our ambulance company, it seems it's all unknown medical. You show up and find out what it is. But this one, we already know. Except truth is, you can go in for a headache and it can turn into a brain aneurysm. Shoulder pain can become heart attack. Common cold can become death. That's the awesome thing about medicine. Everything can change in a heartbeat. Or lack of one.

This call falls into the majority of our calls, which, at least for me, seem to be diabetes, epilepsy, cerebrovascular accident, simple DCAP-BTLS. Those are calls you see over and over and you can repeat "and over" a hundred times here.

DCAP-BTLS stands for deformities, contusions, abrasions, punctures/penetrations, burns, tenderness, lacerations, swelling. If you want to get sick of acronyms really fast, go to EMT school. They'll pound them into your head. P.O.'ed doesn't mean pissed off; it means taken by mouth. S.O.B. means shortness of breath. T&A? That's tonsillectomy and adenoidectomy. And where are we going now? To an ASS. A simple seizure. I've seen preacher seizures, playground seizures, just-crashed-my-car-into-a-bridge seizures, dentist seizures, and, the second most common of them all, Walmart seizures. The most common? That's your standard nightclub seizure. Drugs, heat, strobe lights—it's like dance clubs are designed specifically with the epileptic in mind.

We walk up to the mobile home. In this "Manufactured Home Community," as it's billed, ten people have died in the last month. It's Florida. People die in Florida. But the good thing about a seizure is patients tend not to die, which I like. I like living patients. My favorite patient, personally, is a living, breathing, unconscious patient with perfect vital signs. Nothing better.

The reality is always different.

My partner has gloves on, a mask on. He looks prepped for surgery.

He did this for our last epileptic too. Apparently it's common to have seizures with ebola, so apparently any time we get one of these calls, he's going to PPE like a neurosurgeon. You can't explain to him that the ebola patient count in central Florida has the undeniably low number of zero.

We knock on the door. No lights on. No sound inside. I used to deliver pizzas. People would wait for me outside for a pizza. But an ambulance is coming and half the time they don't even think to put a light on.

We stare at door. If I had to diagnose the door, it has ichthyosis vulgaris, its paint looking like dead skin cells, thick dry scales. Door eczema. I knock again and dandruff falls to the floor like a tiny blue snowstorm.

"Morons," my partner says. His name's Luke. He says it's short for leukocytes, short for leukopenia, leukotriene. He hates if you call him "Luke-emia." He looks like the healthiest human on the planet. He's an arachnophobic Haitian triathlete who hates when we go to houses that aren't clean, which is the majority of the houses we go to.

The door opens, but not how you'd think. Someone from the inside picks the door up and moves it to the side, the entire door not actually connected to the hinges. For a second,

I thought I was in *Inception,* something so Christopher Nolan about it.

The patient stands in front of us—overweight, over-tan, over-medicated. There's a certain lethargy that comes with polypharmacy, the common occurrence of patients taking so many prescription drugs that they seem to be operating in slo-mo.

Humans, I've learned from being an EMT, have the ability to mutilate, explode, burn, amputate, and overdose themselves in ways you can't imagine.

She's also lacking in the hygiene department. I'm sure that—without exaggeration—the woman hasn't showered in a month or two. Her hair is cobwebbed. I can't help but talk to her hair. "What seems to be the problem, ma'am?"

Her voice is so smoke-damaged that when she says, "Other room," it sounds like her letter o's have carbon monoxide poisoning.

We follow her down a hall with more than fifty things to trip on. One of the common calls for the elderly is for falls. She has landmine after landmine to avoid—part of a stove, magazines with actual titles of *Crappie World* and *Bassin',* yarn, coupons for yarn, indescribable things made of yarn, a mattress, a hubcap, a globe painted completely black, a hopefully empty gas can.

We get to a back room and no one's there. She points. At emptiness. That is, an emptiness if you ignore the boxes and pharmacological bottles and upside-down table and stack of chairs. An emptiness of patients. I've never treated an invisible patient before. I've had invisible people in the room before, seen by our letter *P* patients, meaning the ones on peyote, PCP, psilocybin.

The woman points to the floor. The worry is that there is a husband buried under the piles.

Luke says, "La sécurité des lieux."

The beautiful thing about having a Haitian partner is we can talk French in front of patients. We have to be careful because they might speak French or they might be able to figure out the French or they might not like that we're speaking French, but the more we do this, the more we don't care. If we ever get a formal complaint, we've vowed to explain that we were just using medical terminology and the patient thought it was French.

"La sécurité" is Luke's reminder that my number one priority is keeping myself alive, the number two priority is keeping Luke alive, and then third comes the patient.

The woman says, "He's drowning."

"Who's drowning?"

She points, motioning to the floor. "At least that's what it looks like to me."

Anyone there would be drowning in boxes.

I lean over to see better. And then I see a poodle in full-blown grand mal quivering on a pile of T-shirts. Its teeth are showing, eyes all white, reaching towards me for help.

My EMT training kicks in full force. Luke, on the other hand, sees it's a dog and says, "We're not vets."

I'm making sure the dog doesn't hurt itself, clearing away anything that could fall on it, while Luke says, "Animals don't have the same bodily systems as humans, so we really don't have a clue what to do when it comes to animals."

I tell the woman to put on the air conditioning. I spot a fan in the pile, so I shove pillows and blankets and towels and a TV to the side until I find an electrical outlet and plug it in.

While I flick switches trying to get the fan to work, Luke says, "We had someone who called us once because of a skunk she saw as road-kill and wanted us to do some kind of miracle to bring it back to life."

"You *should* bring it back to life," says the woman, as I push the fan out of the way and find the main light switch, turning it off.

I talk calmly to the dog, stroking the entirety of its body from top of the head to back paw, telling it that it has to be the ugliest cutest thing I've ever seen and that it's going to be all right.

Luke looks down at me, angry. I ask the woman how long the seizure has been going on. She doesn't respond so I say, "Do you have a guess?"

"Since Anthony Bourdain ended."

"Which is?"

"I was about to tell you." She looks at the light switch. "Why's off?"

"Why is it off? For the dog."

In the shadows, for some reason it feels like I'm on the moon. A vulgar amount of manganese-like tin foil around the old TV's antennas. A volcanic pile of boxes. The feel like I'm nestled into a crater.

"How long exactly?" I say.

"How long?"

"Yes."

She thinks and says, "Why?"

"Because if it's only a few minutes, that's not a major issue, but if it's been an hour, well, that's life-threatening."

"Tonic-clonic," says Luke.

"An hour," says the woman.

"It's been an hour?"

"More. Off and on." She turns on the light. "I can't take that. Not with me alone with two men. It's ridiculous."

I try to decide what I should do. I'm trained to ask the patient questions and find myself wanting to ask the dog if it can describe its pain, if it's on any medications, if the owner has a tendency of yanking its chain aggressively.

She says, "It can't die, can it?"

I tell Luke to put on the air conditioning and the woman tells me there is none.

"It needs to go to the vet."

"What vet?"

"Any. It needs to go now."

"I'm not a millionaire," she says and holds out her hands as if to imply that I should look at the house, the room, her clothes, everything to take in the fact that this is a true statement.

"The dog's going to get brain damage if it's left to seize like this."

"Then take it," she says.

"We can't," Luke says.

"It's overheating. The temperature, I'll guarantee, is over 104," I say. I look to Luke, "Brain tissue doesn't regenerate. Once it's gone, it's gone."

"Sortons d'ici," he says.

"Non."

"Putain, c'est bordélique."

"J'essaie de bosser putain."

"Je m'en fous."

"Va chier."

"Va te faire foutre."

Luke leaves. We basically have exchanged a series of vulgarities in front of the patient, all in French.

The woman looks at me like she's hungry. "Done?"

"I can take the dog?"

"Have it."

"Can you write that on a piece of paper?"

"Take the dog."

"I need it on a piece of paper. You're the owner, correct?"

She leaves the room.

I pick up the dog. It's still seizing. It's pressing into me, cuddling into me like it knows it's going to die.

"I'm here," I say, "I'm Superman."

I put my face into the fur of his face. You should never do that, not with an unfamiliar animal. I don't care.

I step through the minefield of clothes and kitchen appliances and antiques.

Outside, I see Luke in the ambulance. I motion a knob turning. He rolls down his window. I whisper-yell, "Air conditioning, crank it!" He rolls up his window.

I hear things falling behind me.

The woman holds out a page ripped from a *People* magazine with Hillary Clinton on the cover. Across Hillary's face are written the words, *You can have my dog,* followed by the woman's full name and signature.

"Can you date it?"

She goes to a wall, scribbles the date.

In the back of the ambulance, I put the dog on the gurney.

The air conditioning is on, weakly.

I make sure the dog isn't going to move, go up front, and say, "If you don't blast that air conditioning, things are going to get very ugly."

I pick up my stethoscope and hear the air conditioning come on, along with AC/DC on the radio, not quite loud enough for me to complain.

On the drive, I do a full rapid assessment, head to paw. I chart everything. We have hundreds of patient care report sheets. One can be used for a little dog. I get breath sounds, breathing rate, heart rate, pupil condition, ears, nose, throat, abdomen, doing just about everything I'd do on a human patient, except blood pressure. But mostly I just pet the thing, soft, whispering that it'll live, that it'll be fine.

I feel my partner watching me in the rearview.

The seizure has stopped for awhile now. The dog, tired.

I stop petting and immediately he reaches for me with his paw, so I keep petting it all the way to base station.

Once we park, the back doors open and a paramedic and the watch supervisor are standing there.

The paramedic tries to take the dog, but I hold him closer.

"Give her the dog," says Smith, the watch supe, her hair spiky and short, her jawline like two precise scalpels.

I give her the dog.

"You're out of commission," says Smith.

"*I* am?"

"The ambulance is."

"Why?"

"Do you know the types of diseases dogs carry?"

I pick at my fingernail.

She grabs my hand, makes me stop.

"This whole thing needs to be bleached."

I start walking back to the staff break room.

"Now. It needs to be bleached now."

I keep walking.

"That's an order."

"I'll do it," I say over my shoulder and go inside.

I see the medic on the couch with the dog in full seizure again.

I go to the break room, get a bowl and fill it with water, come back and put it by the dog's head. The dog doesn't drink.

"Can we IV it?"

"No," says the medic.

"Can I?"

"You don't know how."

"Teach me."

"You want to IV the dog?"

"I saw vomit at the house. It has to be dehydrated."

The supe walks in. "Do you understand what I mean when I say an order?"

"Please," I say, "just ten minutes."

"We have people to serve. Clients."

"Ten minutes," I say.

"No."

I pet the dog. "What if I quit?"

"Then you have to leave the premises."

"With the dog."

"No, not with the dog."

The medic says, "Do we have any calls right now?"

"No."

"Then can we give him ten minutes?"

"No."

"Five."

A lighthouse painting is on the wall. We're in the direct center of Florida, no lighthouses for miles.

"Five minutes," says the supe.

She leaves.

The medic tells me to get the IV tubing, the catheter, gloves, the non-latex tourniquet, alcohol wipes, gauze, sterile pad, the IV fluid. I run, get everything, come back, and she talks me through it.

"Introduce yourself to the patient," she says.

I look for a spot on the dog for the IV.

"Don't touch the patient until you've introduced yourself," she says.

I speak to the dog, "Excuse me, you cute little thing. I'm EMT Renaud with MedLine. I'm going to insert an IV into you, OK?"

The medic says, "The dog gives its OK. Now what we want is a calm patient. When a patient is nervous, the veins may constrict. That's what?"

"Vasoconstriction."

"Which makes it harder to start the IV. So—"

I start petting the dog again, whispering to it.

"Good. Now, next thing is ask the patient if they've had any trouble with IVs in the past."

"OK, I did," I say.

"OK, we'll move along to get this little honey some fluid in him."

The medic helps me prep the tubing.

"Thing is now we have to be careful with making sure we remove any bubbles in the tubing. Or what can happen?"

"Embolism."

"And that can do what?"

"Bad things."

I go through all the steps: puncturing the IV bag, and finding a catheter that works, sterilizing.

"Find a vein," she tells me.

I try, but can't.

"Do the cephalic," she says.

"Where?"

"You don't know the cephalic?"

"The dog's all fur. There aren't any veins."

She tells me to pet the dog, tells me to watch. She explains that we would shave the dog's leg at this point, but she's going to put the IV in without doing so. She's good, smooth, calm, professional, amazing.

The dog is all of those things as well.

I ask the medic if she was ever a veterinarian before. She just shakes her head no.

In the window to the break room, I see five paramedics and EMTS looking through the glass.

"We're well over five minutes," says the medic.

"Two more," I say.

"You better get out there before she bleaches you."

"Can I just have two minutes with the dog?"

She gets up, pats me on the back, and walks out.

I give the little dog a kiss on the head.

I've had one seizure in my life. A freak one. At my parents in Leesburg. Christmastime. I remember hitting the coffee table. The soreness afterwards that seemed to last for months. My back completely thrown out. The ceiling. The sensation that I smelled like saliva. The fear.

I look down at the dog and realize that life goes into seizures at times, that sudden surge of electrical activity that can happen with existence, chemical changes with time itself.

They say that if you have a second seizure in your life, you're eighty percent likely to have more. I look at the dog and hope that this is his first and only, that both of us will escape statistics. I pet it and realize it's going to be in my life now. Permanently. The raging beauty of that.

Robert Sachs

A Death

I stop for gas outside Indianapolis at one of those complexes one sees on the Interstate that not only pump gas, but sell you toys, camping equipment, radios, cell phones, soft drinks, packaged foods, perfume, and razor blades. There are showers for the truck drivers. This one has a Pizza Hut and a fried chicken drive-thru attached. I wander the aisles just to stretch my legs and immediately start thinking about getting a gift for Linda.

Once, when we were dating, I gave her a stuffed panda for her birthday. "Something to sleep with when we're not together," I had said. She had given me a disdainful look.

"What?" I asked.

"Nothing," Linda said. "It's cute. I'll put it on my desk." It was clear she was upset at my comment and the next time I was in her apartment, the panda was neither on her desk nor anywhere in sight. "So she didn't like me taking our fucking for granted?" I asked myself. No good deed.

That reminded me of the little girl who walked by me on State Street in Chicago years back carrying a thin wooden stick with a light green balloon attached to its tip. She was holding her father's hand. I smiled at the girl and playfully flicked the balloon with my finger, hoping the wiggle would please her. But the balloon popped. The girl was stunned for a moment and then started crying. The girl's father, with his free hand, pushed me against the wall of a bank building, holding his forearm against my chest. "What kind of an asshole are you?" he said. His face was flushed, his neck taut. The girl was shrieking.

"I didn't mean to break it," I said. "It was an accident." I looked down at the distraught girl. "Please forgive me. Please."

The father took his arm from my chest and punched me hard in the stomach. I hunched over in pain. "Sorry," the man said. "Accident." He grabbed his daughter in his arms and walked away. The few people who witnessed the incident looked at me as if I had molested the girl.

"It was an accident," I said, holding my stomach. I could hear the little girl's cries almost a block away.

I sometimes wonder now what kind of adult she grew to be and whether the incident—it must have been forty years ago—affected her view of men. I've tried to convince myself it faded from her memory and had no lasting effect on her life. And lately, I've begun questioning whether it happened exactly the way I remember it. It's possible I simply walked by the child, thought about flicking the balloon, but didn't. Like my relationship with Linda, it was so long ago, it's hard to know for sure. But there is a clot of regret inside me that has yet to fully dissolve.

•••

I'm standing at the rear of the funeral parlor, waiting to see if I'll recognize anyone or if anyone will recognize me. It's been almost forty years since I've lived in Chicago. After a few minutes, I see the back of Linda's head and shoulders. Her hair is no longer auburn, but I know it's her. She's seated in the front row, next to her two children. It doesn't look as if she's crying and I decide it's a good time to pay my respects. Happily, the casket is closed. Linda stands and embraces me.

"Thanks for coming, Michael." she whispers. "Here, sit next to me. Mason, Ellen, you remember Mr. Tupper." They nod, but how would they remember me? Ellen was only a couple of years old and Mason was in utero the only other time I saw them. I shake their hands as Linda motions for them to move down a seat.

I feel I shouldn't be sitting with the family; I'm an outsider. It's a fraud. But what can I say? Herb and I were no longer friends? I came here more to see you than to pay my respects? None of this would be appropriate. So I sit, assuming the role of a mourner. Linda takes my hand.

"It's been difficult," she whispers.

"Of course," I say, not really knowing if she's talking about Herb's death, the divorce that preceded it by a year, or—and here's where I worry I'm going crazy—being without me.

Herb's suicide was a shock. I hadn't heard from him in several years. He had seemed fine then. He had retired from the IRS and was adjusting. I know this is what you tell strangers or friends you don't often see: Things are fine; everything's great. But I believed him.

Our relationship had long since drifted into coolness. We had become old-time acquaintances rather than friends. Ask me, before the funeral, the names of Herb's children and I couldn't tell you. I was the one who had moved away, but neither of us bothered to pick up the phone and call the other. Email helped some, but it's not real communication, especially not with someone you've known since kindergarten. However, we both seemed okay with it. Herb would forward jokes or his right wing revelations about the president's birthplace, with notes saying it had been checked out at Snopes. I would send him jokes about old people and sex, things that had been forwarded from a libidinous friend on the West Coast. I also sent links to stories written about our old neighborhood.

Even though I thought the relationship with Herb had devolved from friendship to something less, on those occasions when we did get together it took only a few minutes until the old familiarity bubbled to the surface and we fell into relating to each other as if we were still in high school. Kidding each other. Remember when we did this or that?

I noticed, however, that I remembered little of the things that now, in Herb's mind, seemed to define our relationship, things that more often than not embarrassed me. Herb told people about the time I threw up in science lab, for example, or the time—as Herb recalled it—I lost the touch football game by dropping a last-minute touchdown pass. Whether these things happened as he suggested was disputable and also not the point. It's just that Herb assigned an importance to them I didn't share.

After some years, I heard from a mutual friend that Linda had left Herb. Maybe that had something to do with his suicide. I wanted to know. I was hoping it was because he found out he was going to die of some painful, incurable disease and not because Linda walked out on him. It was something we shared, Herb and I: having been discarded by Linda. I had been young and resilient. Unfortunately, Herb was old, ailing, addled, and defenseless.

•••

Now the place is filling up. A line forms to pay respects to the family and I am obliged to stand there as a mourner. People I don't know are shaking my hand, telling me how sorry they are. I adopt a mournful look and nod. Who must these people think I am? Herb's brother? Linda's brother? Her new boyfriend? Ha! I recognize a few from high school.

If they're surprised to see me sitting between Linda and her children, they say nothing. I need to talk with Linda, find out why she wants me sitting next to her, why Herb killed himself. A lot of whys. Talking now is impossible and all the crying, the Kleenex, is having an effect on me. Tears well up in my eyes. I feel like a method actor. I don't actually mourn Herb's death, but I'm doing a good job convincing myself that I do. This is not a personal trait I admire.

The line of well-wishers traces down the aisle, up to the back of the parlor, and out into a large lobby. It seems to me as if they could be there all day. The children, both in their thirties, seem to take no notice of me. The four of us are busy shaking hands, hugging Herb's friends, his old co-workers, his relatives. I keep eyeing people as they shuffle past the children and on to me. Which one will ask me what the hell I think I'm doing standing next to the aggrieved ex-wife?

But it doesn't happen. Linda insists I accompany her in the long black limo to the cemetery and then on to Herb's house, her house, the same house I had visited those many years ago, where now the meal of consolation will be served.

•••

Linda was someone I had fallen in love with and dated soon after college. She was my first serious affair. One evening we were having a quiet dinner at my favorite Indian restaurant and she said, "Michael, something's happened. I'm involved with someone."

"Involved?" I said.

"It just happened. An account executive at work. I know this is terrible to say, but I've got to give the relationship a chance to work."

I leaned back. "There's a relationship?"

"Michael, please. It just happened."

"You said that. And I'm trying to figure out how this relationship 'just happened' while you've been fucking me."

"Shhh," she said, "Keep your voice down."

"I'll do better than that," I whispered. And I got up and walked out. I didn't make a fuss. I didn't see myself as the type to plead with a woman to take me back. Still, I sometimes wondered what would have happened if I had.

Herb was helpful then, not allowing me to brood. He fixed me up with young women who were captivated by my pain. God knows how Herb built that up to them. But in the end, I measured them all against Linda, with the foreseeable conclusion. Surely I wasn't the only one who thought there was something special about a first love.

A year after our breakup I moved to Louisville, and a short time later I heard that Linda and Herb were engaged. Apparently, the account executive didn't work out. The news came via a mutual friend and I supposed then that Herb felt too guilty to call me himself. In my mind, there was nothing to be guilty about: Linda and I were history, but maybe Herb thought I would think something had been going on between them while we were dating. Which got me thinking that maybe there was. I don't remember obsessing about it, but I knew at some level I deeply resented Linda marrying Herb. Maybe anybody, but definitely Herb. I didn't drive up for the wedding, sending a substantial gift instead.

•••

The summer before the start of college, Herb and I had purchased an old clunker and drove west. We argued most of the way about this and that, nothing consequential, but if there was a theme to that trip, it was our arguing. We made it just past Billings, where the car stopped running. The mechanic shook his head the way they must teach them at mechanics school and pronounced it dead. We stayed at a cheesy motel for three days while trying to figure out a way to get back home. The rental car company turned us down and we ended up taking a train and a bus. It was at the motel that Herb really started getting on my nerves, and I supposed I was getting on Herb's as well. "I shouldn't have let you talk me into buying that piece of junk," Herb said. The whine in his voice reminded me of the sound the engine had been making the last hundred miles before it sputtered and died. As I remembered it, Herb had a need to assign blame for just about everything and an annoying way of sidestepping blame for anything. On the bus from Billings to Rapid City, we didn't speak. Things warmed up a bit on the train to Chicago after we met two young women and there was a need to appear affable.

Years later, on one of my visits to Chicago—we must have been in our late thirties by then and I was engaged to Betty—I called Herb. Linda answered. Herb was out of town on an audit but why didn't I come by for dinner? She sounded cheerful and I accepted. I was anxious to see how she looked after all those years, and brief fantasies blossomed in my brain about being alone with my old girlfriend. I suppose every guy thinks about the one that got away, the old flame. If she came on to me, how should I respond? What if she said she married the wrong man? I wanted to think that through. How I would react. Is it likely we could carry on an affair without Herb finding out? Upsides, downsides. I drove over there having decided nothing.

She met me at the door, very pregnant, with a two year-old hanging onto her skirt. She looked worn out, face flushed, hair undone, no makeup. Which is to say she looked fabulous. She kissed me quickly on the cheek. "Come in. This is little Ellen. Ellen, say hello to Mr. Tupper. Glad you could make it. Herbert will be so sorry he missed you. He talks about you all the time."

I wondered when she started calling him Herbert.

It was a nice evening, just not the one I had invented. Linda was friendly, but made no romantic overtures. It was as if she was showing me, maybe once and for all, there was nothing between us; that I needn't bother trying to rekindle this sodden match.

She surprised me by saying Herb talked about our trip west as the highlight of his bachelor years. One rollicking adventure after the other. "Why didn't you ever tell me about that?" she asked.

How could it be that Herb's memory of our trip was so completely different from mine? Was Herb being honest with Linda? With himself? Or was I the one with the faulty memory? Did I unconsciously change the facts after finding out Herb and Linda were engaged? The thought, now, makes me uncomfortable. If I'm able to do that, who knew how much else I was misremembering? I guess we each build up our own myths, which harden, like the tempering of steel, in the repeating. A slight exaggeration becomes an unassailable truth.

• • •

At the house, someone, Linda probably, had laid out old photographs of Herb. There is even one of the two of us from about the seventh grade. We were both crossing guards, with our white belts and AAA badges. I saw this as my certificate of authenticity. I would bring people to it. "That's Herb," I'd say, pointing. "And that's me. We started kindergarten together." It turns out nobody there knew Herb longer than I did and I imagine people saying, "Oh that's why he was sitting with the family."

After the crowd goes, I am sitting with Linda on the couch. "So how did he do it? And do you have any idea why?"

Linda starts crying again. The "how" is death by bicycle. "About a month before his death, he took up riding a bicycle," she says. "He'd go off on his own for an hour or two almost every day. He'd call me in the morning. 'I'm on the bike,' he'd say, and I encouraged him. It was getting him out of his house. Now I know he was preparing to kill himself. He got on Skokie Boulevard that morning, waited for the right time, and swerved into an oncoming truck."

"You're sure it was suicide?"

"He left a note." She goes to a table next to the front door and takes a sheet of paper out of a thin drawer.

Goodbye, Linda. My life is over. I might as well make it official.

"It's typed," I say.

"Vintage Herbert. The 'why' is complicated," she says. "Am I black widow, Michael? I don't think I could live with myself if I thought I drove him to it. After he retired, he lost all interest in life. He'd sit in front of the TV, a vegetable. I'd try to get him to do things. We'd argue. I was going crazy. He refused to get help. Eventually I left him. Had to, to keep my sanity. The kids were great: Always calling him, stopping by to see him. But he didn't respond to them any more than he did to me." She puts her hand on my knee. "Have you ever forgiven me for leaving you?"

"You dumped me for some guy you worked with," I say.

"Oh, Michael. I don't remember anyone from work. Are you sure?"

"For a long time I didn't forgive you."

"But now. I mean now after all these years."

"Of course," I say. "It's in the dim past."

"And you had Betty for all those years," Linda says.

"Widow and widower. We have that in common."

"Are you seeing anyone?"

Is this just talk? This is a woman who moaned during our lovemaking, told me she loved me. I try picturing her body, her breasts. So long ago. And here I sit, holding her hand after her ex-husband's funeral, thinking about touching her, kissing her. Sick, I know, but there it is.

"I've had some relationships. But now I'm comfortable living on my own. I see a few women. If I was younger, you might call it dating."

"I think we met too young. I know I was immature. I thought you were getting serious and, to be honest, it scared me. I didn't think I was ready to settle down."

"You hooked up with Herbie pretty damn fast," I say.

"Herbert was like a father figure. Solid. Dependable. You know."

"Were you seeing him before you broke up with me?" I hadn't intended to ask the question, at least not so baldly and it takes me by surprise as much as it does Linda.

"Michael. Of course not." Her face flushed. "He was our friend. Yours and mine. Did he secretly love me back then? He's intimated as much over the years. But…"

I touch her shoulder. "I'm sorry. That just slipped out. None of my business really."

"I just don't want you to think I could have done that to you. I couldn't have."

I want to believe her. I do believe her. "I should head out," I say. "It's a six-hour drive."

Ellen and Mason come in about then and sit next to us. Linda squeezes my hand and lets it go. I tell them I'm driving back to Louisville. "Shame you can't stay longer," Linda says, again taking my hand.

Politeness or something more? I realize I'm hoping she'll implore me to stay on for a few days, a week. But I'm not about to invite myself to stay. If she wants… whatever, she's going to have to make the first move. Getting back with Linda in what's euphemistically called our waning years makes a lot of sense to me. I realize it was the reason I drove up for the funeral. I never really got over her, and now that both Betty and Herb are gone I think we can be happy together. But I'm not going to make a fool of myself by pleading this case. I always thought sooner or later she'd realize we belong together. Sooner is long gone and now it's later and I think by showing up at the funeral I'm giving luck the best chance of success.

"I'll be in touch," I say.

She nods and leaves it at that. She walks me to the door, kisses me on the cheek, and says, "You don't know how important it was to have you here."

I almost say that I've decided to stay on for a few days, but I worry she'll view it as a weird come-on. So I say nothing.

The door closes and I think I hear Linda say something like, "Now that was weird." It could have been something else, and even if I heard correctly, her meaning was ambiguous at best. On the drive home, I comfort myself with the thought that after a suitable period of mourning, she'll call.

Terry Sanville

Scents

Ava stared into the mirror that hung on the wall behind her counter. Flecks of makeup had fallen away from the creases below her eyes. She retrieved her compact from her purse and dusted her face with light beige powder from the pharmacy. Ms. Shoemaker would make her mid-afternoon rounds in less than an hour and all her girls in the fragrance section had better look perfect, and act properly superior to New York City's great unwashed.

A figure appeared in the mirror just as Ava finished her toilette. She turned and adjusted her blazer. A middle-aged woman with ash blonde hair stood at the counter, fingering the spray bottles of expensive cologne. She wore huge glasses that made her eyes look like a Margaret Keane painting, Passionate Pink lipstick, and last year's off-the-rack clothes.

"Can I help you with something?"

"Yes, can you spray me with some of your best perfume?"

"Do you have a particular fragrance in mind?"

"No. I've...I've never been here before. But you're on the first level, right off the Avenue, so I thought...."

Ava nodded, the woman obviously some Manhattan office gnome out for an extended coffee break.

"Well, here's an amber cologne we've just received from Spain."

"It's not too sweet, is it? I hate that sweet stuff they sell in the drugstores."

"No, it's not sweet at all...more like a sandalwood...a bit of spice, but not too strong."

"All right, give me a shot."

Ava sprayed a blotter paper and handed it to the woman, who sniffed loudly.

"I like that, but I don't think it's right for me. It's too...I don't know...too high class."

"I'm sure," Ava murmured.

The woman frowned. "Do you mind if I try some of these others?"

"Go ahead, but be careful not to spray too much. They're expensive and cost a lot of money per ounce."

Ms. Big Eyes glared at her. "If I was some rich bitch, you'd be spraying the entire store with this stuff."

Ava tilted her chin up and stared down her nose. "Not at all, madam. I suggest that all my customers behave in a responsible and considerate—"

"Ah, that's what you're doing, being considerate." Ms. Big Eyes' face had transformed into an angry mask. She began sampling the array of spritz bottles.

Two women slid in next to her, having obviously come from a three-martini lunch somewhere off the Avenue, their voices high and girlish, their heels clacking against the polished marble floor. They moved with authority, asked questions that only boasted of their own knowledge, picked up bottles and sprayed, and gave critiques of particular fragrances using the most literate language.

"So what do you have from Louis Vuitton? Or maybe Mauboussin? One of my girlfriends was wearing a cologne that smelled delightfully floral."

Ava selected a bottle from the glass case. The woman held out her wrist and Ava spritzed it. The woman sniffed and smiled. "Yes, that is very close, but a bit too sweet, wouldn't work with my skin chemistry. Do you have others?"

The mid-thirties socialites continued their discourse, exclaiming about their husbands' long workweeks, their busy social calendars, their children's latest accomplishments, all the while spritzing, sniffing, and critiquing.

Ava awaited their decisions, if in fact there ever would be any decisions. But the women knew their scents, and she expected credit cards to be flashed eventually. Other women crowded in to sample fragrances and share their olfactory experiences. Ms. Shoemaker passed along the aisle and smiled at her girl's engagement with the customers. With all the commotion, Ava didn't notice Ms. Big Eyes' departure but just shrugged it off, figuring the neighborhood pharmacy would have what she wanted.

As the crowd thinned, she saw a navy blue leather bag on the counter, with "Made in Italy" embossed in gold near its clasp.

"Excuse me ladies, does this bag belong to any of you?"

A woman in an embroidered floral jacket answered, "I think it belongs to that woman with the glasses that just left."

"Really?" another of the ladies exclaimed. "That bag is expensive Italian. Where would *she* get the money to—"

"Now Rachael, don't be so catty."

"It could be a knockoff...like the ones they sell at those shops in Chinatown along Canal Street."

"No, it's the real thing. Look at the stitching, and the clasp looks like genuine gold."

"I still don't believe it, not *that* woman."

Ava frowned. She considered herself observant and her failure to notice the exquisite bag made her, in some slight way, regret her treatment of the big-eyed woman.

"I'm sure she will soon return to reclaim it," Ava told the ladies.

She lifted the surprisingly heavy bag and moved to the other end of the counter. The leather handles felt soft to her touch. Resting it on top of the thick glass, she fingered its clasp. *One quick peek inside won't hurt anything. Besides, I can look for an ID.* For a moment, Ava thought about making off with the bag that probably cost a month's salary. *Nah, Ms. Big Eyes is sure to come back for it...plus the other ladies saw me take it. But how can anyone leave behind something this gorgeous?*

From the other end of the counter the high bird-like chatter continued. A haze of perfume and cologne drifted toward Ava, mixing in the air to create a miasma of conflicting smells. She dabbed at her watering eyes with a tissue then tugged at the bag's golden clasp. It resisted. She pulled harder. With a soft click, the purse yawned open. Inside lay a bundle of tubes and wires surrounded by plastic bags filled with nails. A red digital display counted down: 6...5...4...3... Ava screamed. With frozen smiles, the lip-glossed ladies stared at her as the end of all scents arrived.

Timothy Schlee

The Translator

A man came to her, desperate, soaked, and disheveled from the storm that was raging outside. He had a manuscript, a roll of parchment from ancient Egypt, he said, whose signs and symbols were a road map to a long-lost treasure buried with the body of a Pharaoh (one of the Ramses, he believed, though he wasn't sure which—there were so many). He was a handsome man, and in another world they might have been lovers, but of course he had more important things to attend to. She lit a cigarette and got to work. In a week he had found the treasure he was looking for. In a week he was fabulously rich, though he didn't even make it out of Egypt before someone clubbed his head in and stole it. Such was the nature of her work.

•••

She could translate anything, it seemed. The military was always knocking at her door. There were Russian intercepts they needed her to translate. There was Iranian babble, and gibberish from North Korea. They had their best guys on it, but it went too slowly. They needed her, and they would pay handsomely, but she always turned them down. Her favorite stuff was the quotidian, the ordinary, the everyday. She would rather translate blueprints from the Czech architecture firm she freelanced for. They were simple people. They were nice. She tried to shut the door quietly when they came to request her services, but those military men always stand so rigid and close that she always felt she was slamming the door in their faces.

•••

People brought in dogs and asked her what they meant when they barked. She listened carefully and told them truthfully what the dogs had said. Usually it was, "I'm hungry," or, "I have to pee." Something along those lines. Not unlike a human, she thought to herself, though the owners always seemed somewhat disappointed.

•••

"It's really quite simple," she told the crowd at the lecture hall. "If you know one language, you know them all. You just have to move the sounds around a bit."

•••

The first thing she ever translated were some Runic scripts she saw on vacation in Norway when she was eight. Her parents didn't realize what she had written on the back of the receipt for the drinks they had bought at the hotel bar the night before, so they tossed it out without a further thought. That could've been a blow to her ambitions, if she had let it, but she didn't. By thirteen, she had translated the entirety of "The Iliad," set to a flowing prose that far exceeded any version yet produced in English. She published it years later and it was a wild success, praised by the New York literati and bought by a sizable portion of the American middle class who cared whether people thought they were educated or not. There was no language she couldn't tackle. She even translated the ancient Zhuangzi, and everyone agreed that she had nailed it quite exactly.

"What does this say?" her boyfriends would always ask her. She grew to hate that question. Why couldn't they just read it for themselves?

•••

She sometimes got couples who spoke, to all appearances, the same language, yet never seemed to be able to communicate. They would ask her to translate. "He always tells me he's tired," the wife would say when talking about sex. The translator would sigh, then explain that he was no longer attracted to her, that he fantasized vigorously about younger women he interacted with at his office, often masturbating in the shower while picturing their supple breasts. The couples didn't like it when she was honest. They often stormed out, men and women alike, and left her with an hour still to invoice, if they ever bothered to mail her the check.

•••

She met many people in her job. There was the embarrassed head of a Classics department, not sure how to translate the text he had promised to read at that semester's party. There was the lawyer who wanted to decipher, as an anniversary gift, an old letter from his wife's grandmother who had perished in the Nazi camps in Poland. There were the heads of various international NGOs, always looking for a bit of free work to pad their RFPs. And yet, through it all, she was distinctly lonely. She seemed incapable of communicating just how the world was for her. For all that she could translate, that was something that eluded her. She was still unmarried at fifty, and she told herself that this wasn't a problem, but it was. Deep inside, it gnawed.

•••

She was offered posts at all the prestigious colleges, but she never left her modest office in Brooklyn. That was her home, she decided. That would be her home. The door dinged as people entered, and she kept all her records on paper. She wasn't used to email yet. She loathed the Internet and its gaudy, imprecise translations. She wasn't a machine. You couldn't just enter text into a search bar and find what it said in a different language. There was an artistry to it. There was a human element that simply couldn't be replicated. That is why she never left. She valued the human. She valued, perhaps too much, the lives of those around her.

•••

A young child asked her, "Why does my father hit me? Translate this for me. Tell me what he means when he does such a thing."

"He does it because he cares," she said, "in his own way." She paused and then said, "He does it because he doesn't know how else to say that he loves you."

Kyle Summerall

Where We Come From

The crowd settles down around three, leaving stacks of glasses, mugs of cold coffee, and tables scattered with leftovers to clean. The headache is coming back, like an old stray cat that'd been fed out of pity the night before. The rush of truck drivers hadn't left any room in my mind for it, but now that the night's winding down, I'd have that throbbing, and a couple of dollars to take home.

I hadn't had a chance to stop, let alone sit down, so when I slide into a booth to grab a bowl of half-eaten grits, I take the moment to stretch my toes, feeling the tips ache and swell. The women in the back are laughing behind saloon doors, trying to out-gossip one another. They never seemed to care about the change left on the tables, the leavings after a customer broke a dollar, but I didn't mind corralling the coins into my apron. Rarely could you find a whole bill, and when you did, that's when one of the other waitresses would pipe up about how they refilled that guy's coffee or how that man meant it for her. Two dollars was never worth fighting over, so I'd hand it to them and they'd stuff it under a bra strap or in their back pocket. No one had to worry about counting that. The number was printed in every corner and that somehow made it worth more than the change pulling on my waist.

I usually didn't warrant anything solid. Most everyone could tell I didn't want to be here. I never bothered flirting with the men hiding their eyes under baseball caps, fresh off the road and lonely. I'd watch those women come out of the back with pots of coffee that'd been sitting on the plate, burning and reburning, flashing a gap-toothed grin and leaning in, trying their best to seem like more than just a hung and beaten old rug. Some would follow a man back out to his truck, then come back only to mock him as he made his way to another truck stop for his scrambled eggs.

The highway outside the wall of windows is dead for a while, until the sun starts to resurface like a bobber over the trees. Widowers start to pull in and take up the booths, the same ones I see every morning. They take off their coats and hats before greeting all the others and sitting down to talk over the fresh coffee I'd just brewed.

It's easier, despite the exhaustion taking root like a bad hangover. The old men are nice, chatty, and more than willing to take up every second you have, making it easy to find a groove.

A short Indian man with silver braids tucked behind each ear walks in and sits at the bar while I wait for Mr. Strain to get done telling me about this song he wrote back in the forties that some famous singer bought from him. I act like I'm hearing it for the first time, all the while listening to the Indian man tell one of the waitresses that he's waiting for me.

I round the bar. "Did he come home?" I ask.

He had. "Sometime a few days ago, in the middle of the night. I woke up and found him passed out on the couch, still in his work clothes. He's avoiding me, though," Joseph tells me. "And when he is there, he's either asleep or on his way out the door."

"Why now, you think?"

"Money probably. I've had to put everything in a safe, just to make sure," he says. "I don't want that girl getting none of it."

Joseph stops and looks at me. "All your color is gone."

He's looking at my hair, now a colorless, washed-out white. I pull the ends, the bit that still holds any memory of what it used to be, over my shoulder. Some of the split ends are red, blue, and, in places, brown where all the colors have run together. I pick at the edges, not meeting his eyes, making me feel secure enough to ask, "You going to call the sheriff?"

"I have. I called the sheriff months ago. After I watched him walk out the door, and I just let him. I thought I wouldn't see him again. So, I told the police where he was, what I thought he was doing. They said their hands were tied. They could bring them in, but they'd be out in six months, and that's if it was even pursued beyond a warning. If they aren't wandering the streets, out driving at night, or breaking into houses and killing a family for what little their lives are worth, they don't care."

His face ages another ten years. "It's not his fault."

He goes on for a few more minutes, long enough to drink a cup of coffee and leave a twenty under the empty mug while my back is turned. He's not out of the parking lot good before I'm spinning the dialer on the phone. It rings eleven times before it disconnects. It rings eleven times again and again. A few more people come in and I assure them that someone will be with them in a second. He answers the phone about the time they start giving me dirty looks.

"Hello?" he says.

"Hey."

I had seen Clip in those months he'd been gone, but I couldn't have told his daddy that. I'd drive east of town after school on days I didn't have work, knowing good and well where he'd gone. The Silas House was where Michael and Clip used to drink on Friday nights while everyone was at the football game. It was also the place where he'd go after lying and telling me he was going somewhere else. There weren't always people everywhere but after awhile they were all on the place; on the porch, in the grass, and passing by glassless windows. I'd sit with Clip and watch as Michael handed out pills to everyone else so that he could turn around and refill his syringe. Michael wrapped his truck around a tree not long after that. Clip and I started fighting, about the time I started seeing him less, about how it was time to go home. About how there was nothing left at that house but addicts. He told me to take my own advice and go home. The fighting stopped when I stopped seeing him. I hadn't even talked to him until the phone rang a few weeks ago.

I'd called in sick for the second night in a row because I was tired of it. I hadn't considered the fact that I was so used to staying up all night that I wouldn't be able to sleep, so I was awake when the phone rang. I heard Momma cuss from the room next door. Miranda stirred for a moment, then the phone stopped. I think everyone was waiting for Jamie to start crying. When the phone started ringing again, he did. Miranda came unglued. I wasn't sure if she was even fully awake when she bolted out of bed, hollering about how she couldn't get a second of goddamn sleep.

The floor popped as Momma stormed down the hallway and yanked the phone to her ear. *It's Choctaw,* she'd yelled.

I took the phone from her while she reminded me that she had work in the morning, and about how she couldn't just call in when she didn't feel like working as she waddled off back to her room.

Clip sounded far away when he said my name. He told me he was scared. He told me that they'd left him somewhere. The rest I had to pull out of him while he complained about being cold despite the unflinching humidity that had settled in until November.

After he finally tells me where he was, I grab my keys and head out the door. I drive forty-five minutes to a Love's truck stop lit up like Vegas on the side of the highway and find Clip leaned against the ice cooler. His pupils are the size of silver dollars and the color in his cheeks are gone. I help him back to the car. He's light, hollow feeling, as I steady his steps. His eyes stay closed and each passing streetlight catches in the sweat slicking his face.

We pull into the driveway around four a.m, under a black sheet scattered with the shrapnel of stars. He'd never been inside, I'd thought, before dragging him across the worn-out welcome mat. I'd always been too ashamed to let him get this far, because although he'd complained about his house and how bad it all was, his stories couldn't hold a candle to mine. He never did believe when I tried to tell him. He'd just say that we were both gutter flowers waiting on a big gust of wind. That made us more similar than different. I try to concentrate on that, instead of the hoard in the living room and the shallow roots we grew from.

He shakes, his fingertips cold, his eyes closed even after I have him in the bathtub, dabbing at his forehead with a warm cloth. His lips keep bleeding from being so dry and there is a tint of brown ruin starting to trace his gums. His heart beats hard against his chest, like something feral caught in a cage.

I tell him that he's got to stay away from all this, move back home. I tell him that I missed him, and that Helen wasn't worth all this. I tell him that I am going to find whoever left him out there. I tell him I'd go to their house and burn it to the ground if it meant keeping him away. The fire would spread to neighboring farms and they would burn too, acre by acre, corn row by corn row, cotton field by cotton field. Families would be just as ruined as his and mine by the devastation. I lose the anger in my voice somewhere along the way and my throat fills with worry as I talk about the cows burning in the pastures, their tails flicking at the flames like flies until they couldn't take it anymore and dropped, melting in the blaze. They'd see the flames for miles, I said as I push his soaked hair off his forehead and re-wet the cloth. People four counties over would get up for their late-night piss and they'd think daylight had come. Their hearts would jump as they ran to check their clocks to find a few hours left before dawn. There wouldn't be enough water in the world to put it out.

Not knowing how long it was going to take for him to come down, I get him to stand and we take it easy into my room. Miranda is on her back, mouth wide as a bass, and snoring like a boat motor.

I ease him down onto the double-stacked mattresses. I look around at the single closet that Miranda and I share, the sliding door gone. Clothes and papers from school are pushed into its bottom. A fat-back TV sits next to a stereo twice its size on a cheap particle board cabinet that looks about as close to real wood as the paneling striping the walls.

I crawl into bed with him and pull the covers high, hoping that Miranda won't care enough to look over when she gets up. It's the first time we'd been in a bed together, an actual bed. Not a sleeping bag we'd snuck into some abandoned building or laying in the back of his truck on blankets. I lie on my back, looking up at the popcorn ceilings where me and Miranda used to string together pictures in the bumps, points, and divots like trying to find a constellation in the stars. There was the witch's face, a swirl that resembled the sun, and a snowman that had been melting since we moved in. That was before I knew what trash was. Back before all those girls stopped coming to the house that one day a year I wanted them here most. I'd spend days cleaning before birthdays, finding places for things that didn't have a place to go. I'd clean the laminate walls and floors in the bathroom, wipe the dust that clung to the lighthouses my momma kept on shelves, and dust away the buildup off the fan blades. It didn't make a difference though. Momma wouldn't help and Miranda sure as hell wouldn't lift a finger. It was okay to ignore it. That's what made us trash. It wasn't the house or the way people saw us, but the way nobody gave a damn about the rust-colored rings in the tub or the rolled-up pieces of paper stuffed around the base of the ceiling fans that kept them from rocking on summer nights. It was the fact that we'd just pick around the gnats caught in the butter after it was left open overnight, instead of throwing it out.

I stare at the blades spinning slowly, then beyond them to the perfect circle completely void of anything due to the fan's constant motion. Just outside the blades' reach though, the rest of the ceiling is spotted with dust. That'll be the first thing he sees when he wakes up, I think before rolling over. Then he'll see everything else.

•••

He sighs, waiting for me to respond. "What do you want?"

"My car. It won't start and I don't know anyone else who can help me."

"And you call here?"

"I was hoping to get your dad. I know he heads out early," I lie.

He's quiet.

"Just come look, please? Or give me a ride home."

"I'd have to be up in an hour anyway. I'll be there in a few." He hangs up and I rush out of the front door, to the car. I pop the hood and pull the first hose I see until one end pops free before tugging the other end out. I toss it in the trunk, sure I had enough saved up to fix something that seems so minor.

I screw up a few orders while I watch the parking lot.

Clip pulls into the lot and parks next to my car. I don't bother writing in my time when I leave, knowing that I can just pencil it in my next shift.

He's in the shadow of the open hood when I walk up, not even bothering to raise his eyes.

"Want me to just take you home? I don't know anything about this."

"You fixed it last time," I say.

"I replaced the bulbs in your headlights," he says.

"Yeah, but I couldn't have done that."

He looks at me for the first time and it's nothing like I'm expecting. His face is trim, his cheek bones sharp and high, creating hollers underneath. It's like looking at a painting that had been balled up then attempted to be flattened out again. It's easy to point out all the things that have changed, but what disturbs me are all the things that are still familiar. I look down at my feet. "Can you just look, please?"

The sun isn't even high enough to change from orange to yellow but sweat drips from his nose.

"I'm leaving in a few months," I say.

"Not in this thing. Not unless you take it to someone who actually knows what they're looking at."

"I'll figure something out."

"You ever find a place to stay up there?"

The dorms hadn't worked out. What few scholarships I had managed to scrape together came out to about the cost of a psychology book and a pack of pencils. "No."

"So what? Your mom gonna drive you up there and come get you in the afternoon?"

Ole Miss was five hours away, but it was far enough that it seemed as foreign as places like Hong Kong or London. In my mind, five hours was enough space to create a whole new culture.

"No," I tell him. "I'll get the car fixed and make friends with couches I can sleep on."

"That doesn't sound very conducive to learning," he says.

"Neither does sleeping in my car, but if it comes down to it."

It all tastes so bitter. Talking to him, hearing him say things as if words carried the same weight they held on his tongue. Still not giving a damn. Still acting like this isn't his fault.

"Stubborn," he calls me.

"It's not a flaw."

"It can be." He steps out from under the hood and drops it.

"Not if it gets me the hell away from here."

"Yeah, but why not take a year off? Work, save something, then you can have a place to live?"

He's standing in front of me now, the smell of sweat and bug spray coming along with him, reminding me of afternoons bleeding into nights out by the river with a fire going, the music loud, and everybody laughing. "You changed your mind," I tell him, holding back a sob and the tears that are already too far along to hide.

"I had to."

I bury my face in his chest. "You say that but you can't tell me it's done you any good. They just threw money at you, the brilliant little Indian boy, then your grades were so good, they just kept throwing more and more and I can't get shit and this was our thing."

I know he can't understand a word of what I'm saying and when he pulls back, hair is sticking to my wet face and bubbles form between my lips.

"Go get in the truck. I'll give you a ride home and your sister can help you come get this piece of garbage later."

I get in. There are books everywhere. There are a few titles I recognize, and others that I'd never seen before, but it isn't hard to figure them out, *How to Be a Good Dad, Fatherhood in the First Year,* and *The Big Book of Boy Names.*

I grab the spine of one jammed between the seat and the gear shift.

"I haven't read this one," I say.

"Me, either," he replies. "Not a lot of time to sit and focus."

"I haven't been reading much either. Finals are coming up. It's not too late to come back, you know? Your dad could talk to someone. People like him. And with your grades…"

"Stop."

When he pulls up to my house, he doesn't even pull into the driveway, just stops by the mailbox and doesn't say a word. I don't either when I get out.

•••

Clip had stood out like the first fall leaf, the son of a Chickasaw and a green-eyed woman who would be damned if she was going to stifle that free spirit for a life on the reservation. She'd been barefoot and pregnant when she'd told Joseph about how *important it all was.*

She might as well have not even come home from the hospital, but she had to, so she could pack her things. A quiet man fell silent as his baby cried in the other room. He'd sleep on the couch or in his chair as he spent his hours of daylight working and his nights with eyes glued on the TV, looking for her among the halos of flowers, long-haired men, and acts of protest against the war as Clip grew up, just out of frame.

Ninth grade was when the kids from the reservation were bused into the county to start attending Carpenter High. Any empty seats on the bus or in the classrooms were filled up by boys and girls who didn't seem to even speak the same language as the rest of us. That first year, most sat quiet, eyes down at their desk while the other boys whooped, hollered, and danced like they'd seen the Indians do in *Peter Pan.* I laughed along with them. We talked about all the things our older sibling had done when they were our age, the pranks on the red kids that we always tried to outdo.

We'd found a dead black bird one day outside the building and I watched a kid shove it in Clip's bag. We watched as he unzipped the bag after lunch, all giggling, trying to stifle a rawr of laughter but he showed no effect. He pulled out his biology book and closed the bag. A note got passed around the room later on, until it found Clip's desk. On the inside it read, *Thought you could use the feathers.* I remember not laughing that time.

I sat down next to him months later, after the girls I rode the bus with stopped inviting me to their houses when we were old enough to start distinguishing who was poor and trash from the rest of the girls. They talked about what they remembered, how messy my house was when they'd stayed over when we were kids.

There was a sack lunch, still full, sitting in front of him while he read a worn-out copy of *Winesburg, Ohio* by Sherwood Anderson. We didn't talk, and it went on like that for a week or so; each day the only thing changing were our clothes and his book. I'd thought about what to say. I thought about asking him about his book, about why he never ate his lunch, but one day it just came out. "So," I said loud enough to draw his eyes. "What's your spirit animal?"

•••

I wake up with the same headache I fell asleep with.

The afternoon light plasters the walls, ignoring the bedsheet thumbtacked over the window. I close my eyes, holding them tight, trying not to let any of it in when I hear Miranda's Pinto rattle into the yard, the undercarriage threatening to drop out like the insides of a gutted horse. Her car door slams, then the front door, then the clinking of the curtain on a shower rod we use as a bedroom door. The throbbing moves from the back of my head to the front when I sit up. Miranda is sitting on her bed, pillows propped up in the corner, her knees to her chin, her eyes on me, wide with desperation for some kind of relief.

"Where's Jamie?" I mutter, my hand navigating my nightstand's cluster of open Coke cans and scattered plastic jewelry for a ponytail holder.

She keeps looking at me, shrinking somehow. "I can't find the stereo remote."

I look around at the mess and am not surprised. Rolling off the mattresses, I kick one of her bags to her side of the room. "Did you look?"

"Yeah."

Liar.

"Couldn't tell you where nothing is in this mess," I tell her.

There is a hamper sitting at the foot of the mattresses, full as indulgent tick, then there is another pile in front of the closet. Some things are a day dirty, others worn a few days too long. I take the hamper and dump it out onto the bed, taking a shirt from the top and a pair of jeans from the middle before pushing it all back in. The window rattles when her car back-fires. "Why is your car still running?"

She has a makeup mirror in her palm and a mascara tube in the other. "I left Jamie in there. He's been crying since I picked him up and I can't stand it. It never stops."

"Go get him."

"I am when I think he's calmed down." She looks at me when she realizes the tube is empty. "This was mine."

"Because you need makeup on to sleep?"

She tosses the tube at me and springs up, passing me and slamming the front door on her way out. My guitar, propped up in the corner, slides free, the neck skidding across the wall before hollowly hitting the floor. That's probably the closest thing to being played it's been in years. I remember begging Momma for it at Walmart. She'd said we didn't have the money then bought it anyway, just so she could complain about it later. I'd promised I'd learn to play, unaware of how hard it would be. I gave up after a day, but like the stuffed animals and clothes that don't fit anymore, I kept it.

The window rattles again and my head pulses with the thrum of her pounding music. I throw on what I have in hand and walk out the door. I ask her for a ride back to the diner.

•••

Graduation had come with the dogwood blooms and the honeysuckle. Clip hadn't bothered to come, and I had to sit through the whole ceremony with Michael smiling at me. There was a memorial set up to the left of the stage dedicated to those who were in too much of a rush to get somewhere else. Eight of the nine photos were kids killed in wrecks, six of them driving drunk, two hit by drunk drivers, and one who'd shot herself over Christmas break. But Michael had been the school's biggest loss. That's why he was front and center. That's why his parents, a sheriff and a housewife who raised a son who could do no wrong, got an honorary diploma that would have been his. I hated him while everyone else mourned, but none quite as hard as Clip. Michael sold Xanax, Vicodin, and Demerol to kids who'd gotten bored with just sitting around and drinking, and at his wake I watched a ninth grader named Helen, with a too-full belly and Oxycodone eyes, cry into Clip's shoulder. It wasn't too long after that, Clip told me that he'd changed his mind about college. That he never even filled out any of the applications, and that he didn't see the point.

"It's just another place where they can tell us what to do. At least here, we're free," he'd said after he'd told me that Helen needed him now that Michael was gone. That he could help her kick that shit and maybe the baby would have some kind of chance. That he felt responsible now and how doing that meant something.

"Free to have nothing, you mean?"

"We should all be used to it by now," he said.

"That's not how you get out of this place, Clip. That's how you get stuck, and if having nothing and being free means that you wrap your truck around a tree because you're too fucked up, then I don't want it."

"You'll come back," he told me. "You just haven't realized it yet. You still got family here."

"We can both leave. I can change what I'm going for. I can be a nurse or something. I can support us both. We just have to stop and think. Plan something."

We didn't talk again until after he'd left his dad's house.

Leaving, I pass kids posing for pictures with their families. Mine didn't come. No one to watch Jamie was what Momma had told me. I told her she didn't have to come. It's just easier to stay at home and let Miranda sleep while someone else tries to ignore the constant squalling. I have work afterwards, anyway. At the car, I take the cap and gown off, exposing the diner uniform underneath.

•••

I drive the five hours there and back once a week, my schedule worked out to where I don't have classes on Fridays. I work doubles at the diner to make up what I'd normally make in a week in the three days that I'm home.

I pull out books thicker than the bible Momma kept on her nightstand when I find those rare moments to try and study, and toss them on the bed. Miranda looks at them with fear while she nurses. It's never quiet, not with Jamie crying all night and my sister screaming at anything that will listen, just to get some of the frustration out. Every time I go to pick up a book to read a chapter or take notes, I skim a few lines before having to fold it closed again.

My grades suck and my nights are spent laid out in my cramped backseat, the muscle relaxers easing me into a dead sleep. I used to not be able to sleep, but the pills help. I miss a lot of classes because I just can't get myself moving, but no one seems to care. No one asks me why my grades are the way they are. No one asks me about why I look the way I do. And home is no better.

I can hear Jamie squalling before I even open the front door. He's sitting in his high chair while Momma and Miranda work on dinner, green snot smeared all over his face and hands. I can't remember a day when he wasn't sick.

No one bothers to look up when I go by, not until I take a seat at the table. Miranda turns, "Are you just gonna let him sit like that? Go get something and blow his nose."

I stand, "Sorry for wanting to sit down." I pull a few paper towels off the roll.

"You've been driving. I have been on my feet all day, get home, then cook, and I don't get to sit down for shit," Miranda says.

"You also can't wipe your damn baby's nose for shit either."

She looks at Momma, who's stirring what smells like beef stew. She doesn't even look up, just says "We all have to pull our own weight around here."

It sounds so rehearsed, like a reflex built on the foundation of not giving a damn. I can't help but look at her, her hair a mess of silver and black, her cheeks sagging. She's still in the same sweatpants and shirt she was in when I left. When did she give up, I wonder?

Was I here? Did I see it but just not notice? Or did it happen before me, before Miranda? Maybe somewhere in between? Maybe even before Daddy's accident at the timber mill that set him up in Woodlands Retirement Home for the rest of his life. God, I couldn't even remember the last time we went to see him, but she sure was proud of that check she got each month. The *sorry about your damn luck* check that wasn't even enough to hide the bottom of the barrel from our eyes. *I'd love to have a house where each of you could have your own bedrooms,* she'd told us growing up, but at some point that didn't matter anymore and the mattresses on the floor became good enough.

"Sit down," Momma tells me.

"Why?" Miranda asked. "Make her help."

I was so selfish. I'd been hearing that all my life but now I knew it and was proud of it. They never bothered to ask how school went. No one cared that it was harder than I could have imagined, and no one knew that I didn't have any friends to spend the weeks there with so I sat in my car with no air then came home to this. It made me miss the back seat a little until I was there again for another four days.

I tell her she can have my portion. "Maybe if you put some meat on your bones, they wouldn't have to nearly kill you cutting the next one out!"

I go to our room and pull a duffel bag out from under the pile of shit and fill it with everything that is mine. I have to stop from falling apart when it only fills half the bag. I toss the bag out the window and walk out of the room. Miranda is nowhere to be seen and Momma is standing on the porch, blowing smoke out over the railing. "Going to work?"

"Yeah." She doesn't even care about what happened, so why should I? I walk around the house, pick up my bag, toss it in the passenger seat, and drive until Momma and the house are nothing but a glare in the taillights. I drive into town, stop at an ATM, and empty what I've got. It's not nearly what I thought it was, but I take it and drive back to the husk where I knew Clip was living.

There is a fire as tall as the house burning in the field, while people dance around it. I kill the engine and shoulder my bag.

I don't see him among the people humming out of tune and laughing so I head towards the house.

Tyler, Michael's brother, is standing just inside the doorway, his wide eyes glowing. He takes a step back inside and hollers, "Hey, Clip, there's some college girl here for you. Said she's bringing you the homework you missed."

I step inside.

People lie scattered on the floor, while others sprawl out on ripped-up furniture. The smell is hard to stomach. Chain link is rolled up in bundles and tossed in the corner of the room like carelessly placed firewood and there are handfuls of copper wire rubber banded together all over the place. Needles and tin foil are just as common as pill bottles and bent beer cans. The kitchen is hidden behind sheets of foggy plastic stapled to the ceiling. Tyler sits next to an Indian girl with fluttering eyes and kisses her, never taking his eyes off me.

Clip walks into the room and up to me but I don't meet his eyes. The only thing coming to mind is how ruined he is.

He looks at Tyler. "I hear you walk on water now."

"What?"

"You got out," he says. "But what did I tell you about having to come back?"

I swallow the burning flavor in the air. "I never left. I'm still at Momma's."

Clip steps past me and walks to the open doorway before leaning on its frame. "Are you happy you came?"

"I will be if you come back."

He shakes his head.

"I have enough money saved up, we can get an apartment in Oxford. I can do school and you can work construction or something and I can work at night."

"And it'll be hard at first but if we work at it, it'll all work out.... Yeah," Clips spits.

I should have been more prepared for this, but I'm not. He's not even happy to see me.

Tyler speaks up behind me, "You worried 'bout the wrong one, blonde. He's the one taking care of us. Without him, there ain't people sprawled out all over the place. Hell, I ain't been past the damn mailbox in a week. Just when I think I'm coming out of this fog, he comes out ringing the dinner bell and it ain't like I'm just not gonna eat."

I hear somebody screaming in another room, followed by crying, shrill and sharp.

"The baby is here?"

Clip tells me that Helen had no place to go. "Better here than in the ditch where its grandparents threatened to put it if she'd left it with them."

"But here?"

"You act like there is no one here to take care of it. There is always someone here sober and we get it food and milk before we even think about anything else. It wouldn't have stood a chance where it was."

"And it does here."

Helen walks into the room with the baby on her hip. She's so small. I think about that wide scar carved under Miranda's belly, sure Helen has one too.

They walk past me together, with Tyler and the Indian girl behind them, out into the yard. Every breath I take is heavy.

Why was I so tired?

I walk out and find Clip. "You are going to come with me to Oxford like you promised?"

His eyes slide side to side while everyone stops dancing to the rhythm of the flames to stare.

"I'm not taking no for an answer."

He looks into the fire, reaching into it, lost in it for a few seconds, before saying, "You're better than this place."

It wasn't the first time that I'd thought I wasn't good enough. The idea had been there for a while.

I glance at the car before thinking about Momma, miserable because she married a man who worked too hard, a man she wanted home more, but when she got her wish she turned out to be too busy to blend his food or even sit and talk to him even though he never talked back. I think about Miranda and about how she'd end up marrying some son of a tradesman who Momma or Daddy had gone to high school with, someone else who'd had kids before they could pick the highest ear of corn. Their life would be hard so he'd go to where the money and hard work was. I think about Jamie, growing up thinking that yelling was love.

I think about all the things he'll have to do without. It makes the decision easier.

Pulling off the bag, I undo the zipper and dump all of it onto the grass. I toss my keys on top of the mound that means nothing in comparison to the size of the fire. I drop next to Clip, crossing my legs.

Tyler takes a seat in the grass next to me and folds his legs like mine. He reaches into his pocket. "Well, I sure don't mind sharing."

Eric Twardzik

Plastic

The day before Halloween, Mom took us to Aunt Edie's house so she could see our costumes. Aunt Edie's house was once Uncle Dan's house too, but now Uncle Dan was dead.

That day at school was the Halloween parade. That meant that all the kids got to go to St. John's in our Halloween costumes, and after lunch we walked around the outside of the building in a line so all the parents could see our costumes. Mom had made our costumes, and she was very proud of that.

I was a knight, and had a long white tunic with a red cross on the chest. Mom had cut the tunic out of cloth for me and stitched on the cross. The only parts of the costume Mom didn't make were the plastic sword and the plastic helmet. The helmet had a visor that kept closing on me and stopping me from seeing things.

I thought it would get me the third grade prize for best costume, but the prize went to Jimmy Wisnewski instead, even though he was wearing a Darth Maul costume his mom bought at the mall. I complained to Mom about it. She said something about how teachers didn't give prizes out based on who actually had the best costume. Instead, they gave them to kids who had problems at home. I didn't know what Jimmy's problems were and Mom said I wasn't allowed to ask.

Mom brought my little brother, Paul, to Aunt Edie's too. Paul was in first grade, and he had wanted to be a vampire. Mom made him a costume with a cape and fangs and everything, but when she showed him how he looked in the mirror he got too scared and took his fangs out. That meant my costume was better, because Paul wasn't even a real vampire anymore.

Aunt Edie lived in a house that was much smaller than ours. It was really just one half of a house, what Mom said was a "row home." After Mom knocked on the door we heard Aunt Edie's voice, but it took a long time for her to open it.

She was tall, taller even than Mom. She wore a black sweater and a pair of pants that were really high. Her hair was grey and stiff looking, like the ends of a paintbrush that no one cleaned after art class. Her glasses were big and strange. They made me think of a cat.

Aunt Edie hugged me first. Her smell reminded me of flowers, but also of cleaning the chalkboard erasers at school.

We hadn't been to their house in a long time, not since Uncle Dan died. That happened a year ago, when I was in 2nd grade. Paul and I were downstairs playing with our new Lego castle when Mom came and told us. It was the first time someone in our family had died. I didn't have too many feelings about it.

Mom was on the phone with people that whole night. I remember walking into the kitchen for Oreos and hearing some of what she was saying. She was telling someone that Aunt Edie wanted to die. I'd never heard of someone wanting to die before. The next day in religion class I asked Mrs. Baxter if that was a sin.

I was wondering whether or not Aunt Edie still wanted to be dead when she let me go and went to hug Paul. I was just standing there until Mom told me to go inside.

The living room looked the same as when Uncle Dan was alive. Everything in it was dark, from the carpets to the furniture. I walked over to the big red chair that Uncle Dan used to sit in. It made me remember what it was like to be in his lap. It still smelled like the pipe he smoked, which made me think of cherry candy. I hopped up in the chair and thought about what it'd be like to be grown up and smoking a pipe.

Mom was still at the door talking to Aunt Edie, so I started thinking back to how I'd asked Mrs. Baxter that question and what had happened the day after. I was at recess eating the Fruit Roll-Up mom packed me when Jimmy Wisnewski walked over. Jimmy said he told his mom about my Aunt Edie wanting to be dead. And Jimmy's mom said that meant Aunt Edie was going to hell. I told Jimmy that his mom was stupid like him and he pushed me. I pushed him back and we both got detention for it.

Now Mom and Paul were inside, and they were following Aunt Edie to the kitchen. Mom told me to come along.

The kitchen was nothing like the living room. It was bright and shiny, with white tiles for a floor and big windows that looked out to the backyard. Aunt Edie asked us if we were hungry and Mom said yes before I had a chance to answer. Aunt Edie said she'd make us grilled cheese sandwiches, which I liked. Mom told us to take a seat at the kitchen table and tell Aunt Edie about school while we waited. I was hoping she'd make Paul go first, but she chose me. I had to talk about times tables and Christopher Columbus and Jimmy Wisnewski winning first place for being Darth Maul. While I was talking Aunt Edie took bright, yellow squares of cheese out of her refrigerator. They looked different than the cheese mom used at home.

We had to wait a long time for the sandwiches. Aunt Edie moved slowly, like everything she did hurt. Mom kept asking if she needed help, but Aunt Edie said no. Finally Aunt Edie took the sandwiches out of the press and brought them to us on paper plates.

The first bite was okay. The bread was warm and toasty, and the cheese was melted and gooey how I like. But after my second bite I felt something strange. It was chewy, though not chewy like a grilled cheese should be. I knew it had to be something that wasn't supposed to be there, like the time I found a big lunch lady hair on my Swedish meatballs at school. I knew this wasn't hair. I looked over at Paul, and saw that he had a funny look on his face.

Mom must have seen it too, because she went over to Paul and picked up his sandwich. She peeled apart the bread, and when she did the melted cheese stretched like a commercial for Pizza Hut. Something else was stretching out too, something that wasn't bright yellow but clear like glass.

Plastic, Mom said. She asked Aunt Edie if she'd forgotten to take the cheese slices out of their plastic wrappers.

Mom started laughing, and we all started laughing too. But not Aunt Edie, who kept apologizing and seemed really embarrassed. She didn't stop apologizing until we left the house. She gave us heavy bags of candy (with lots of Reese's Peanut Butter Cups, my favorite) to take home.

That was the last time I saw Aunt Edie. She died just before Christmas. Mom walked into our room and told us as we were getting ready for bed. She asked us to say something for Aunt Edie in our prayers.

It took me a long time to fall asleep that night. All I could think about was Aunt Edie and Uncle Dan's house, and how no one would ever be inside of it again. I kept imagining their living room and their kitchen and dark rooms upstairs with no people. I had to stop because I was making myself scared.

We were too little to go to the funeral when Uncle Dan died. But now Mom said we were both old enough for Aunt Edie's, even Paul. Before the funeral happened there was something called a viewing, and we'd be going to that too.

I put my First Communion suit on, which had gotten too short. I was nervous to see Aunt Edie at the viewing. I'd never seen someone dead before.

The funeral home wasn't spooky. I always thought the inside would be like the Haunted Mansion at Disney. Instead it was a bunch of white rooms and flowers. All the old people were wearing suits. I'd never seen so many people wearing suits before.

We were all standing in line. Mom said we were supposed to kneel in front of the casket like we were at church and say some prayers. Then we could look at Aunt Edie and say goodbye.

Except I couldn't see Aunt Edie. There was just the big black box, and it was getting closer and closer until it was right in front of me. Then mom and dad put their hands on my shoulder and told me it was okay to go.

There was a kneeler in front of the box, just like at church. I kneeled on it and said a Hail Mary with my eyes closed. Then I opened them and looked into the box.

Aunt Edie was wearing a shiny white dress. It made her look like one of the angels in our religion textbook, except old. Her hair was in curls and looked very fancy. I'd never seen her with such fancy hair when she was alive.

Something was really wrong about Aunt Edie, and it wasn't just that she was dead. She didn't look like herself, like a person. Her face was tight and shiny like her dress.

I got the idea that Aunt Edie wasn't really dead. Maybe it was a mix-up, like the sandwiches before Halloween. I stuck my hand into the box. I was scared, but I wanted to touch her cheek to find out if it was really Aunt Edie.

The next thing I remember is being on the ground in the funeral home, surrounded by the faces of old people. Mom, Dad, and Dr. Gorshaw were right next to me, and Dr. Gorshaw was holding something funny-smelling in front of my nose.

On the drive home Mom said that Paul and I wouldn't have to go to the funeral the next day. Dad said something about us not being ready after all, but I think it made Mom mad so he didn't say anymore.

Paul went right back to the Lego pirate setup we'd made before we left. He didn't even get out of his suit. But I didn't feel like playing.

When Mom tucked me in that night she said I could talk to her about what had happened at the funeral home, but I didn't want to. After she left I stayed in bed thinking. I moved my hand up to touch my face. It was still warm, and soft.

Essays

"Baby Chair, Abandoned Motel,"
photograph by Christopher Woods

Richard Compean

"What's That Sound": My Vietnam War

It always starts with the same sound and brings to my mind's eye the same picture. And it always takes me back. I hear two guitar notes, reverberated and repeated, joined by quiet drumbeats, then the unforgettable voice of Stephen Stills calmly letting us know "There's something happening here." Even before he can add that "there's a man with a gun over there," the picture, too, enters my mind—the indelible, Pulitzer Prize-winning photo of young Mary Ann Vecchio kneeling over victim Jeffrey Miller at the Kent State Massacre of 1970. Song and photo always bring instantly to mind the role the American Vietnam War has played in my life and in the lives of my contemporaries.

With the release of *The Vietnam War,* an in-depth documentary by Ken Burns and Lynn Novick, Americans are talking again about a war that deeply divided us in the 1960s and continues to do so to this day. It has taken over forty years to acknowledge the deep and painful wounds of this war, fought not just in Vietnam but also in the streets of American cities like New York, Chicago, and San Francisco.

It is a war that America should not have fought, could not win, and in fact did not win, whose shameful loss in 1973 is hushed and ignored. And it is a war that defined a generation of young men, including myself.

Because I turned eighteen after I started college at the University of San Francisco (USF), even though I had grown up in Los Angeles, I registered for the draft in San Francisco. At that time U.S. military forces in Vietnam were only there, as my ROTC commander assured us, in an "advisory" capacity. But when U.S. involvement increased dramatically, more U.S. soldiers were needed and draft status became vital. Draft deferments for married men and for students, routine during my first year, were taken away, and any able-bodied man between eighteen and twenty-six became obligated to serve. This war now struck home for me and my friends at USF. It became real, and because it became real, resistance against America's involvement in this war and demonstrations against it grew, especially in urban areas.

Early in 1967 I was still an undergraduate at USF, still taking Theology and Philosophy from the Jesuits and doing the required ROTC parading every week. (I would discover later that USF made money for each "student cadet.") Meanwhile, plans were being made in New York and San Francisco for the first-ever mass demonstrations against the war in Vietnam. The Spring Mobilization Committee to End the War chose April 15, 1967, a Saturday, and over half a million people in New York and San Francisco marched that day. In New York, the nearly 500,000 demonstrators included Martin Luther King, Jr. and renowned pediatrician Dr. Benjamin Spock. In San Francisco, the 60,000 demonstrators included me.

Initially, I was reluctant to join the demonstration. I was not crazy like my friend Bruce. He had boycotted all of his ROTC classes, and on the final parade day, when a lieutenant colonel from the Presidio of San Francisco would be reviewing all the USF cadet troops, Bruce planned to emerge from a car near the parade grounds dressed in black Viet Cong pajamas and a coolie hat and personally hand him a plastic hand grenade. To talk Bruce out of this caper, we had to persuade him that some of the top brass from the U.S. 6th Army at the Presidio that day would likely have live rounds of ammunition and might shoot first and ask questions later.

No, I was not as crazy as Bruce, but when I woke up that April 15th morning, I knew I had to join the demonstration. I had heard there might be a few USF students, so I took a MUNI bus downtown and found the only three other USF students and two professors, both part-time lay Philosophy instructors. We marched from Second and Market to Kezar Stadium in Golden Gate Park, a route that took us very close to USF. What we got from USF fraternity boys and others along the way was a lot of heckling and jeering. A few years later, at my USF graduation, the Jesuit president would actually congratulate USF students for NOT protesting the war. "Here we were," he would say, "sandwiched between radical UC Berkeley across the Bay and riotous San Francisco State to our west, and we chose not to demonstrate." His words of pride came across to me as embarrassing words of shame.

The summer after the Spring Mobilization, my younger brother came for a visit, and when we played a friendly game of tennis, I won and foolishly tried to jump the net—foolishly because I didn't make it and, in trying to brace my fall, injured my left elbow. A doctor told me I may have done permanent damage and may never be able to straighten that arm completely. Surgery was a possibility (50/50), but I wouldn't be able to play golf or, most importantly, shoot a rifle. Even if my elbow could be corrected, he suggested I wait until after I became twenty-six to even try. And he guaranteed me a 4F (unable to serve for medical reasons) military deferment.

This doctor even wrote me a letter, which I took with me to the Selective Service Oakland Induction Center when I was ordered to go. Men on my bus had all kinds of plans and schemes to avoid getting classified 1A (fit for military duty) and being sent off to Vietnam. Some carried contaminated urine, some were taking drugs of various sorts, some were practicing acting psychotic or gay (yes, that worked back in the 1960s). We were processed through nineteen different stations, each specializing in one medical test or another—blood, urine, eyes, ENT, and endless others. At the final station we met one-on-one with the chief medical doctor and were given one last chance to answer a final question: "Is there any reason you cannot serve in the U.S. Army?"

At this final station I showed him my letter, which he quickly read, then went into an absolute rage and stormed out. I was sure his anger was targeted at me and fully expected him to have me shipped off then and there directly to Vietnam. When he came back, he threw the letter at me and told me to "get the fuck outta here!" As I left I heard him muttering about those goddamn doctors and saying something about someone with my same condition having gone through weeks of training, costing taxpayers a fortune, only to be released.

It took three months, but finally my letter from the Selective Service officially categorizing me as 4F arrived. Thus I was able to finish college and eventually go on to graduate school in English, still hearing daily from Walter Cronkite on the *CBS Evening News* about how horrible the Vietnam war effort was going, both abroad and with increasing resistance in the U.S.

When I visited home the summer after my USF graduation, my father asked me, as "the college graduate," for advice on whom to vote for in an upcoming election. I looked directly at him and said, "Dad, you're the one who taught me about 'Tricky Dick' Nixon and how he smeared Helen Gahagan Douglas as a pinko commie in the 1950 California

Senate election." He and I did not know then that presidential candidate Richard Nixon had treasonously dispatched an aide to the South Vietnam embassy to persuade South Vietnam to withdraw from the Paris Peace Talks and thus prolong the war to help him win the 1968 U.S. presidential election.

The Vietnam War dragged on until 1973, but its impact on me and my generation continued, even as it does now. Such great films as *The Deer Hunter* and *Coming Home* (both 1978) captured the experiences of men who fought in this war, as did Francis Ford Coppola's *Apocalypse Now* (1979) and *Good Morning, Vietnam* (1987), with a great performance by Robin Williams, and more recently *The Post* (2017).

And then there was the music. I still hear it today in my mind's ear.

In early 1967, Buffalo Springfield released "For What It's Worth," and three years later, when the Ohio National Guard injured nine and killed four unarmed students at Kent State University, this song became forever associated with that tragic slaughter. The song spoke of "battle lines being drawn," of "people in the street / singing songs and carrying signs," of "something happening here" that "ain't exactly clear." It also implied that young people, at home on American soil, were being killed for "speaking their minds" about the Vietnam War.

The killings at Kent State happened in spite of eloquent pleas in 1969 by John Lennon and Yoko Ono to "Give Peace a Chance." They happened in spite of Country Joe McDonald's mocking invitations at Woodstock just a month later, for young men to "put down your books and pick up a gun" and for mothers and fathers to "Be the first one on your block / To have your boy come home in a box."

In 1971, Marvin Gaye, having heard about his own brother Frankie's experiences in Vietnam, lamented the crying of too many mothers and the dying of too many brothers as he asked "What's Going On?" and pleaded that "War is not the answer." Although the Vietnam War ended in 1973, its consequences continued, some of them expressed by Bruce Springsteen in his 1984 song "Born in the U.S.A." Eleven years after the war, the veteran protagonist of this song sings of how he was sent off to "kill the yellow man," of how he had a brother killed at Khe Sanh who left behind "a woman he loved in Saigon," and of how now his country, represented by his "V.A. man," can do nothing for him.

In the English classes I now teach, I often include Tim O'Brien's great 1986 story about a platoon of soldiers in Vietnam, led by young Lieutenant Jimmy Cross, "just a kid at war, in love." Titled "The Things They Carried," it is an increasingly deeper exploration of both the tangible things soldiers in the platoon carried (weapons, ammunition, equipment) and the intangible things they carried (love, responsibility, fear).

In my own Vietnam War, I carry not only this story but also my USF ROTC, my 1967 San Francisco anti-war march, and my Oakland Induction Center experiences. I carry memories of my father and the Vietnam movies and songs I have mentioned. I find all of these things to be not burdensome, but liberating, ultimately remembering that war is never the answer and that my country not only sometimes makes mistakes, but it also might be able to learn from one of its biggest ones—the War in Vietnam.

Andrey Gritsman

Poetic Meridian of Paul Celan

Russian Perspective
To hear the axis of Earth, Earth's axis
(Osip Mandelstam)

The first time I heard about Paul Celan was many years ago, back in Moscow. There was a remarkable publication by a well-known translator of German, Solomon Apt, in a popular literary magazine, Foreign Literature. There was a brief introduction and several poems translated by Apt from Paul Celan. I remember a feeling of recognition, as if I saw some sign; I felt something very important for poetry and philosophy, different from anything I had ever experienced reading about a poet and some of his poetry. Paul Celan's metaphors were flashing from the pages of the magazine and have stayed in my soul, in my heart, for my entire life.

For me, those were the years of youthful wastefulness of time, also of preparation to emigrate, to escape from the suffocating air of the Soviet Union. Later—the first years of emigration, kind of sleepwalking years, entering a new life, settling down. Then, in a few years, already in the United States, I started writing poetry in English. However, during all those years, the poetry of Paul Celan was calling me, living in me, and didn't let go. Sort of as a lasting desire for a narcotic, incidentally tried once in my youth. Therefore, much later, I decided to come back to his poetry in earnest. At that time, as I started an MFA program at Vermont College, I began reading everything about Celan in English I could get my eyes and hands on.

An unexpected connection with Celan turned out to be a wonderful Romanian-American poet, Nina Cassian. Nina apparently was a friend of Celan from the early period in post-war Bucharest. It was really one degree of separation, through one handshake. Interestingly, Celan himself, in his letters, compared a poem with a handshake; that is, with a gesture, expression, and direct speech—handshake. This could be one of the definitions of poetry. Nina Cassian was, in her own right, a great, famous European poet from Romania who made her home in America quite late and started writing in English in her late fifties; an unusual, amazing phenomenon. She became a well-known American poet of European origin, a leading, so-called *bilingual poet,* an eternal "displaced person" in American culture.

Once I was walking up Lexington Avenue on Manhattan's Upper East Side. It was a humid autumn day in October and I was on my way from Lenox Hill Hospital, where I worked. I noticed Nina Cassian's name on the announcement of a poetic seminar in the Unterberg Poetry Center at 92Y. I read some of her poems in *The New Yorker* and was very interested in her poetry and in her personal story. A little later I read one of the books about Paul Celan, about his youth and early art, and in the footnotes I noticed Nina's name. She was mentioned as a close friend of Celan in Bucharest in the late '40s. They both were in the same social circle of young artists and poets who survived the war. Nina was a young poetess and, as she told me later, at that time she unfortunately didn't understand the special place and significance of Celan's figure in the art. The direct relation to Celan's persona amazed me. I particularly value direct speech, personal communication, and one-handshake separation. In those footnotes I noticed the citations of some of Celan's expressions, words, what he said to her, and she to him. I find such touching personal feeling precious.

Shortly after, I called New York City information and—amazingly—immediately received a telephone number for Nina Cassian. She lived on Roosevelt Island, between Queens and Manhattan—a strange, somewhat artificial bedroom community. Roosevelt Island reminds one of a ship made of stone landed in the East River between the two large living spaces of Queens and Manhattan. As Nina answered the phone, she was at first apprehensive and cautious. But after she heard my explanations and strange, heavy Russian accent, which she immediately recognized, she invited me to visit. She sounded abrupt and matter-of-fact. Over the phone I didn't tell her anything about myself or what I do, but, as if she guessed, she issued a command: "And don't forget to bring your poems."

At the moment I went to see Nina with one purpose—to feel some direct connection with Paul Celan. I didn't have any special hopes related to our meeting and discussions. I thought that, as an older female American poet, she would offer some decaf tea with crackers, and I wouldn't be able to smoke for a couple of hours, but it would be certainly worth it. Unexpectedly, everything turned out quite differently. Nina was a whisky drinker and a heavy smoker. So we drank a whole bottle of whisky (Teacher's, Nina's household scotch), filled an entire ashtray with cigarette stubs, got into a quarrel, and after that became close friends. We got into an argument, first of all, because Nina really admired Marina Tsvetaeva and I liked Anna Akhmatova better. We even managed to exchange some sharp words about our own poetry, mine being too cerebral (not at all!) and hers too feminine, Tsvetaeva-like (not at all!). Later we changed our opinions completely, both in the opposite directions.

Our encounter impressed me so much that as I was driving out of Roosevelt Island, I didn't notice a sobriety stop on the Queens side. It was a roundup by the NYC Police Department. However, as I opened my window, I had such a reflective, thoughtful expression on my face that a police officer couldn't even imagine that a person with such an expression had a half bottle of whisky in his body. Magically, he let me go.

By that time, Nina Cassian had lived in New York for more than ten years, writing very successfully in English and continuing to write in Romanian. She escaped Bucharest in the last years of the horrendous dictatorship of the Ceausescu couple. The story goes that as the secret police of Romania were searching the apartment of her old friend, they found his diary with some satirical verses by Nina addressed to the Ceausescu couple. At that moment, however, she had already been in the United States for a year, teaching at New York University. Still, she got the information that officers of the Securitate were beating her old friend in prison. There were rumors about mortal bleeding caused by liver rupture. It became obvious that, for Nina, there was no way back to Romania. She got stuck in New York, and in several years had become a well-known American poet.

She was talking about Celan and her meetings with him for a couple of hours. It was a magical connection of details, direct speech, and their live conversation. It is most precious in literature. She told me about her last encounter with Celan in Paris, shortly before his death by suicide. Quite possibly, she was the last person of his circle who saw the great poet alive. During this meeting he was editing her translations of his poems from German to

Romanian. Unfortunately, she didn't remember the details of his comments and his precise advice related to choosing the right words and corrections to the text. According to Nina, Celan's concentration on the text was amazing, despite the deep depression that afflicted him during this last period of his life. She remembered that they'd had some red wine and ham sandwiches. She noticed that the face of her friend had become somewhat heavier and puffier.

Paul Celan is a rare phenomenon in art. He is unique not only because of the power of his genius, but also because of his place as the eternal "artist-foreigner," which he willingly or unwillingly occupied. He didn't completely belong to any culture and, at the same time, benefited from several cultures because of his unusual sensitivity and depth of feeling. A very important feature of his art is an ambivalent relation to his native German language, the language of his poetry.

Celan was raised in a middle-class Jewish family in Bukovina, Chernovtsy, in the central part of Eastern Europe. Until 1918, it was part of the Austrian-Hungarian Empire. During Celan's life this region was under the jurisdiction of several different governments: Austrian-Hungarian Empire, Romania, Soviet Union, German occupation, Soviet Union again, and eventually part of Ukraine. Celan was bilingual; his native languages were German and Romanian. However, while his literary and cultural upbringing, like Franz Kafka's, was mainly related to the German culture, he also heard Romanian and Ukrainian languages around him in that region. Therefore, Celan lived at the crossroads of three cultural traditions: Jewish (his origin), German, and Romanian, with some influence of the Hungarian culture. For the last twenty years of his life, until his premature death in 1970, Celan lived in Paris (his French was absolutely fluent). He was married to a French woman, a Catholic of noble origins. This was a wonderful graphic artist, Gisele Lestrange.

The twentieth century gave us several great writers, thinkers, and philosophers who belong not only to a certain culture, but to the entire world: Franz Kafka, Vladimir Nabokov, Samuel Beckett, Joseph Conrad, Robert Muzil. One can add, with some comments and remarks, Joseph Brodsky to this list. These are the representatives of the world's Acmeist (or, rather, post-Acmeist) culture.

These writers occupy a special place in the world culture because of their unique features and the greatness of their gifts, but also because of the special historical situation that occurred in the twentieth century. Each of these artists had his own historical and personal circumstances, but here was something common to all of them: they were moved, shifted from their native cultures elsewhere, and they created their art not necessarily in their native tongue, or else in a language different from the one surrounding them during their creative life. The most important thing is that they were immersed in their own inner world, having created it from several layers of language and culture. Therefore they achieved deep spirituality, almost independent of the surrounding culture and language.

Samuel Beckett didn't write in his native language, and although he apparently experienced some fear of the "second language," he skillfully used it to achieve his artistic goal. This conflict emphasizes the poetics of his artistic speech. Celan's experience is closer to the experience of James Joyce—that is, creation of his own language, but with penetration into the extreme depth of his native language. Both these geniuses used all the resources and facets of the language with the creation of their own artistic language out of the native one.

In some ways these are antagonistic, ambivalent relations with the native language. Thus James Joyce created his new English language, and similarly Paul Celan created his new "anti-German," "anti-Nazi" German.

Jewish origins played an important part in Celan's art and in his mentality. He received a serious Jewish education in Chernovtsy, although he was never formally a religious Jew. But Hebrew words and Jewish mysticism and symbolism are very significant in his art. It is enough to remember "Psalm," one of the most known poems by Celan, based on Jewish religious symbolism.

In his earlier years in Chernovtsy, and also during the relatively short period of his life in Bucharest after the war, Celan was also writing poetry in the Romanian language. Interestingly, later on he didn't accept his early poetic exercises in Romanian. Again, we have to be thankful to Nina Cassian, who translated those early Romanian poems by Celan into English, and they were recently published as a separate book.

In essence, Celan was a multilingual writer: German and Romanian, fluent English (translations from Shakespeare and Emily Dickinson), and French (twenty years of teaching at the college in Paris). He was also proficient in Russian and translated Mandelstam, Esenin, and Lermontov. Letters to his wife were written in French.

Curiously, Celan felt negatively about creating poetry in two languages, which is strange, considering his developments at the cultural crossroads and knowledge of several languages, and his unique talent as a translator. In the '60s, he gave an interview to a French literary magazine in which he expressed his distress over poetic creation in two languages. Celan identified poetry as a "unique moment in language." However, according to Nina Cassian, his earlier poems in Romanian showed his ability to write live and unique pieces of art in the Romanian language.

Celan finished his life in Paris at the age of forty-nine, throwing himself into the Seine from the Mirabeau Bridge. It was not far from the place of his last resort, his last apartment, the place where Nina Cassian visited Celan. There were several strange circumstances related to his death. First of all, it is well known that Paul Celan was a very good swimmer, growing up on the banks of a rather significant river (Prut). He was a strong man who liked hiking in the mountains of Bukovina. The choice of the method of suicide is yet another mystery; however, perhaps that choice was not incidental. Let's remember the gas poisoning of Sylvia Plath and the "typically American" death of Ann Sexton, who committed suicide by slamming her car into the garage door of her own house on a quiet, peaceful New England street. Remember Mayakovsky's bullet and the hanging of Esenin.

Nina Cassian wrote an extensive essay about Celan that was published in the end of the '80s in *Parnassus,* an American literary review magazine. Nina mentioned that Celan lost a dear friend in his youth—a woman who drowned in the Black Sea by the seafront of a Romanian resort. The shadow of this tragedy was cast over Celan's entire life.

Interestingly, Celan was influenced very little by the fabric of everyday life around him, including the landscape and other daily things. The real images around the poet, for instance in the poems "Koln, Cathedral" and "At the Station," are only the backdrop for the internal drama of the poet. With his poetic vision, Celan saw in a landscape, in his surroundings, the layers of drama and tragedy superimposed on the flow of time. We can call it "poetic archeology." To a certain degree it is similar to Joseph Brodsky's art. It is the relative autonomy of Brodsky's English language poetry related to the surrounding American reality. Apparently, it didn't interest Brodsky too much and, again, served mostly as a backdrop to the philosophy and development of the internal conflict. Paul Celan mainly existed and created in his own inner world, in his own developed poetic German language.

Fame came to Celan in a relatively early period of his artistic activity. Interestingly, it occurred not so much because of his innovations in the German poetic language and his astonishing, unique eschatological lyricism. It happened mainly because of the political significance of his poetry, related to the circumstances of the mid-twentieth century (his famous poem "Death Fugue"). Quite probably, Celan would be less well-known if not for this poem, the most anthologized German poem in the twentieth century. The appearance of this poem right after the war coincided with the period of "denazification" of Germany. Therefore, Celan was glorified as a famous "poet of the Holocaust." This apparently reflects only a part of his significance in the literature of the twentieth century. Celan's achievements in the development of a unique poetic language are unprecedented. The weight of a word in his poems is very substantial. He managed to achieve a powerful poetic effect with a minimal set of the most precise word-metaphors. This is a rare situation, when a poetic emotion is delivered not only with the right words and with the use of the instrument of metaphors; but, as the German language allows such a construction, emotion-word-metaphor becomes itself a poetic event.

The most significant German poet for Celan was Rilke; in Russian poetry—Mandelstam. Celan translated an entire book of his poems. His translations of Shakespeare's sonnets and Emily Dickinson from English are well known, as well as Mallarme from French.

There are some dominant themes in Celan's art: a memory of his mother, who perished in a Nazi concentration camp; the Holocaust; the poetry and figure of Osip Mandelstam. There is an interesting and characteristic guess by Paul Celan that Mandelstam perhaps survived Stalin's concentration camp, was released, and later perished at the hands of Nazis in the occupied territories during the war. This is quite characteristic for Celan's mentality: understandable fixation on the theme of the Holocaust and, to a certain degree, remaining, possibly subconsciously, trending to idealization of Soviet Russia.

It is well known that in the beginning of World War II, Celan, as well as many other urban educated Jews, greeted the Soviets in the zone of "liberation" by the Red Army. While attending university in Chernovtsy, he was part of a sympathizing circle. Years earlier, in high school, Celan distributed underground materials in support of international brigades in Spain against the Fascist regime of Franco. However, unlike many of his contemporaries who later found themselves in Stalin's Soviet concentration camps, Celan sensed where the wind blew and, after the war, escaped Bucharest, which was under Soviet rule. It was in the end of the '40s when he first went to Vienna but became desperate in this desolate, anti-Semitic, imperial postwar city. He moved to Paris, where he lived the last twenty years of his life, teaching at the college, lecturing in *École normale supérieure.*

•••

"Death Fugue," a famous poem by Celan, although written by a very young poet (in his early twenties), nevertheless shows an incredibly high control over the poetic form in combination with a maturity and depth of focus. This poem uses the structural principle of the fugue—imitation of the superimposition of several voices, which become combined into one central theme. In this great piece of art, besides the obvious main theme—the Holocaust and the loss of his mother, to whom he was very close—there are other, less visible, deep layers: an idea of a diaspora, not belonging, and searching for the Almighty. At the same time, acceptance of the absolute loneliness and estrangement of man: "You'll have a grave in the clouds."

Undoubtedly, the deep crisis in Celan's art was related to the loss of his parents, the complete loss of the world of his childhood, and also the entire collapse of European Jewry. In a certain, albeit negative, way, it served as a powerful emotional and energetic source for his art. However, it's important to remember that the poetic creativity and intuition of a poet are autonomous phenomena and are only partially subject to influence from the outside world. We can remember Joseph Brodsky's words about Mandelstam, saying in one of his essays that Mandelstam was the greatest poet in the period of his first book, *Stone*; that is, before the Revolution and Russian Civil War, before all those horrors that he lived through in the consecutive years. In other words, the art of the great artist develops despite destructive and suffocating influences of the horrible circumstances in the artist's life. The same relates to Marina Tsvetaeva and Anna Akhmatova, although these circumstances certainly influence the coloration, tone, and especially choice of themes in their art.

The rationale of Celan's suicide is not quite clear. It is known that the poet lived through a clinical depression, was hospitalized for some time, and was treated with electrical shock and other methods of the time. He also experienced a longstanding eschatological complex related to the events of the war and the postwar years. This was the psychological backdrop of the main period of Celan's art. We don't know if depression influenced his creative process, especially in the last period. Nina Cassian claims that Celan was always writing in his "clear" periods, when he was completely in control of his writing. This was the conscious and sober work of an experienced writer. It is known that Celan continued his translation work even in the psychiatric hospital. It is very unfortunate that Celan had to live through a period of an unfair accusation of plagiarism by the widow of French poet Ivan Goll. Even though the accusation was unfair, the widow threatened Celan with court proceedings, there were incriminating articles in the press, and there is no doubt all this worsened his depression.

His depression was likely exacerbated also by the atmosphere of increasing anti-Semitism that was developing in Europe about ten to fifteen years after the war. There is a known event when Celan found a disgusting anti-Semitic note on the lectern at one of his public readings in Germany. His psychological condition was also influenced by his close friendship and constant correspondence with another great German poet, Nobel Laureate Nelly Sachs. She originated from a well-to-do Berlin Jewish family, before Nazi rule, with a steady household and a large house in the center of Berlin. Nelly managed to escape to Sweden, where she suffered from a paranoia of prosecution in quite serious form, related to anti-Semitic threats. In the postwar period, the Swedish Nazis were quite active and capable of creating a significant anti-Semitic campaign of threats.

Later on, in the '60s, Celan developed an almost ambivalent relation to his greatest poem, "Death Fugue." At the time in Germany, this poem was used as almost a pedagogical instrument of the denazification and rejuvenation of society—in other words, as a political tool. There is a well-known expression by Adorno: "Poetry after Auschwitz is impossible." However, the experience with "Death Fugue" shows that poetry is possible after concentration camps, provided that it's created at such a high poetic and emotional level.

"Death Fugue" is not to be considered only as an anti-fascist poem on the theme of the Holocaust. All Celan's poems related to the Holocaust bear deeper psychological, cultural, and philosophical meaning. They cannot be considered only as strong poems written on a certain "topic." Celan was always trying to detach himself from the excessive politicization of poetry. For him, for understandable reasons, the events of the war and the catastrophe of European Jewry equaled the end of an entire era, the collapse of civilization. This was because of the unimaginable quality of the so-called "telescope effect" in his art; that is, the transition and unexpected changes of the "landscape" of a poem related to the masterful use of the shift of the "point of view": close vision, farsighted vision of the time and subject of consideration. Therefore, the shifts in vision and appreciation of time in Celan's poem are difficult to comprehend from the point of view of "normal" human understanding. What he was doing in his poems apparently can be discussed, analyzed, and interpreted from the point of view only on the biblical and philosophical levels and not in the aspect of the regular historical-sociological analyses.

Celan experienced a feeling close to admiration for Martin Heidegger, who, as is well known, was a member of the Nazi party and a dean of the university and, even in the postwar years, never publicly turned away from his prewar activities.

Some of Celan's collections were illustrated by his wife, Gisele Lestrange, a French Catholic graphic artist. She insisted that the significance of the Jewish themes in Celan's art should not be exaggerated by literary circles. This was happening after the poet's death, during various symposia and seminars related to his work.

The Jewish theme naturally played a significant role in his art: Celan's interest in Israel; his immediate translation of a famous Yevtushenko poem, "Babi Yar," from Russian into German (it was published in Germany in 1961). Eventually, after long delay, Celan visited Israel. This visit touched him deeply, and he was even planning to move to Israel. However, it never happened. The reason was probably his fear of likely isolation, of not being able to adapt to the Israeli culture.

Celan was interested in the writings of Martin Buber, especially in his Hasidic tales. Celan grew up in Bukovina in Eastern Europe—the region of the original development of the Hasidic culture. Therefore, he felt some historical and cultural relation to their roots. Celan was disappointed with his futile attempt to establish a connection with Martin Buber in Israel. There is a strange paradox: his unsuccessful connection with Martin Buber and established, long-term liaison with the philosopher Martin Heidegger, who had some Nazi background. Celan and Heidegger corresponded for years, which culminated with a visit of Paul Celan to Heidegger's university (University of Freiburg). In 1967, Celan delivered a lecture and a reading in front of an audience of one thousand, an event obviously organized by Martin Heidegger. The next day they also met in private, when Celan visited Heidegger at his "hut" in the mountains. It will always remain a mystery what they talked about during their lengthy stroll in the mountains, but the very fact of this conversation is symbolic and metaphorical. Mountains played a significant part in Celan's psyche.

Arguably, Celan was the greatest German language poet of the second part of the twentieth century, or perhaps of the entire twentieth century. However, the German language of his poetry is rather a translation from the regular German into a nonexistent language created by Celan—his own, internal German. This is the opinion of translators and Celan scholars George Steiner, Pierre Joris, Michael Hamberger, and John Felstiner. This is an unusual case in the history of poetry—translation from the translation. Hence, the special method used by Celan: his famous new word creation. This is perhaps an attempt to detach from the regular, everyday, orderly German language of the Nazi period.

The cultural phenomenon of Nazi Germany represented a much broader historical and philosophical event than simply the official political newspaper language of Nazi Germany from 1933 to 1945. The spirit of it and, naturally, language as a reflection and part of the national spirit existed much longer—appearing long before the establishment of the Weimar Republic. So it's not surprising that such an artist as Paul Celan developed a love-hate relationship with the German culture of the beginning and mid-twentieth century. Naturally, it occurred first of all on the level of language and its usage in poetry.

There is a special link, similarity, and likeness in the career and destiny of Paul Celan and Franz Kafka: personal, historical, and in their strange position of not belonging completely to any culture. This was regardless of the fact that they were developing in a quite specific culture—the German language culture. But in that milieu, their unique, autonomous genius "mutated," first of all in their relation to their native tongue. George Steiner, in his classic work *After Babel,* remarks that as a writer, Kafka is placed between the Czech and German languages, but his creative world had very close links with the Hebrew and Yiddish languages. As a result, Kafka developed profound feelings for the opaqueness of the language and, in some sense, of the conceptual impossibility of direct human relations on the level of language. Here we can add that perhaps this is the origin of Kafka's development into a genius metaphorical poet, although utilizing a seemingly prosaic method. It is known that Kafka called this method "illusion of the speech."

Celan expressed his views on poetry probably best in his two poems "In Variable Keys" (1945) and "Standing in a Shadow" (1967), as well as in his brief essay "Meridian." The latter he delivered as a speech on the occasion of receiving his Georg Buchner Prize in 1960. Celan compared language with a meridian extending through human personal and communal national conscience. Both of the above-mentioned poems expressed Celan's search for the deep core of poetry—"above the language."

In his poem "Landscape" (*Atemwende* collection), Celan renders, with a great artistic, surrealistic power, the feeling of the oppressive atmosphere of the petty everyday life of common people on the original artist. The poem shows the landscape being transformed into monstrous creatures and body parts. Actually, Celan was rather close to the surrealistic artistic movement of the middle of the twentieth century and not infrequently used images related to that school.

•••

It is known that Celan actively participated with a group of young Romanian surrealist artists in the first postwar years in Bucharest. Apparently, he was not formally included in the group but socialized with them and, to a certain degree, was probably influenced by this development. This circle was connected with the Andre Breton Artistic School in Paris. Once this group of Romanian artists visited Andre Breton in Paris at the end of the '40s and early '50s but without Celan. Celan, in his poetry, approached the deepest structures of the subconscious of the language, the so-called "Universal Units" of pre-language subconscious information. According to Noam Chomsky, the concept of these Universal Units supposedly related to all languages, or at least to certain groups of languages related to each other. To a certain degree it was also developed by George Steiner in his well-known book *After Babel*.

It is important to emphasize that Celan operated within clearly recognizable language structures, observing all the norms of syntax and grammar. However, he used a characteristic approach—the creation of new combinations of words, "double words." Such operations with language are more natural for German; still recognizable as German, unlike English or Russian. The characteristic examples of such new language formations could be found in his poem "Fadensonnen" in the collection *Atemwende* ("Breathturn"). In this poem, Celan used two words of new formations—"sunrays" (not characteristic for German) and "light tone." This is typical for Celan—combining in one word the subject, the object, and movement related to that object; sometimes two distant entities, sometimes conflicting with each other and therefore mutually enhancing each other. As a result, he produced a unique method in poetry: the creation of a one-word metaphor. This is a situation when a word itself becomes a metaphor without additional explanations or comparisons, a method quite uncharacteristic for talkative and suggestive Russian language and, therefore, poetry.

The poet utilized the syntactical pliability of German (which possesses that hard sound) and brought it to the extreme. He successfully used the strong rhythmic effect, ideally rendering the breath of a poem. This was achieved by frequent unexpected shifts from one line to another, especially when he used the confluence of simple words into one complex word; for instance, in the title of the collection—*Atemende* ("Breathturn")—in one word.

Therefore, Celan, with his precise poetic intuition, utilized unique qualities of the German language, that of being able to maintain the main recognizable, logical line of a poem. That is where the difficulty of the translation of German poetry originates, especially Celan's poetry. Each Celan poem is so unique that any one of them could be called most characteristic of him. Celan lived not only through the Holocaust, but through the entire preceding German history and development of the German language.

Paul Celan is a great master at using pauses and silences in his poetic language. This untranslatable silence is felt not as a lack of sound but as a pause in speech directed straight at the listener or reader. This is the silence or pause that harbors the deepest potential of poetic speech. This is Mandelstam's "sound remote and dull" in his early poem: a pause in the street noise, silence of the ocean during the calm, of the ravine before one can hear the fall of a rock.

This is the expectation of truth and the possibility for the reader to interpret the silence in any way with a mathematically endless number of variations of the meaning. This is a meaning that the author kept in mind, perhaps subconsciously.

It is not incidental that most of Celan's poems are fairly short. They condense a large amount of information concentrated in sounds and complex words. The weight of one word is great, unlike words characteristic of Russian poetry—talkative, extensive, and excessive. German language gives such an opportunity to condense meaning into a smaller number of words. An example is the entire story and view of the whole era concentrated in a relatively short poem: "Koln, at the Station."

Interestingly, this system of using pauses and poetic silence is not generally characteristic for Russian poetry. Language itself is perhaps more important here; Russian is less hard than German or English, more inflective, organically reflecting the curves of "the Russian soul."

The metaphorical qualities of Celan's poetry are phenomenal, practically incomparable and unrepeatable. The deepest layers of poetry in his work surface and become extremely effective. Usually, in the works of other authors, these deep layers are masked by the layers of the cadence, rhyme, and metaphors. In Celan's work, word connotations and semantics of the metaphor frequently do not have a direct, simple explanation or even an obvious meaning. However, an attentive reader could feel that despite the opaqueness, this is the most precise and, as a matter of fact, the only possible combination of words that leads to the completion of a poem. This impresses the reader tremendously as something completely "logical" and, on the subconscious level, unique and singularly truthful. The reader feels, along with the author, the emotional energy of a poem, a power stream, regardless of the abstract images present in a poem.

In Celan's poetry, the reader can find unpredictable images or metaphors in almost every line. It is curious that Celan used, not infrequently, anatomical images and metaphors related to the body. Quite likely that has something to do with the beginning of a medical career in his early years in France. Celan entered medical training in Tours before the war. He went there from Chernovtsy and spent some months, perhaps a year. It is possible that the usage of medical terms stemmed from his intuitive, precise feeling of the semantic difference of these "medical words" from "common poetic language." This gives a different metaphorical coloration to the poetic language.

The most commonly used words in Celan's poetry are blood, snow, and stone. These are the main word-symbols for Celan, and also eye, retina, and heart. There is probably some connection with the selection of words and metaphors in Rilke, like in Rilke's poem "Exposed on the Mountains of the Heart."

The word "stone" is possibly related to a profound affinity of Celan to the poetry of Mandelstam. His translations of Mandelstam's poetry render its central position of the notion of stone and architectural features. Hence, the architecture in his poems: mountains, "hills of Toscana," "cool mountain air," etc. Perhaps it mattered that Celan spent months during the war in a labor camp, working on construction and repair of the stony mountain roads and in the quarry. That was forced labor during the German Occupation during wartime with other young Jews from Chernovtsy. Older people, including Celan's parents, were sent to special camps in Ukraine, and most of them perished there. It's amazing that Celan continued his writing work and translations in the labor camp.

Famous Russian literary scholar and linguist Yuri Lotman, in his book *Analysis of the Poetic Text,* noted that the power of poetry is characterized by the high level of information that is achieved by unexpected sharp shifts of the poetic stream. Therefore, what awaits in the next line, in the next stanza, should be unpredictable for the reader. The dynamic tension is achieved by a link between the relative regularity of the cadence and the unusual use of language and metaphors.

Precisely these qualities are characteristic of Celan's poetry. Probably it is related to the title of one of his last collections, *Atemwende* ("Breathturn"), 1967. In fact, this is probably a definition of his method. That implies the poet probably operated on the level of the primordial units of the language, intimately connected with the physiology of breath, and breath during speech.

In his later years, his last period of artistic work, Celan's method becomes even less traditional and metaphorical, his language more economical, tight, but at the same time, unpredictable and unexpected. Celan's method significantly changed and developed from the first collection, *Mohn und Gedachtnis* (1952), including the famous "Death Fugue," to the last collections, *Schneepart* and *Seitgehoft,* published posthumously in 1971 and 1976. One could notice the use of unusual lexicon and his avant-garde approach in the early works. However, they were still closer to traditional poetry and sometimes represented almost a poetic narrative: "Memory of France," "In Memory of Paul Eluard," "Schibboleth."

In the later period of work, Celan's poems become shorter and occasionally represent one long sentence and lines representing one or two complex, newly created words. German language allows such syntactical and grammatical experiments, which create an extremely unusual type of poem. Celan's images become more abstract and represent unexpected and amazing structural units of the language. One has an impression that these later poems are concentric circles, composed of three intimately linked units: language—thought—emotion, the circles becoming narrower and tighter.

> "I hear the axe has flowered.
> I hear the place can't be named.
> I hear the bread that looks at him
> heals the hanged man,
> that bread his wife backed him.
> I hear they call life
> the only refuge."
>
> (Adapted by A.G.)

Paul Celan found his last refuge at "the place that cannot be named" in 1970 at age forty-nine. The tremendous significance of his poetic heritage becomes more and more actual and relevant in the process of the cultural and linguistic exchange in our era of globalization and migration of people and souls (era of DP). Paul Celan was one of the few artists who expressed the dark spirit of the time and understood the meaning of the twentieth century with great and tragic precision.

Rachel Rinehart Johnson

Beauty in the Spice of Life: An International Playgroup

> When God created humans,
> He was the artist.
> His art work was perfect.
> His choice of colors was perfect.
> God's purpose for color was beauty,
> not separation.
>
> —Richard Johnson

I had tried three playgroups, all white Americans, all mothers, and all looking for friendship for themselves and playmates for their children. 1. La Leche League… we all sat in a loose circle on the floor, babies and toddlers, and preschoolers running around or lounging across their mothers' laps, playing with their mom's beaded necklace or nursing. The women discussed attachment parenting, co-sleeping, selling handstitched slings, and making their own baby food or diapers. 2. A Christian playgroup where I saw babies slapped and toddlers spanked; I left early. 3. A local group of suburban moms, and this meeting was for parents only to plan and schedule the year in advance; I grabbed a Styrofoam cup with lemonade before taking an aisle seat in the middle of the room and listened to the announcements, the invitation and instructions for joining, and the activities planned, but not one person spoke to me during the entire evening. I squared my shoulders and walked back out the door with my head held high.

Obviously, I needed to look elsewhere. I didn't belong to any of the groups and felt like I was back in high school where I didn't fit in with the hippies or the Christians or the popular kids. So, where could I find a place for both my daughter and me to make friends?

•••

Lexi and Tomás hold hands, dancing round and round in circles to *El cocherito Leré,* while Sanju reads Bablee a story from the magazine *Chandamama.* Gautam and Parham play with the playdough as Adarsh and Paloma eat chapatis. Thomas, the youngest, toddles around, stumbling over our shoes at the door before heading back to his mom. Rama, María, Priya, the rest of the mothers, and I sit in the middle of the floor conversing and watching our toddlers. A year before, I met a few of them on the playground at our apartment complex in Columbia, Missouri. Our kids started playing together, we began talking, and soon I'd created this playgroup that met at least once a week.

"I'm really going to miss the massages." Priya, eight months pregnant with her second child and recently returned from India, tells us that women stay in the home for a month or two after giving birth and someone comes into the home to give daily massages to the mother and baby.

"The equipment are very wonderful, but they [doctors and nurses] don't really know what's happening without it." Elham interjects. "We experience it through the patients not the equipment." Her son, Parham, rushes straight at her. She catches him, places him face-down on her lap, and begins slow circular rubs along his back.

After a short pause, I ask the women from India, "What's something you think sets your culture apart from others?"

"Parents are really involved in their children's education. It's not a passive thing," Sudha replies. "They really spend a lot of money to send them to school. Take time off to teach children in evening."

Gladys hurries to the playroom to check on some commotion as Maria asks, "What's a popular book you read to toddlers in India?"

"We don't read to them. Maybe at five or six years, but not younger," says Sudha. She sits cross-legged on the floor in her brick-colored sari. A dot drawn in the middle of her forehead sparkles as she turns her head.

"You don't?!"

"My grandpa told me stories," Rama shares as she hands each of us a cup of Indian-style tea spiced with cardamom and cloves along with the milk and sugar.

"Of course—the oral tradition." I blow on the tea and take a sip. "Telling stories must build a strong bond."

"Grandparents like to spend time with grandchildren," Sudha states as Gautam plops into her lap and hands her his Play-doh creation. Sudha, like the other women from India, is wearing a sari—a bright, colorful cloth draped around her body. "I started working again when Gautam was three months and my mother was with him all the time."

"The extended family is very important, then?" Becky asks. Dark-haired Becky, an American like me, is my best friend from college. We met during my sophomore year when we were both living in the same dorm, and I love that I can share this experience with her.

After my first three failed groups, I finally hit on what I was after and created what I needed.

"Yes," Sudha tells us. "The moral support from our parents is much more. They're always there for us. Especially when we're pregnant. Every time my mom was there. When doctor said I had to have cesarean, I never had time to think of the surgery. My parents and friends visited the whole time." As she talks, Gautam runs up and pulls on her arm, asking for food. She stands up and heads to the kitchen, where she picks up a baggie filled with Indian snacks. She hands him one, and he stuffs it in his mouth before darting back down the hallway.

"And we would always take care of our parents. The elders here are independent with active, busy lives, but there [in India] they just want to be with the children," Rama adds. I wondered how they coped here in America so far away from their extended families. I wondered how I was coping so far away from my family. I wondered how Americans, so scattered, so busy, were coping.

I enjoyed those discussions so much. Much better than when Lexi and I tried the all-white, middle-class playgroup the year before because then we only talked about children, whereas in this international playgroup, we had so much to share with each other about our different cultures, about the reality of everyday life for us.

"Aaahhh!" A loud squeal from my daughter jerks me back to the present.

"DADDY!" Lexi's eyes light up with delight as Tomás responds with this scream. He loves the sound of that word; thus, it has become part of their special greeting.

Tomás is definitely Lexi's best friend; they connected from the very beginning, even when they couldn't understand each other. From the first day, they held hands and ran around the room, always together.

Tomás quickly learned English while Lexi learned a little Spanish. He would ask his parents, *"Como dice Lexi agua?"* (How does Lexi say water?)

••••

How do we teach our children diversity and acceptance? How can we help them see beyond color and language to people and their hearts? As recent headlines show, these are still important questions in the twenty-first century.

It all starts with what we pass down through the generations; I am grateful that I learned these vital qualities from my parents through conversations, books, movies, music and then passed them down to my own children, using love, exposure, and conversation.

••••

We enjoyed the playgroup so much that we wanted our husbands to experience it, so we decided to have a dinner each month where we each brought a dish from our country.

The first night, parents and children from India, Spain, South America, Iran, and the United States crowd into our two-bedroom apartment, and freshly prepared dishes from each country cover the kitchen counters. Paella is set beside Biryani, which is next to chips and salsa and kebabs and radish curry and lentils. Hints of garlic, ginger, cinnamon, cardamom, shrimp, and steak tease our noses as screaming toddlers dodge around adults and charge down the long hallway to the bedrooms where they love to play. Laughter and conversation flow smoothly, even with the broken English. Several of the men take the chairs at the table while the women and some Indian men carry full plates into the living room and bedrooms and sit on the floor to eat while supervising playing children.

"Sudha, I love your curry! It's so good! You gotta give me the recipe."

"I'll show you make it sometime."

"What's in it?"

"Coconut, coriander powder, ginger root, cloves, cilantro, cinnamon sticks, green chilies..."

"Where do you get all that?

"The Indian store."

I laugh. "You're gonna have to teach me how to shop for curry before you teach me how to make it."

Later that week, we visit the Indian store. Lexi and Gautam pull everything off the shelves as we search for the exotic ingredients. Bollywood movies line the walls, and fresh fruits that I've never heard of before line the counter at the register. We walk up and down the aisles as I explore all of the new options, such as gigantic bags of jasmine and basmati rice. I buy spices, rice, and Indian snacks and load up my car.

During playgroups, we start making recipes they know by heart. They show me how they chop onions and tomatoes, how to make sure the oil is just hot enough, how to mix the spices and veggies to make curry from scratch, how to make yogurt with cucumbers, how to smash the flour dough just so. I pitch in, taking time to write down the recipes on colored notecards as we cook. Now, I know how to make chicken curry, potato and pea curry, paella, bonda, Indian mashed potatoes, chapatis, and palav, and I have handwritten recipes that I use to this day.

In this group, we were learning to pass it along, generation upon generation, through love, exposure, and conversation. Children have an innocence that automatically welcomes and that can be nurtured. When my children were toddlers, I started an international playgroup and exposed them to food and kids and clothes from around the world. I read books to them about other cultures, and we talked about the differences and similarities. Even when they were babies, I bought a board book that is simply the song, "Jesus loves the little children, all the children of the world," and is illustrated with children from various cultures. I bought my daughters white American Girl dolls that looked just like them, but I also bought them Native American, African American, etc. dolls as well. I took them to local International Festivals every year and took photos for their albums. We watched movies about Dr. King, Rosa Parks, the Civil Rights Movement, women's rights, Gandhi and so on. When my children became teenagers, we hosted foreign exchange students every summer, and my daughters now have French and Spanish sisters.

•••

"Surprise!" María walks through our apartment door, expecting a quiet dinner with our two families, to see the entire playgroup there for her going-away party. After being with us for almost a year, María and Tomás are returning to Madrid.

Leaving.

How do you explain to a two year-old that her best friend won't be around anymore? Tears flow down María's cheeks as she opens her gift, a framed photo of all the moms and toddlers. She hugs each of us, and we take a whole roll of film, trying to somehow capture and save this wonderful experience and feeling. These beautiful friendships, frozen in time by the camera, will live forever in the shadowy corners of my mind to be recalled at odd moments in bittersweet remembrance.

Tomás gives each of his friends a tape with Spanish songs, and they give him a tape with American songs. How long will they remember this time together when they connected without words? All of them giggling, squealing, holding hands, and dancing in circles. Totally accepting.

Beautiful!

•••

A few years later when I was the one leaving, the women got together and gave me my first rice cooker. Every time I make rice, I think of them and smile. They taught me much more than how to make authentic curry because they welcomed me and my children, accepted us, and loved us. If the kids ever had an argument or issue, they worked together with me to resolve it for everyone. No one was left out or judged or bullied. Together, we cooked. Together, we talked. Together, we worked through anything. In the end, this group revealed the importance of unity, difference, community, and the innocence and acceptance of children. Our lives are enriched when we reach beyond the common white bread of our culture into the difference, diversity, yet oneness of others.

Susan Doble Kaluza

Bruises

The day our dog, Baiya, ran out into the path of a truck, I'd been scrolling through videos submitted on YouTube dealing with child abuse cases. It seemed, at first, like a sordid venue, as though the easy path one took down the sequenced line of videos made the process of acquiring information somehow cheap and untrustworthy. Still, I could not deny what I saw in the photographs posted within the videos. Further, I was shocked at the inordinate number of accounts detailing children with emotional and physical wounds inflicted by people they knew or who were related to them. As a general interest columnist for a local paper, my plan was to write a succession of articles, starting with op-ed pieces and then eventually featuring stories for bigger newspapers. It appeared to me that little was being said in the press about an epidemic that was spreading faster than—at that time—the bird flu or AIDS in Africa. There were footraces all over the country raising millions for breast and prostate cancers but nobody was running for the four-year-olds being used as punching bags. Before viewing the YouTube videos, which displayed sad and bruised toddlers with cigarette burns and cuts on their bodies, I felt strong and forthright like an avenging angel, but though, in theory, the pen be mightier than the sword, my own quiver full of linguistic skills on this issue would fail more often than not to hit its mark.

After discovering the *next* button disclosed still another endless sequence of nightmarish testimonies, I felt only anger, the hot prickly kind that crawls up the back of your neck and sticks at the base of your skull like an unquenchable migraine.

•••

Baiya was discovered at a stop sign during a blizzard in late February. As seemingly remote and un-metropolitan as it is, Montana is not immune to vagrants both animal and human. Situated against the backbone of the Continental Divide, it's as though this town was the end of the road for some, the "last best place" to lay one's head. But animals that attempt this kind of muddling through fare far worse than their human counterparts, having no use for one's spare change and unable to speak beyond the telltale signs of starvation and neglect. Baiya had hailed countless motorists, according to my daughter, who claimed the other drivers at the intersection had gunned their engines as the dog slid off the side, yelping.

So, it was out of pure impulse, out of a deep-souled need to rescue another living thing from the bitterness of her circumstances, that Baiya landed wet and shivering on our kitchen floor. Though, despite being loved in her new home, she was covetous and ill-mannered, grabbing food out of our hands and racing downstairs like a raccoon scurrying away from a ransacked garbage can. She was wild-eyed and quick-footed, a delight to watch in action with her antelope speed and gorgeous spotted markings. But she belched and passed gas like an 80-year-old with a sluggish digestive system. For two years, household necessities like brooms and mops and vacuum cleaners could not be used in her presence. She was beautiful but troublesome, leading our older dog on wild jaunts that landed them both, two or three times, in the local pound. Once, on a fishing trip with my husband, she picked a fight with a porcupine. Again, with her older counterpart in tow, she'd borrowed trouble and lost.

•••

I stand in the kitchen and weep as a maintenance man works feverishly to shut off the main valve to our water supply during a bathroom renovation. My sorrow seems bottomless, and even in public, my efforts to dry the tears are akin to a childhood fairy tale I once read of a man given the task of draining the ocean with an hourglass and a thimble. For days I gather half-chewed bones and stuff them into a ziplock bag. The discovery of her plush toy—a pink rabbit in the corner of a downstairs bedroom—drops me to my knees, and I wait for the sound of her whining, her cue for me that she has completed another night's sleep and is ready to go out and use the backyard facilities. I wait, but the basement door stands agape. And the space between me and it is empty. All is quiet on the Baiya front.

I imagine things because I wasn't there, because the incident, blurred by the rapidity with which each action took place, was told to me by my husband whose mountain bike excursion with both dogs ended almost as soon as it began. Baiya's plight began with another dog being walked by a man on the opposite side of the road. I imagined her crazy spotted ears had shot up, and her raccoon face formed a permanent smile. With her eyes scoping the distance between her and her newfound friend, she bolted out. This is where I stammer in the recantation of events, where my mind spirals like heat rising from the searing asphalt in front of the black pickup truck. I replay her actions as though they, too, had appeared on YouTube, as though they'd been intricately recorded to memorialize the snap decision that ended her life. In this video I have in my head, she has already been hit. She limps back across the road, her right shoulder a sack of splintered bone, the ribbon of tongue unfurled between her teeth like a windless flag. They come to kneel beside her—the two women from the truck—they cry and apologize as the thin film that precludes whatever light beams down on the dead begins to form in her luminous eyes.

•••

Meanwhile, the story of a four-year-old boy named Ethan had caught my attention. It certainly was not that his story was any more troubling or gruesome than the dozens of others I'd rifled through. My obsession with it had more to do with a flu bug that, while I was compiling notes on Ethan, converged upon my youngest grandson like one of the seven Egyptian plagues. I remember from the first wet burp and choking gulp to the last soaked towel, soiled diaper, and red bottom of this then one-and-a-half year-old boy, the horrors of that feverish night. I believe that he, now seven, has long since forgotten that bitter twelve hours—the cocktail of bile and strawberry Pedialyte—but I am forever undone.

I am no less affected when, even now, I freight back to pictures of Ethan Stacy, his glasses slightly askew, his hair spiked with a clear gel, his smile both a mask and a plea for help—the depth of which lies far beyond my own wherewithal to uncover or even to comprehend. In reality, my applied poetics and attempts to reconstruct what played at the edges of his mouth bring me no closer to the truth. I had once read a statement about four-year-olds. I can't remember what the criteria for the study entailed, but it claimed that we, as humans, laugh more heartily and with greater intensity at age four than at any other time in our lives. My oldest grandson—who incidentally escaped the same flu that gripped his little brother— was four at the time I had read this, and judging by him, I knew it to be true. I applied this same knowledge to pictures of Ethan posted on YouTube, and tried to imagine through the broken smile and missing teeth what scrap of his brief existence on this earth had contained something so funny that he laughed until his stomach hurt. I could sense his zest for the adrenaline rush that comes from running fast, hitting a ball, bolting across the street.

Strangely though, Ethan's story had eluded my attention on the evening news. Perhaps it had escaped—though I can't imagine how—the tale bearings and tongue lashings of Nancy Grace. I have no idea, but I do know that the police documentation of his abuse survived online for approximately a week before it was one-upped by Jesse James' inability to restrain himself from dating "skanks" while married to screen goddess Sandra Bullock. By the time the Hollywood sect had lavished hours of airtime on the burning question surrounding the "shocking" infidelity, Ethan Stacy was being mutilated posthumously for purposes of camou-flaging his true identity. All the reasons I've bowed out of pursuing a career in criminology were included in the online police report, including details of Ethan's physical hunger and compulsion to eat his own feces. According to the online police documents, his mother, Stephanie, and her then fiancé, Nathan Sloop, had locked him in a bedroom while they planned and celebrated their wedding. They left him alone with injuries that Nathan had caused and which caused Ethan's brain to swell, while they carried on a lurid romance, even documenting their mutual endearments in letters too nauseating to read more than a couple scattered lines at a time. Although I had read the police reports, had seen with my own eyes the documentation of one torment after another, I was only able to process the obvious with a minimal degree of professionalism in order to write a balanced, even a coherent, account. I began to resort to name calling, swaggering between profanity and active verbs as though drunk on my own words.

Thinking that *snake in the grass* was too noble a term, I bumped Nathan Sloop farther down the food chain to the realms of pond scum and reveled in turning Stephanie into a tangible rendition of her metaphysical self—spineless—pondering how she could attract a man at all in her condition, let alone garner the adjectives "beautiful" and "hot" that were lavished upon her like an expensive wine. My only defense was to continually refer to "the boy" by his personal name, and keep the bullets of my wrath firing against the empty page. I was off on tangents most of the time, imagining what was not told, the worst possible scenarios, having no faith that Ethan's pain had been the least bit adhered to. I attributed his helpless cries to days on end dehydration and starvation so severe that the fast food dinners allegedly set before him had been nothing more substantial than dust blown from the furnace vent.

•••

I squat down in the pickup bed as the mid August heat bears down; and Baiya's body, though warmed by the sun, has grown hard, and a coldness from deep inside her creeps into my touch. I recite in broken syllables a prayer for healing as though I'm hovering over a dead little boy with geek glasses and baby teeth, waiting for the tooth fairy. There is a sudden acrid smell, and a thin pool of blood and water trickles from beneath her chin. I rock back on my heels as though physically struck by the sun, by the universe with all its power to thieve and destroy.

For days I feel detached except for my body sleepwalking through appointments and mundane chores. In a lull from the storms of my imagination and regression into child-like sobs, my husband and I attend a local music festival. My thought is that the jolting energy of the stage and food court crowds is potentially better than re-living the impact, the horror of broken bones. But I find the musicians loud and intrusive, and the festivalgoers repulsive in their phony over-exuberance, screaming their pleasure toward the stage as though it was everyone's first outing since grammar school. At one point a girl and her boyfriend elbow in, pushing us nearly over in their pursuit for a front row view. The girl stands in front of me, allowing her knotted ponytail to swipe my face as she whips from side to side. To say that she lacked manners dates me back to a one-room schoolhouse poised in defiance against a widowed school teacher wearing an apron and a pencil in her hair bun. Or it sounds like an endearment. *The ill-mannered Baiya bolting out into the street.* This girl was ill-mannered at perhaps age twelve, but now she is hateful, and arrogant. *Arrogant.* The word with its hard consonants and air of superiority conjures images of Stephanie Sloop out dancing with her new husband while her son drowns slowly in his own vomit. I want to grab the girl by her ratty ponytail and toss her against the stage. I feel the weight of violence rising up inside me, settling in around me like a toxic cloud. For the first time in my life I feel like every shred of good I'd ever exhibited could be sacrificed to some indiscriminate demon fettered to the wounds inside my soul. Through the tambourines and the wailing of a deep South vocalist, I see Baiya's spots in the crushing impact of the truck's front wheel. How could she have known that a simple daily jog would take her from a familiar road to the blurred entrance of the earth's black core in less time than it takes to tell about it. And Ethan? Where were his neighbors, what was wrong with us that we danced and sang while children died in homes that looked normal, even comfortable, from their front doors?

•••

We buried her in an obscure patch of Aspen off a road she used to run. It was a road that I was fond of running due to its kindness to my hips and shin bones. Baiya loved it because it had been an inhabitable paradise of rain puddles sequestered in miles of brush that hid deer and all manner of pursuable birds and rodents. There had been no match for her happiness as she bobbed up and down through the patchwork of Aspens, and I knew, at her deepest level, she would always be a transient scratching for that elusive "elsewhere" which existed always in the present moment. And so it was on this road that my daughter and I stood in the rain with our tattered Kleenex and spoke of her like a sainted aunt, even her amusing bent toward hoarding—the day she died we found thirty-six chew strips stuffed in a downstairs couch and various assortments of yam and chicken wraps arranged in a long line behind an old television set—undone by some internal compass pointing the way out.

•••

Because the story of Ethan had evaporated from the press as quickly as it had appeared, the consequences of his death, the debts being paid, have long since dissolved into the shimmer of regrets that I, myself, have saved. My mind continues the hunt for safety against what I once heard called "the screwing motion of the world," where there is nothing with which to measure love in its many capacities, even where it resides unmet in its truest attempts to survive. Despite what we believe about the progression of our own civilization we live in a world where two people stop to revive a misguided mutt while another person trades her four-year-old for the affections of a killer.

Here I must pause, hating the lengthy digression that must follow, or else must follow me through the hallways of my conscience and convict me forever. I believe that people are not throwaways, not even the bad ones. As much as I loved scaling down through the food chain to attach a form of vile bacteria to the person of Nathan Sloop, and to Stephanie, the term *spineless*—hitting bottom at *heartless bitch* and *whore*—I cannot easily dismiss the thought that his and her own childhoods may well have been entrenched in similar types of hell. What rarely arises from the fog of our own ambivalence, our quickness to judge and label and condemn, is the acceptance—or not—of this one dirty little cliché: Hurting people hurt other people. The degree of damage may vary, but wounds imprinted upon the human soul lie vagrant and ugly and in darkness until the agony, much like a physical wound, is symptomatically treated, or healed completely.

Nathan Sloop, according to a police affidavit, suffered from multiple personality disorder, which included a personality that was angered easily when intimidated. We rarely see humanness—and certainly brokenness—outside our own skins, nor do we care to empathize with those weird or other-worldly we've absent-mindedly (to whit, stupidly) typecast from *Friday the 13th* movies, and in addition, applied only a trite Halloween version of gore to what must assuredly be cruel reality for a battered child.

Despite this, I shudder to think what echoes out from a life that sees fit to punish others in the way that he or she was punished. I believe the human soul, which we are taught to imagine is some mystical entity hovering above our heads like invisible eye candy for the devil, is actually tangible—just as thoughts are tangible—and can be wounded and bruised as quickly and as noticeably as an arm or a leg. To forgive adults for their offenses against children, I must first think of them as children who once, themselves, were afraid of the dark; who choked back vomitus or squirmed under a tetanus shot; who, despite parental warnings, poked around in campfires with willow sticks sharpened for roasting marshmallows; and who waited out the eternity between Thanksgiving Day and Christmas morning. I know that mental and emotional sickness cannot be explained away as easily as it can be brandished like a weapon on the next generation.

•••

Ethan was buried near Hollow Mountain, Utah, en route to his mother's stopover at a 7-11 for a Slurpee. His grave was, of course, unmarked. I rooted around in the pile of blankets that contained Baiya's hair, and pulled out a quilt large enough to wrap around her twice. With the sun bearing down, I lifted her head off the tailgate of the pickup and began to swaddle her one taut muscle at a time—all her color, black on white, white on black, her spots in tarnished disarray that divulged Blue Heeler breeding way back somewhere… her wild seed, her raccoon face—until she disappeared.

Contributors

David Anderson has published in *NonBinary Review*. He lives and writes outside of Tucson, Arizona.

Roy Bentley's books include *Boy in a Boat* (University of Alabama), *Any One Man* (Bottom Dog), *The Trouble with a Short Horse in Montana* (White Pine), *Starlight Taxi* (Lynx House); and *Walking with Eve in the Loved City*, a finalist for the Miller Williams Prize, just published by the University of Arkansas.

Byron Beynon lives in Wales. His work has appeared in several publications including *Kentucky Review, The Interpreter's House, The Yellow Nib, Crannog, London Magazine,* and the human rights anthology *In Protest* (University of London and Keats House Poets). Collections include *Cuffs* (Rack Press), *Through Ilston Wood* (Lapwing Publications) and *The Echoing Coastline* (Agenda Editions).

George Bishop's work has appeared in *The Carolina Quarterly, Flare,* and *Cold Mountain Review*. Bishop won the 2013 Peter Meinke Prize at YellowJacket Press for his chapbook, *Following Myself Home,* and his second full-length collection, *One Dance,* was published by FutureCycle Press. He attended Rutgers University and now lives and writes in Saint Cloud, Florida.

Z. Z. Boone is the author of *Off Somewhere,* a 2015 Indie Award nominee for Best Short Story Collection. Since that time, his work has appeared in *New Ohio Review, Bird's Thumb, 2 Bridges Review, Smokelong Quarterly, Kentucky Review, Eleven Eleven,* and other terrific places. Z. Z. teaches creative writing at Western Connecticut State University and is married to novelist Tricia Bauer.

Jesse Breite, native of Little Rock, Arkansas, lives in Atlanta, Georgia. Jesse's poetry has appeared in *Prairie Schooner, Spillway, Crab Orchard Review, Tar River Poetry, Terrain,* and many other journals. He has been featured in *Town Creek Poetry* and *The Southern Poetry Anthology, Volume V: Georgia*. FutureCycle Press published his first chapbook, *The Knife Collector,* in 2013. Jesse has taught high school English for all of his professional life and currently works at the Westminster Schools in Atlanta.

Roger Camp is the author of three photography books, including the award-winning *Butterflies in Flight* (Thames & Hudson, 2002) and *Heat* (Charta, Milano, 2008). His work has appeared in numerous journals, among them *The New England Review, New York Quarterly, North American Review,* and *Southwest Review*. His documentary photography has been awarded Europe's Leica Medal of Excellence.

Wendy Taylor Carlisle lives in the Arkansas Ozarks. She is the author of two books, *Reading Berryman to the Dog* and *Discount Fireworks* and five chapbooks, most recently *They Went Down to the Beach to Play* (2017). Her work appears in the new contest anthology, *Untold Arkansas* (etAlia Press, 2018). Her new book, *The Mercy of Traffic,* is due out in 2019. For more information, check her website at www.wendytaylorcarlisle.com..

Bill Carr's short story "Exquisite Hoax" was published in the *Scholars and Rogues* online literary journal. His short story "Execute Eric Smith" was published in *The East Bay Review*. Two other short stories, "The Beginning of the End of the Draft" and "One Accord," appeared in *The Ham Free Press* and the *Central American Literary Review,* respectively. His work has also appeared in the *Menda City Review* and *The Penmen Review*. Carr received his master's degree in English from Brooklyn College, and currently serves as chairperson of the North Carolina B'nai B'rith Institute of Judaism.

David Chorlton is a transplanted European who has lived in Phoenix since 1978. His poems have appeared in many publications online and in print, and often reflect his affection for the natural world, as well as occasional bewilderment at aspects of human behavior. A recent collection of poems is *Bird on a Wire* from Presa Press, and The Bitter Oleander Press published *Shatter the Bell in My Ear,* his translations of poems by Austrian poet Christine Lavant. A new book, *Reading T. S. Eliot to a Bird,* is out from Hoot 'n' Waddle, based in Phoenix.

Douglas Cole has published four collections of poetry and a novella. His work has appeared in anthologies and in *The Chicago Quarterly Review, The Galway Review, Chiron, The Pinyon Review, Confrontation, Two Thirds North, Red Rock Review,* and *Slipstream*. He has been nominated twice for a Pushcart and Best of the Net, and has received the Leslie Hunt Memorial Prize in Poetry and the Best of Poetry Award from *Clapboard House*. Visit douglastcole.com.

Richard Compean currently teaches English at City College of San Francisco and has published stories in *Menda City Review, Forge,* and *Pour Vida Zine*. His experiences of ROTC during the draft call-ups for the Vietnam War were not unlike those depicted in the now classic film *Animal House*. Richard has been inspired not just by favorite classic poets and writers like John Donne, Andrew Marvell, and Jonathan Swift, but also by modern singer-songwriters like Leonard Cohen and Bruce Springsteen, who has himself written and sung about the impact of the Vietnam War on Americans.

Barbara Crooker is the author of eight books of poetry, including *Les Fauves* (C&R Press, 2017). *Radiance,* her first book, won the 2005 Word Press First Book Award and was finalist for the Paterson Poetry Prize; *Line Dance,* her second book, won the Paterson Award for Excellence in Literature. Her writing has received the WB Yeats Society of New York Award, the Thomas Merton Poetry of the Sacred Award, and three Pennsylvania Council on the Arts Creative Writing Fellowships. Her work appears in a variety of literary journals and anthologies, including *Common Wealth: Contemporary Poets on Pennsylvania* and *The Bedford Introduction to Literature,* and has been read on *The Writer's Almanac* and featured on Ted Kooser's *American Life in Poetry*. She has been a fellow at the Virginia Center for the Creative Arts, the Moulin à Nef, Auvillar, France, and The Tyrone Guthrie Centre, Annaghmakerrig, Ireland.

Gareth Culshaw lives in Wales. He first collection, *The Miner,* was published in 2018 by FutureCycle Press. He hopes to achieve something special with the pen.

John Danahy resides in New Hampshire. He enjoys writing, reading, photography, and travels with his wife and family. His work has appeared in *Aim Magazine, Alembic, Amarillo Bay, Art Times, Desert Voices, Forge, The Griffin, Haight Ashbury Literary Journal, The MacGuffin, North Atlantic Review, Penmen Review, RiversEdge, Salt River Review, Sanskrit, Schuylkill Valley Journal of the Arts,* and *Valparaiso Fiction Review*.

J. P. Dancing Bear is co-editor for the *Verse Daily* and Dream Horse Press. He is the author of fourteen collections of poetry, most recently, *Cephalopodic* (Glass Lyre Press, 2015). His next book, *Fish Singing Foxes,* will be released in early 2019. These poems are part of the book *Of Oracles and Monsters,* due out from Glass Lyre Press in mid-2019. His work has appeared in *American Literary Review, Crazyhorse, The American Journal of Poetry, DIAGRAM,* and elsewhere.

Alena Dillon is the author of *Mercy House,* which is forthcoming from William Morrow of HarperCollins in 2020, and the humor collection *I Thought We Agreed to Pee in the Ocean.* "Dashed" is an excerpt from a manuscript about a blue-collar woman in Gloucester, MA, who fights to save her son from opioid addiction, and in doing so discovers confidence and competency she didn't know she had. Alena's work has appeared in publications including *Slice Magazine, The Rumpus, The Doctor TJ Eckleburg Review,* and *Rkvry Quarterly.* She teaches creative writing at Endicott College and St. Joseph's College and lives in MA with her husband, their dog, and, by the printing of this journal, their son.

We are sorry to report that **Mike Faran** passed away in December 2017. He lived in Ventura, CA, as a retired factory worker. He authored *We Go To A Fire* (Penury Press), and his work appeared in *The Midwest Quarterly, Coal City Review, Atlanta Review, The Listening Eye,* and others. He was twice nominated for The Pushcart Prize.

After a teaching career, **Jason Feingold** began writing, with works published in journals, anthologies, and collections. When not writing, he reads, keeps house, is a husband, raises a son, chases dogs, and volunteers as a Guardian ad Litem in his North Carolina home.

Michael Gaspeny has won the Randall Jarrell Poetry Prize and the O. Henry Festival Short Story Competition. His chapbook, *Re-Write Men,* was published in 2017 by Finishing Line Press. A previous chapbook, *Vocation,* appeared from Main Street Rag Press in 2013 as part of its Author's Choice Series. His poetry has appeared in *Brilliant Corners: A Journal of Jazz and Literature, Cave Wall, Kakalak,* and *Flying South*; his fiction in *storySouth* and *The Greensboro Review.* For hospice service in Greensboro, NC, he has received The Governor's Award for Volunteer Excellence. He taught English and journalism for nearly four decades, mainly at High Point University and Bennett College.

Andrew Gent lives in New Hampshire where he works as an information architect. His first book, *[explicit lyrics],* won the 2016 Miller Williams Poetry Prize and is available from the University of Arkansas Press.

Andrey Gritsman, a native of Moscow, immigrated to the United States in 1981. He writes poetry, essays, and short stories in both languages. He authored seven volumes of poetry in Russian and five collections in English, was nominated for the Pushcart Prize several times, and received the 2009 Pushcart Prize Honorable Mention XXIII. His poems, essays, and short stories in English have appeared or are forthcoming in more than 90 literary journals. His work has also been anthologized and translated into several European languages. Andrey edits the international poetry magazine *Interpoezia* and runs the *Intercultural Poetry Series* at Cornelia Street Café in New York. andreygritsman.com and facebook.comgritsman.

Randel McCraw Helms is retired from Arizona State University's English Department. He is the author of five books of literary criticism, including *Tolkien's World, Gospel Fictions,* and

The Bible Against Itself. In retirement, his vocation is making poems, and his recent work has appeared in such places as *Dappled Things, Tipton Poetry Journal, Silkworm,* and *Blood & Bourbon.* His poem about Koko is part of a projected volume of verses about animals.

Mike Horan lives with his family in the desert outside Palm Springs, California. He teaches during the day, writes, and does dad stuff in the evenings, and sometimes manages to practice kung fu in the few moments left over. His work has appeared in *Kindred* magazine from Anchor & Plume Press and *Mad Swirl.*

Joseph Hutchison, Poet Laureate of Colorado (2014-2019), is the award-winning author of seventeen poetry collections, including *The World As Is: New & Selected Poems, 1972-2015, The Satire Lounge, Marked Men,* and *Bed of Coals.* He has co-edited two poetry anthologies—the FutureCycle Press anthology *Malala: Poems for Malala Yousafzai* (all profits to the Malala Foundation), with Andrea Watson, and with Gary Schroeder, *A Song for Occupations: Poems about the American Way of Work.* At the University of Denver's University College, he directs two programs for working adults—Professional Creative Writing and Arts & Culture—with courses both online and on campus. Born and raised in Denver, Colorado, he lives in the mountains southwest of the city with his wife, Iyengar yoga instructor Melody Madonna.

Paul Ilechko is the author of the chapbooks *Bartok in Winter* (Flutter Press, 2018) and *Graph of Life* (Finishing Line Press, 2018). His work has appeared in a variety of journals, including *Stickman Review, formercactus, Sheila-Na-Gig,* and *HeartWood Literary Magazine.* He lives in Lambertville, NJ.

Mike James has been widely published in magazines, large and small, throughout the country. His twelve poetry collections include: *First-Hand Accounts From Made-Up Places* (Stubborn Mule), *Crows in the Jukebox* (Bottom Dog), *My Favorite Houseguest* (FutureCycle Press), and *Peddler's Blues* (Main Street Rag.) He has served as an associate editor for *Kentucky Review* and Autumn House Press, as well as the publisher of the now defunct Yellow Pepper Press. He makes his home outside Nashville, Tennessee. More information can be found on his website at mikejamespoetry.com.

Rachel Rinehart Johnson writes narratives, poems, and children's stories, and her work appears in *Florida English, New Plains Review, Rocking Chair Reader: Family Gatherings, Slippery Elm Literary Journal, The Heartland Review,* and other journals. She earned her MFA at Murray State University and currently teaches composition and creative writing at Eastern Florida State College. In her spare time, Rachel loves to read, travel, and explore nature.

George Kalamaras, former Poet Laureate of Indiana (2014-2016), has published fifteen books of poetry, eight of which are full-length, including *Kingdom of Throat-Stuck Luck* (2011), winner of the Elixir Press Poetry Contest, and *The Theory and Function of Mangoes* (2000), winner of the Four Way Books Intro Series. A lover of dogs—especially hounds—he is Professor of English at Purdue University Fort Wayne, where he has taught since 1990.

Susan Doble Kaluza is the author of a poetry chapbook, *Songs of Deliverance* (Finishing Line Press, 2018). Her work has most recently appeared or is forthcoming in *Tammy Journal, Pure Slush Australia, RATTLE, Lost River Review,* and *Visiting Bob* (a 100-poem tribute to Bob Dylan from New Rivers Press). Susan writes, runs, and rescues horses in Southwestern Montana.

Clyde Kessler has published poems in many magazines, both in print and online. He is also a regional editor for *Virginia Birds,* a publication of the Virginia Society of Ornithology. His book of poems, *Fiddling at Midnight's Farmhouse,* was published in 2017 by Cedar Creek Publishing and illustrated by Kendall Kessler.

Steve Klepetar recently relocated to the Berkshires in Massachusetts after thirty-six years in Minnesota, where he taught literature and creative writing at Saint Cloud State University. Klepetar's work has appeared worldwide, in *Boston Literary Magazine, Deep Water, Expound, The Muse: India, Red River Review, Snakeskin, Voices Israel, Ygdrasil,* and many others. Several of his poems have been nominated for Best of the Net and the Pushcart Prize (including three in 2017). He has also done several collaborations with composer Richard Lavenda of Rice University in Houston, including a one-act opera, *Barricades,* for which he wrote the libretto. Klepetar is the author of thirteen poetry collections and chapbooks, most recently *Family Reunion* (Big Table), *A Landscape in Hell* (Flutter Press), *How Fascism Comes to America* (Locofo Chaps), and *Why Glass Shatters* (One Sentence Chaps).

Tim Krcmarik is a twelve-year Lieutenant in the Austin Fire Department. He runs on Engine 1 downtown and lives in Austin, Texas with his wife and son.

Jennifer Lagier has published fourteen books, edits the *Homestead Review,* and helps coordinate Monterey Bay Poetry Consortium readings. Her newest books are *Scene of the Crime* (Evening Street Press), *Harbingers* (Blue Light Press), and *Camille Abroad, Camille Mobilizes,* and *Like a B Movie* (FutureCycle Press). Visit her website at jlagier.net.

Before moving to Washington, DC, **Raima Larter** was a college professor in Indiana who secretly wrote fiction and tucked it away in drawers. Her work has appeared in *Gargoyle, Writers Journal, Mulberry Fork Review,* and others. Her first novel, *Fearless,* will be published by New Meridian Arts in early 2019; her second novel, *Belle o' the Waters,* will be published in 2019 by Mascot Books. Read more about Raima and her work at her website, raimalarter.com.

Vivian Lawry is a prize-winning author whose short stories and personal essays have appeared in more than fifty literary journals and anthologies. She lives and writes near Richmond, VA. "Lethal Love" is her first fantasy fiction, inspired by her granddaughters who are big fans of the genre. Visit her website at vivianlawry.com and like her on Facebook.

Marie C. Lecrivain is executive editor/publisher of *poeticdiversity: the litzine of Los Angeles,* a photographer, and a writer-in-residence at her apartment. Her prose and poetry have appeared in a number of journals and anthologies, including *Edgar Allen Poetry Journal, The Los Angeles Review, Nonbinary Review, Red Fez, Spillway, Orbis, A New Ulster,* and others. She's the author of several volumes of poetry and fiction, including *Philemon's Gambit* (2016 International Word Bank Press), which is available on Amazon.com.

Kevin J. McDaniel lives in Pulaski, VA, with his wife, daughters, and their menagerie of pets. His work appears in the *Anthology of Appalachian Writers, Artemis Journal, Broad River Review, Cloudbank, Common Ground Review, Evening Street Review, Hawk & Whippoorwill, Pine Mountain Sand & Gravel, Pudding Magazine, Sand Hills, Temenos, The Cape Rock, Main Street Rag, The Offbeat,* and others. McDaniel teaches English composition at Bluefield College. He is author of two chapbooks (*Family Talks,* Finishing Line Press; *At the Foot of a Mountain,* Old Seventy Creek Press) and one forthcoming volume of poetry (*Rubbernecking,* Main Street Rag Publishing).

Robert McGuill's work has appeared in *Narrative, The Southwest Review, The Saturday Evening Post, American Fiction,* and other publications. His stories have been nominated for the Pushcart Prize and short-listed for awards by *Glimmer Train,* the *New Guard, Sequestrum Art & Literature,* and the *Tucson Festival of Books.*

Melissa McInerney earned her MFA in fiction from Bennington College in 2015 and her BA from the University of Texas Austin in 1981. She has written a series of short stories about growing up in boomtown Houston and three novels. Melissa blogs about living with Lyme disease at lifeandlyme.net/blog and is working on a memoir. Her work has appeared in *Logophile, Jet Fuel Review,* and at www.fiftiness.com. A late bloomer, she tolerated the south and its unrelenting heat for years. Now she thrives in Colorado with her grown daughter, three dogs, and a cat. She is reluctantly learning to garden, and it's not as bad as she feared.

Marlene S. Molinoff lives in New York City and on Kiawah Island, SC. She writes about people in transition, either by choice or by chance. Currently, she is completing a novel about a May/January romance and working on a collection of coming-of-age short stories about the challenges faced by a group of people as they approach their sixties and beyond. A former literature teacher and marketing strategist, Marlene has traveled and photographed extensively in Europe, South America, Nepal, India, Cambodia, Bhutan, and Cuba. Her short fiction has appeared in *The Iowa Summer Festival Anthology, Forge, The Alembic, Amarillo Bay, The Edge, Crack the Spine,* and *Steam Ticket Journal.*

Mary Natwick's short stories and poetry have been published in *Rivertalk Anthology* and in journals such as *Forge Journal, Ignatian Literary Magazine, Pennsylvania English, Salamander, Santa Barbara Quarterly,* and *Schuylkill Valley Journal.* Last year, she challenged herself to write 60 pieces (poems, flash fiction, short stories) in 360 days. Always the rebel, she wrote the first 100,000 words of an epic fantasy instead. Now she wonders, should she challenge herself to finish the novel by the end of the year, or will that lead to further rebellion?

William Page's poetry collection, *In This Maybe Best of All Possible Worlds,* won the 2016 FutureCycle Poetry Book Prize. His *Bodies Not Our Own* from Memphis State University Press received the Walter R. Smith Distinguished Book Award. His poetry has appeared in such journals as *Kentucky Review, The North American Review, The Southern Review, Southwest Review, Ploughshares, The Sewanee Review, Valparaiso Poetry Review, Rattle,* and *The Midwest Quarterly,* and in a number of print and online anthologies; it has appeared as the Best of the Net and been nominated for the Pushcart Prize. William was founding editor of *The Pinch,* now in its 38th year of publication. His reading of his poem, "How We Learned," recently published in the *Cortland Review,* may be heard at cortlandreview.com/issue/79/page.php.

Elaine Fowler Palencia lives in Champaign, Illinois, and has published two short story collections, *Small Caucasian Woman* and *Brier Country* (University of Missouri Press) and three poetry chapbooks, most recently *Going Places* (FutureCycle Press, 2015). A scholarly monograph, *The Literary Heritage of Hindman Settlement School,* was published by the school in 2017. Her work has received seven Pushcart Prize nominations. Elaine is the director of the Red Herring Fiction Workshop of Champaign-Urbana and a founding member of The Quintessential Poets.

Chris Pellizzari is a graduate of the University of Illinois at Urbana-Champaign. His short stories and poems have appeared or will soon appear in numerous literary magazines, including *The Awakenings Review, BoomerLitMag, Good Works Review, Counterclock, Amarillo Bay, The Literary Nest,* and *Ink in Thirds.* His novella, *Last Night in Granada,* was published in 2018 by ReadLips Press.

Simon Perchik is an attorney whose poems have appeared in *Partisan Review, Forge, Poetry, Osiris, The New Yorker,* and elsewhere. His most recent collection is *The Osiris Poems* (boxofchalk press, 2017). For more information, including free e-books and his essay "Magic, Illusion and Other Realities," visit his website at simonperchik.com. To view one of his interviews, visit youtube.com/watch?v=MSK774rtfx8.

Andrew Peters is an Egypt-based writer. His short fiction has recently appeared in the *Aestas* anthology, *Theaker's Quarterly Fiction,* and the Earlyworks Press 2018 prize anthology. In 2017, he received an honorable mention in the Glimmer Train 2017 Short Story Award for New Writers; some of his flash fiction was chosen in competition to appear in *The Fish Anthology.*

Fabrice Poussin teaches French and English at Shorter University. An author of novels and poetry, his work has appeared in *Kestrel, Symposium, The Chimes,* and dozens of other magazines. His photography has been published in *The Front Porch Review,* the *San Pedro River Review,* and more than 300 other publications.

Haley Quinton is an MFA candidate at the University of Memphis, where she is the managing editor of *The Pinch.* Haley's works can be found in *Adelaide Magazine* and the University of Memphis's alumni magazine. Haley is a Kentucky native, and often finds inspiration in the richness and complexity of Southern culture.

Clela Reed is the author of five collections of poetry. Her full-length books are *Dancing on the Rim* (Brick Road Poetry Press, 2009) and *The Hero of the Revolution Serves Us Tea* (Negative Capability Press, 2014). Chapbooks are *Bloodline* (Evening Street Press, 2009), *Of Root and Sky* (Pudding House Publications, 2010), and *Word Bully* (Finishing Line Press, 2018). She has had poems published in *The Cortland Review, Southern Poetry Review, The Atlanta Review, Kentucky Review, The Valparaiso Review,* and many others. She lives and writes with her husband in their woodland home near Athens, Georgia.

Ron Riekki wrote *U.P.: a novel* and edited *The Way North: Collected Upper Peninsula New Works* (2014 Michigan Notable Book), *Here: Women Writing on Michigan's Upper Peninsula* (2016 Independent Publisher Book Award), and *And Here: 100 Years of Upper Peninsula Writing, 1917-2017* (Michigan State University Press, 2017). His fiction has been published in *The Threepenny Review, Bellevue Literary Review, Wigleaf, Prairie Schooner, Shenandoah, Akashic Books, Juked, New Ohio Review, Puerto del Sol,* and many other literary journals. Ron's story "Accidents" received the 2016 Shenandoah Fiction Prize and "The Family Jewel" was selected for *The Best Small Fictions 2015.*

Robert Sachs' work has appeared most recently in *The Louisville Review,* the *Chicago Quarterly Review,* and the *Delmarva Review.* He earned an M.F.A. in Writing from Spalding University in 2009. His story, "Vondelpark," was nominated for a Pushcart Prize in 2017. Originally from Chicago, Robert currently lives in Louisville, Kentucky. He serves on the board of Louisville Literary Arts. Read more at roberthsachs.com.

Terry Sanville lives in San Luis Obispo, California, with his artist-poet wife (his in-house editor) and two plump cats (his in-house critics). He writes full time, producing short stories, essays, poems, and novels. Since 2005, his short stories have been accepted by more than 280 literary and commercial journals, magazines, and anthologies, including the *Potomac Review, The Bitter Oleander, Shenandoah,* and *The Saturday Evening Post.* He was nominated twice for the Pushcart Prize and once for inclusion in the *Best of the Net* anthology. Terry is a retired urban planner and an accomplished jazz and blues guitarist who once played with a symphony orchestra backing up jazz legend George Shearing.

Timothy Schlee is a writer based in Kansas City, MO. He attended Truman State University, where he received his BA in English and BS in linguistics. His fiction has appeared in *ink&coda, Rasasvada,* and *Windfall.*

Marvin Shackelford is author of the collections *Endless Building* (poems) and *Tall Tales from the Ladies' Auxiliary* (stories, forthcoming). His work has, or soon will have, appeared in *Kenyon Review, Wigleaf, Juked, Split Lip,* and elsewhere. He resides in Southern Middle Tennessee, earning a living in agriculture.

Bobbi Sinha-Morey lives in the peaceful city of Brookings, Oregon. There she writes poetry in the morning and at night, always at her leisure. Her work has appeared in a variety of places such as *Plainsongs, Orbis, The Wayfarer, Helix Magazine, Oasis Journal 2016, Pirene's Fountain, The Path,* and *The Laughing Dog.* Her books of poetry are available on Amazon.com, and her work has been nominated for Best of the Net. She loves aerobics, knitting, reading, and taking walks on the beach with her husband.

Christopher Stolle's writing has appeared most recently in *Tipton Poetry Journal, Flying Island, Edify Fiction, Contour, The New Southern Fugitives, The Gambler, Gravel, The Light Ekphrastic, Sheepshead Review,* and *Plath Poetry Project.* He works as an acquisitions and development editor for Penguin Random House, and he lives in Richmond, Indiana.

Kyle Summerall is the author of "Juke" (*ThugLit: Last Writes,* 2016), as well as "What If We Were Strangers" (*The Dilletanti,* 2016), "Mud Bottom" (*Flash Fiction Magazine,* 2016), and "The Surface" (*WritingRaw,* 2015). Summerall lives on the Gulf Coast while he writes about home in West Point, MS. He hopes to follow in the footsteps of those who also call the South home, like Larry Brown, Ron Rash, William Gay, David Joy, Barry Hannah, and Michael Farris Smith.

Carine Topal's work has appeared in *The Best of the Prose Poem, Greensboro Review, Iron Horse Literary Review, Oberon, Caliban,* and many others. Twice nominated for a Pushcart Prize, she was the recipient of residencies at both Hedgebrook and Summer Literary Seminars in St. Petersburg, Russia. Her collection *Bed of Want* won the 2007 Robert G. Cohen Prose Poetry Award. In 2008, *In the Heaven of Never Before* was published by Moon Tide Press. In 2015, she received the Briar Cliff Review Award for Poetry and also won the Fourth Biennial Chapbook Contest from Palettes and Quills for *Tattooed,* voices from the perpetrators, victims, and survivors of Auschwitz Concentration Camp. In 2018, the Pacific Coast Poetry Series published her book *In Order of Disappearance.* She lives and teaches workshops in La Quinta, CA.

Eric Twardzik is a graduate of the creative writing program at Emerson College and resides in Boston, Massachusetts. His fiction has previously been printed in *Kentucky Review, The Emerson Review,* and *Glass Mountain* and has appeared online at Ivy-Style.com and alonelyriotmag.com. He frequently writes about food, travel, men's style, and spirits; his nonfiction work can be found online at erictwardzik.com. Eric is partial to Green Chartreuse, autumn weather, and button-down collars.

Vivian Wagner lives in New Concord, Ohio, where she's an associate professor of English. She's the author of *Fiddle: One Woman, Four Strings, and 8,000 Miles of Music* (Citadel-Kensington), *The Village* (Aldrich Press-Kelsay Books), *Making* (Origami Poems Project), and *Curiosities* (Unsolicited Press).

Martin Willitts Jr. has 20 chapbooks including the winner of the Turtle Island Quarterly Editor's Choice Award, *The Wire Fence Holding Back the World* (Flowstone Press, 2017), plus eleven full-length collections including *The Uncertain Lover* (Dos Madres Press, 2018) and *Coming Home Celebration* (forthcoming, FutureCycle Press, 2019).

Jesse Wolfe is an English professor at California State University, Stanislaus, where he serves as Faculty Advisor to *Penumbra,* the campus's student-run literary and art journal. He is the author of one scholarly book—*Bloomsbury, Modernism, and the Reinvention of Intimacy* (Cambridge U Press, 2011)—and is the recipient of a grant from the National Endowment for the Humanities toward work on his second book, currently in process. His poetry has recently appeared, or will soon appear, in *The Tower Journal, Red River Review, Mad Swirl,* and *vox poetica.* He lives in Turlock, CA, with his wife Alex and their twin daughters, Diana and Vivien.

Christopher Woods is a writer, teacher, and photographer who lives in Chappell Hill, Texas. He has published a novel, *The Dream Patch*; a prose collection, *Under a Riverbed Sky*; and a book of stage monologues for actors, *Heart Speak.* His work has appeared in *The Southern Review, New England Review, New Orleans Review, Columbia,* and *Glimmer Train,* among others. Christopher's gallery of photographs can be seen at christopherwoods.zenfolio.com.

About FutureCycle Press

FutureCycle Press is dedicated to publishing lasting English-language poetry books and anthologies in both print-on-demand and Kindle formats. Founded in 2007 by long-time independent editor/publishers and partners Diane Kistner and Robert S. King, the press incorporated as a nonprofit in 2012. A number of our editors are distinguished poets and writers in their own right, and we have been actively involved in the small press movement going back to the early seventies.

The FutureCycle Poetry Book Prize and honorarium is awarded annually for the best full-length volume of poetry we publish in a calendar year. Introduced in 2013, our Good Works projects are anthologies devoted to issues of universal significance with all proceeds donated to a related worthy cause. Our Selected Poems series highlights contemporary poets with a substantial body of work to their credit; with this series we strive to resurrect work that has had limited distribution and is now out of print.

We are dedicated to giving all of the authors we publish the care their work deserves, making our catalog of titles the most diverse and distinguished it can be, and paying forward any earnings to fund more great books.

We've learned a few things about independent publishing over the years. We've also evolved a unique, resilient publishing model that allows us to focus mainly on vetting and preserving for posterity the most books of exceptional quality without becoming over-whelmed with bookkeeping and mailing, fundraising activities, or taxing editorial and production "bubbles." To find out more, come see us at futurecycle.org.

Made in the USA
Middletown, DE
18 January 2019